T0207387

Building an Effective Data Science Practice

A Framework to Bootstrap and Manage a Successful Data Science Practice

Vineet Raina
Srinath Krishnamurthy

Apress®

Building an Effective Data Science Practice: A Framework to Bootstrap and Manage a Successful Data Science Practice

Vineet Raina
Pune, India

Srinath Krishnamurthy
Pune, India

ISBN-13 (pbk): 978-1-4842-7418-7
https://doi.org/10.1007/978-1-4842-7419-4

ISBN-13 (electronic): 978-1-4842-7419-4

Managing Director, Apress Media LLC: Welmoed Spahr
Acquisitions Editor: Aditee Mirashi
Development Editor: James Markham
Coordinating Editor: Aditee Mirashi

Cover designed by eStudioCalamar

Cover image designed by Freepik (www.freepik.com)

Distributed to the book trade worldwide by Springer Science+Business Media New York, 1 New York Plaza, Suite 4600, New York, NY 10004-1562, USA. Phone 1-800-SPRINGER, fax (201) 348-4505, e-mail orders-ny@springer-sbm.com, or visit www.springeronline.com. Apress Media, LLC is a California LLC and the sole member (owner) is Springer Science + Business Media Finance Inc (SSBM Finance Inc). SSBM Finance Inc is a **Delaware** corporation.

For information on translations, please e-mail booktranslations@springernature.com; for reprint, paperback, or audio rights, please e-mail bookpermissions@springernature.com.

Apress titles may be purchased in bulk for academic, corporate, or promotional use. eBook versions and licenses are also available for most titles. For more information, reference our Print and eBook Bulk Sales web page at http://www.apress.com/bulk-sales.

Any source code or other supplementary material referenced by the author in this book is available to readers on GitHub via the book's product page, located at www.apress.com/9781484274187. For more detailed information, please visit http://www.apress.com/source-code.

Printed on acid-free paper

Table of Contents

About the Authors

Vineet Raina is a Chief Data Scientist at GS Lab, India, and has led the effort of setting up a data science group at GS Lab which has now successfully executed data science projects in diverse fields like healthcare, IoT, communication, etc. He has also led research projects in Computer Vision and Demand Forecasting and developed new data science algorithms/techniques in areas like model performance tuning.

Vineet is a computer science engineer from Pune University with a master's degree from BITS Pilani. For most of his 17-year professional career, he has been associated with data science projects and has two US patents in his name. Prior to joining GS Lab, he worked at SAS for seven years building data science products. He has presented papers in global conferences and has given talks in colleges on topics related to data science. He has also been associated with universities for research projects in the field of data science.

Srinath Krishnamurthy is a Principal Architect at GS Lab, India. His key responsibility has been to bootstrap, and now to lead, the data science capability in GS Lab. A TOGAF9-certified architect, Srinath specializes in aligning business goals to the technical roadmap and data strategy for his clients. His typical clients are software technology companies that depend on data science or enterprises looking to leverage data science as part of their digitalization programs.

Srinath is a computer science graduate from Pune University. During his 17 years of professional experience, he has primarily worked on data mining, predictive modeling, and analytics in varied areas such as CRM (retail/finance), life sciences, healthcare, video conferencing, industrial IoT, and smart cities.

About the Technical Reviewer

 **Jojo Moolayil** is an artificial intelligence professional and published author of three books on machine learning, deep learning, and IoT. He is currently working with Amazon Web Services as a research scientist – AI in their Vancouver, BC, office.

In his current role with AWS, he works on researching and developing large-scale AI solutions for combating fraud and enriching the customer's payment experience in the cloud. He is also actively involved as a tech reviewer and AI consultant with leading publishers and has reviewed over a dozen books on machine learning, deep learning, and business analytics.

You can reach out to Jojo at www.jojomoolayil.com/ or www.linkedin.com/in/jojo62000.

Acknowledgments

The culture of interdisciplinary innovation fostered at GS Lab has been instrumental in providing us with the experiences that formed the foundation of this book.

The editorial team at Apress – Celestin Suresh John, Aditee Mirashi, Jim Markham, and Matthew Moodie – has been extremely helpful in coordinating and supporting the development of this book. Jojo John Moolayil reviewed the early drafts and provided suggestions that helped improve the quality of the book.

Mugdha Hardikar helped create some of the visualizations in Chapter 15.

Introduction

An increasing number and variety of organizations are eager to adopt data science now, regardless of their size and sector. In our collaborations and discussions with technology leaders from various companies, we noticed some recurring patterns:

- They're convinced that their business will benefit from data science, but are not sure of the best way to get started and do not have a sufficiently clear picture of what the overall data science journey would involve.

- They have a few problems that they believe can best be solved using data science, but given the low success rate as reported by numerous publications,[1] they are wary of investing before having more clarity about what they are getting into.

- They've started doing data science but are unsure of whether the efforts are on track toward an anticipated business RoI. Generally, they are seeking ways to make the progress of their data science team more transparent and effective.

Our experience working closely with technology leaders from diverse backgrounds to solve problems using data science – and addressing the previously mentioned aspects while doing so – gave rise to this book.

---

[1] Such as https://venturebeat.com/2019/07/19/why-do-87-of-data-science-projects-never-make-it-into-production/

Who This Book Is For

This book is primarily intended for technology leaders who are considering incubating data science in their organization or are in the early stages of their data science journey: this book is intended to act as a guide for you and your formative team. You would need an intuitive understanding of techniques/technologies of data science, on one side, and, on the other side, the skill to apply this understanding to achieve the business goals. Based on our experience, we believe that it is possible to inculcate this intuitive understanding and the data science thought process as well the skill to apply it to business, without getting into coding or advanced mathematics. This book accordingly aims at imparting all these skills in an intuitive way – a focus of our technical coverage in this book (including the examples given) is to make it easier to grasp the underlying concepts.

We also anticipate this book to be useful to the members of a data science team: you will broaden your awareness of the overall technical ecosystem required to create an end-to-end solution using data science. Also, you can find examples that indicate how the business goals influence the choice of techniques and technologies – synergy between the business and data science is essential to apply data science effectively to the business.

Finally, this book – especially Part 4 – would also be useful to project managers who coordinate end-to-end projects that leverage data science. Similarly, technology evangelists interested in the areas of data and analytics, AI (artificial intelligence), etc., would find this book useful in broadening their horizons.

How This Book Is Organized

This book is organized into four parts as follows:

Part 1: Fundamentals (Chapters 1 to 3)

This part introduces data science and attempts to dispel the terminology chaos around data science. It discusses the applicability and usefulness of data science for business and how the data science culture depends on the business.

Part 2: Classes of Problems (Chapters 4 to 11)

After talking about the general benefits of data science for business in Part 1, this part intends to give a more concrete picture of the various classes of problems that can be solved using data science. It has one chapter dedicated to one class of problem – each chapter establishes a business motive and then transforms that motive to a concrete data science problem and shows how it could be solved. This part is primarily intended to illustrate and inculcate the thought process that goes into mapping a business problem to a data science problem and the steps involved in solving it.

Part 3: Techniques and Technologies (Chapters 12 to 20)

The previous part demonstrates how solving data science problems effectively depends on a good intuitive understanding of various techniques belonging to the field of data science. This part attempts to impart this intuitive understanding of the basic principles of various techniques in data science. It also talks about the technologies (libraries, tools, etc.) that help you apply these techniques. This conceptual understanding is also important for you to understand which type of techniques/technologies could be more applicable to the data science culture in your organization.

Part 4: Building Teams and Executing Projects (Chapters 21 to 23)

After covering the business and technical aspects of data science, this concluding part discusses practical aspects that are important for doing data science *effectively*. It talks about the various skills essential for different roles in data science teams and how such teams are typically structured for effective execution. It also talks about the different types of data science projects that your data science team would work on and various aspects of ensuring data quality that are indispensable for success in data science. It concludes with some legal and regulatory aspects that are important for you to be aware of while working on data science projects, including the recent thrust toward explainable AI.

Note that each part has an introduction that further details the organization of the chapters within that part.

PART I

Fundamentals

This part talks about data science and how it could be beneficial to your business. The three chapters in this part lay the groundwork for the rest of this book.

In Chapter 1, we shall cover our perspective of what data science is and introduce the data science process around which the rest of the book is based.

In Chapter 2, we cover the business aspects around data science. We touch upon various benefits of data science to help understand its importance for your business and, at the same time, cover aspects to evaluate the readiness of your business for data science. This chapter also initiates the notion of how the business needs drive the data science.

In Chapter 3, we introduce the two cultures of data science and how these matter to your business. The cultures permeate every aspect from the technical ecosystem to the processes, as we shall see in the rest of the book.

CHAPTER 1

Introduction: The Data *Science* Process

June 1918. A subcommittee consisting of Prof. Eddington, Sir Dyson, and others made arrangements for expeditions to Sobral in North Brazil and to the island of Principe. The goal of these two expeditions? To collect some data during the eclipse that was to occur on **May 29, 1919...**

> A fellow called Einstein had created a new model of gravitation which he called *general relativity,* which few seemed to understand. Based on this model, he predicted in 1915, that light would get deflected by roughly 1.75 arcseconds when it passes close to the sun. Einstein had created his model based on data collected in the centuries past; his model even explained a puzzling aspect of the motion of Mercury which had not been explained until then by Newtonian physics. But this deflection of light close to the sun had not been observed so far. Hence, the expedition – its sole aim was to collect data about the path taken by light close to the sun. This new data would either validate or invalidate Einstein's model of gravitation.

© Vineet Raina and Srinath Krishnamurthy 2022
V. Raina and S. Krishnamurthy, *Building an Effective Data Science Practice*,
https://doi.org/10.1007/978-1-4842-7419-4_1

...May 29, 1919. What was to become perhaps the most important eclipse in the history of physics. The eclipse allowed the scientists to collect data about the position of certain stars, which would indicate the course taken by the light from the stars as it grazed the sun on its way to us on Earth.

Nov 1919. Analyses of the data confirmed Einstein's predictions. General relativity was established as a more proper description of the laws of gravitation in our universe than the existing standard – Newton's.

What We Mean by Data *Science*

The story of how gravitational models evolved, and how eventually general relativity was accepted, is an illustration of *the scientific method*.

Given certain observations, a scientist first creates a *model* that can explain the observations. While doing so, it is possible that the model is unable to explain *some* of the observations, for example, how Newtonian physics could not explain certain aspects of Mercury's motion satisfactorily. Regardless, such a model may be useful so long as it is practically applicable and is general enough, for example, Newtonian physics was general enough to describe the forces of attraction and resulting motion for most of the common situations here on Earth.

Even if a model is practically useful, the hunt continues for better models – those that can explain the observations better or predict specific occurrences in unknown situations better. This notion of validating a model based on *observational evidence* is one of the cornerstones of the scientific method. A scientist thus continues this cycle of observations ➤ model ➤ observations, and each pass through this cycle results in better models.

Models of gravitation such as Newton's and Einstein's explain the forces of attraction and resulting motion among objects perceived in the universe. Generally, we use the term *model* to refer to any representation of reality that *sufficiently* explains and/or predicts observations.

A much simpler example of a model is an architect's scaled down model of a planned township[1] that shows the layout of the residential and commercial spaces, routes, and other facilities – we can use such a scaled down model to determine distance between two buildings or the time it might take to reach the neighborhood school from a house you're planning to buy. These predictions as obtained from the scaled down model are sufficiently useful and accurate in the real world.

Applying the scientific method to matter in the universe and how it behaves is referred to as physics, and applying the scientific method to living organisms as biology. Similarly, applying the scientific method to any data can be regarded as data science. More practically in current times, data science is characterized by the use of *software* to increasingly automate the steps in this scientific process.

In this book, we refer to **the application of the scientific method to data using software** as **data science**. In our experience, we find this notion to be much more useful practically – it emphasizes the scientific method as the heart of the discipline and software as the primary mechanism/equipment for the science.

This perspective of data science will impact every decision taken in building a data science practice for your business, from the skills required in the team to the tools and technologies that need to be used.

Let us now look at the data science process that is typically followed while applying the scientific method to data.

---

[1] Note that this model is a result of "engineering" rather than science. Though the notion of "model" is not limited to science, in this book, we will use the term *model* to refer to models created by applying the scientific method.

The Data Science Process

For doing data science, that is, applying the scientific method to data using software, the data science team follows an iterative process. In the context of data science, this scientific method is often referred to as the *data science process*.

This process can be broken down into a series of broad steps beginning with the obvious first step of collecting the data (the *data capture* step). This is followed by choosing the relevant data, cleaning, and transforming it as needed (*data preparation*) and then visually exploring and understanding it using charts/plots (*data visualization*). This exploration and understanding are crucial for the next step – learning from the data to build models (*machine learning*) which is at the heart of this process. These models are then used to infer the outcomes for new observations (*inference*). Figure 1-1 depicts these steps which are explained in more detail in the rest of this section.

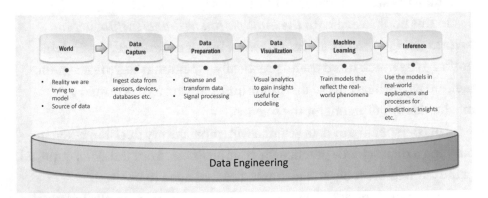

Figure 1-1. *Data science process (iterations are implicit across any of these steps)*

Note that this is a simplistic representation of the data science process, as you will rarely encounter a data science problem which will require you to just follow these steps in a sequential order. Most problems will require going back and forth repeatedly between the different steps – we refer to these as iterations of the data science process. Let us look at a few examples:

- You may realize during the *data visualization* step that a lot of data is corrupt (e.g., sensor readings are out of expected range) so you may go back to the *data capture* step to collect more correct data.

- You may realize in the *machine learning* step that the model you have chosen might perform better if the data that is being fed to it is transformed in a certain way, so you can go back to the *data preparation* step to transform the data in the appropriate manner.

- You may notice in the *inference* step that your model is not predicting outcomes with desired accuracy in the production environment and may decide to go back to the *machine learning* step to try building more accurate models.

As we see, the data science process does not end with creating models – it continues beyond, to ensuring that the models can be deployed to production operations and monitored. This leads to continual gathering of observational evidence to validate or improve the models over time.

The entire ecosystem of techniques, tools, and skills is oriented around this data science process – we shall keep returning to it and see how it is realized as part of end-to-end solutions. This data science process will also form the basis for how we categorize the various techniques, tools, and technologies in Part 3.

Let us look at a few simple examples to separately illustrate each step in the process. We shall start with the step that is at the heart of the scientific method – machine learning – which results in candidate models.

Machine Learning

Let us start by looking at the *machine learning* step in Figure 1-2, because that is fundamental to understanding the other steps of the process.

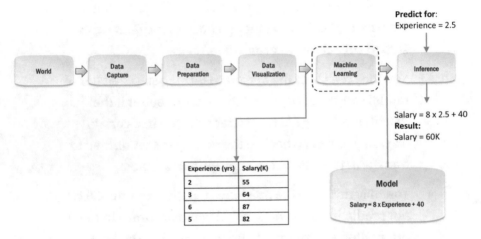

Figure 1-2. *Machine learning: example of predicting salary based on experience*

In the example shown in Figure 1-2, we have data of employees and their salaries within a given industry. In this simplistic example, we assume that we have information about the work experience, and we would like to determine the typical relationship between experience and salary of employees in this industry. Once we know this relationship, it will help us predict the typical salary of an individual based on their experience – this can be useful in, say, hiring processes.

The machine learning step takes the data of experience and salary, and just by looking at the data, it automatically determines[2] that, in general

$$\text{Salary (K)} = 8 \times \text{Experience (yrs)} + 40$$

---

[2] The algorithm in this case is linear regression, which we shall cover in Chapter 16.

This model can now be used in the next step, *inference,* to predict the salary of a new individual. For example, if the individual has 2.5 years' experience (a value that was not present in the original observations), this model will predict their salary to be 60K.

Note that, like all models, this is only a *sufficiently* useful representation of reality – there are bound to be some errors and approximations. For example, from the data, we see that 6 years' experience should result in salary of 87K, but our model will predict 88K, with an error of 1K. But nevertheless, if we consider all the data points together, this model yields an acceptable error overall.[3] If the errors are acceptable, as in this example, the model is useful. If the error is too high, we would continue to search for a better model.

The machine learning algorithm and the resulting model can get increasingly complex in structure. While we have an equation that can represent our model in this case, some other models would be represented as trees or complex graph topologies and so forth. We shall cover these in Chapter 16.

Data Capture (from the *World*)

A model depends entirely on the observations that we have collected from the *World*. For example, imagine if we did not have data about Mercury's orbit – we would not know that Newton's model had some shortcomings or that Einstein's model seems more promising. If our understanding of the World, that is, the system from which the data is captured is lacking, then we may overlook some data that can be crucial to building a good model. Let us look at this with the help of an example.

Figure 1-3 shows a scenario where we have captured sample data about temperature, humidity, and rainfall at a specific location to create a machine learning model.

---

[3] Model performance evaluation will also be covered in Chapter 16 in more detail.

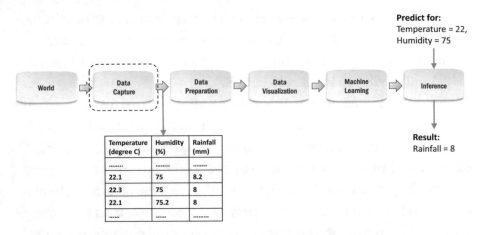

Figure 1-3. *Data capture: example of rainfall prediction*

In this case, our premise is that we would be able to predict rainfall for the next hour based on the current temperature and humidity readings.[4] During *inference*, this model will approximately determine that if temperature is 22 degrees and humidity is 75%, then a rainfall of 8 mm is expected during the next hour.

But in reality, the rainfall also depends on wind speed. Now, it is possible that our data, which we fed into machine learning, was all captured when the wind speed was around 10 kmph – depicted as a grayed out column in Figure 1-4, indicating that this was not captured.

---

[4] This is an extremely simplistic view. But the fundamental formulation of predicting precipitation (rainfall in our example) based on other factors such as temperature, humidity, etc., would be applicable, especially for localized weather predictions, for example, when you have your own weather station on your industry premises.

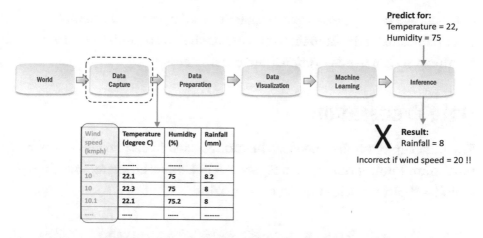

Figure 1-4. *Data capture: rainfall depends on wind speed*

Since the wind speed was not captured and the model uses only temperature and humidity, it predicts rainfall of 8 mm for a temperature of 22 degrees and 75% humidity irrespective of the wind speed. This prediction will be correct only if the current wind speed was also close to 10 kmph. The prediction may be incorrect if the wind speed is very different from 10 kmph (say 20 kmph).

The model does not represent reality sufficiently because it was unable to learn if and how rainfall is impacted by wind speed.[5] The main underlying issue here was that we did not capture all the data necessary to be able to create a model that could sufficiently represent reality.

While this example is rather simplistic, many data science projects in the real world face initial failures due to a similar issue. Data scientists may create models that look good, that is, they have very little error on the data/observations based on which the model was created, but sometimes they mysteriously fail in production. In Chapter 16, we shall cover some

---

[5] We have only mentioned wind speed to simplify the illustration. In reality, there would be other factors such as atmospheric pressure, etc., as well.

data science techniques to guard against this. But the fundamental understanding of the domain to prevent such flawed models due to insufficient data needs to come from the business.[6]

Data Preparation

The data captured often needs to be transformed in certain ways to extract maximum information from it. Figure 1-5 illustrates an example of this which is typical in sales prediction scenarios.

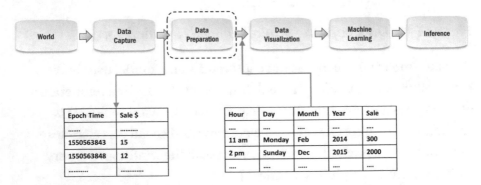

Figure 1-5. *Data preparation: example of converting transaction time to useful data for sales predictions*

In transaction data captured by a system, say a retail store's checkout counter, the time of transaction is captured as a timestamp represented in epoch time, that is, the number of milliseconds since 1 Jan 1970 midnight UTC.[7] The transaction data also captures the sale amount for each transaction. We expect that patterns of sales will not depend on the timestamps of the transactions but will depend on the day of the week and the month. For example, sales patterns on weekends or holidays would be

---

[6] The role of domain experts (business analysts) will be covered in Chapter 21.

[7] This is a conventional quirk of software systems to store a time zone-neutral representation of time.

different from weekdays. Similarly, vacation months such as December would have different patterns than other months. Also, during a given day, sales would be different during various hours.

So, we aggregate the transaction sale amounts to calculate the total sale in every hour. We thus end up with five fields: *Hour, Day, Month, Year,* and the corresponding *Sale*. This will enable us to visualize patterns such as the ones mentioned earlier, as well as allow the machine learning step to determine how sales are impacted by these fields.

Depending on your business, you would determine which fields in the originally captured data contain what kind of useful information. Another example could be that numeric sensor readings are converted into a *High/ Medium/Low* enumeration if that is more relevant to your use case. The machine learning step will accordingly learn from this information to yield a better model.

Data Visualization

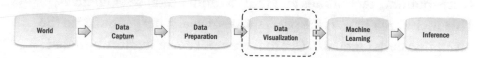

Once a data scientist has prepared data, they first do an exploration of the data and relationships between the various fields. We refer to this step as *data visualization.* Typically, during this visual analysis, the data scientist discerns patterns that enable him to decide which machine learning techniques are likely to perform better.

For example, a linear relationship between two fields, such as Salary and Experience, would prompt the data scientist to try a linear regression model first. Similarly, they can determine based on visual patterns whether there is a correlation between some fields or whether certain rows are outliers. These analyses help the data scientist arrive at the design of the machine learning step. Techniques used for data visualization will be covered in Chapter 15.

Inference

This is the step after machine learning and is executed once the data science team has determined that a sufficiently good model has been created. The resulting model is typically deployed as part of a production system to *infer* information about new observations based on their attributes. For example, if current readings of temperature, humidity, and wind speed are available, the rainfall model can be used to infer rainfall later that day. Or, given a future date, we can use the sales model to predict potential sales.

The act of deploying models into production systems is a transition from the scientific discipline to the (software) engineering discipline. This transitional boundary has its own unique set of challenges and corresponding techniques and tools to address these challenges. This niche area has, in the past couple of years, burgeoned into the discipline christened *ML Ops* that we shall cover in more detail in Chapter 17.

Recall that, for the scientific method, we need to continue gathering information about how well the model performs. Observational evidence that either validates the model or uncovers issues with the model is crucial to improving the model as part of the scientific method. Thus, the observations collected regarding the model are typically persisted and effectively become a part of the *World* for the next big iteration through the data science process.

Data Engineering

All the steps we have seen so far require software engineering techniques specialized toward optimal storage and compute of data. Data science experiments at big data scale often need dedicated engineering support for ensuring optimized and ready access to data – especially when there are multiple applications or sources of data, which is rather common these days.

We shall look at data engineering in more detail throughout Part 3. For now, the key takeaway is that we regard data engineering as the *engineering backbone* that enables the science and thus as a pervasive horizontal within the data science process.

Having briefly covered what data science is, and having an overview of the data science process, let us look at how it relates to some of the other buzzwords rampant these days.

Terminology Chaos: AI, ML, Data Science, Deep Learning, Etc.

Data science, machine learning, AI, deep learning, etc., one is often unsure which term is applicable to a particular problem or use case. As a result, increasingly often now, we see terms such as DS/ML, AI/ML, and so forth as well.

While the terminology and hype games will continue, it is important to understand precisely which kinds of techniques are required to solve what kind of problems in *your* business and to understand what kinds of skills are needed to apply these techniques.

With this motivation in mind, we shall briefly cover what these terms mean to us, referring to Figure 1-6.

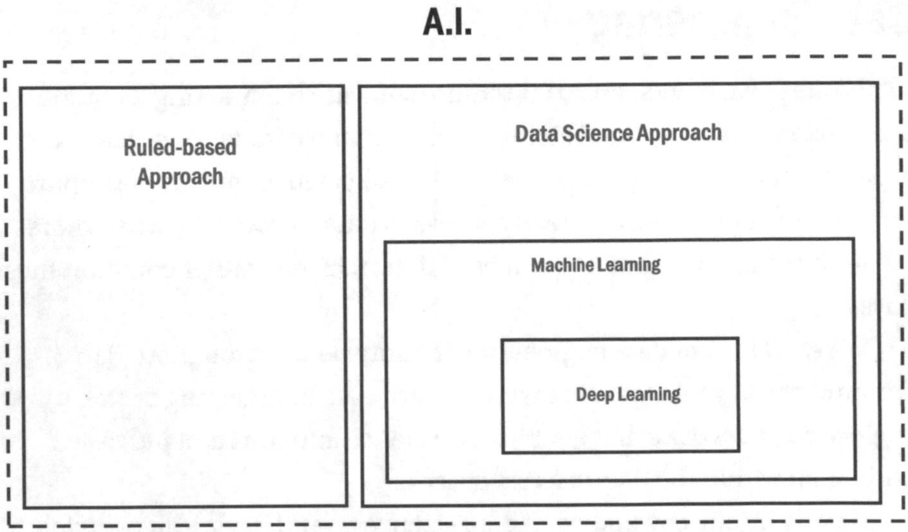

A.I.

Figure 1-6. *Terminology chaos*

AI or artificial intelligence is a rather generic term used to indicate advanced applications or automations that seem to behave intelligently as humans would in similar situations.[8]

Let us consider an *AI engine*[9] that can detect whether an email is spam or not. At a high level, there are two possible approaches to solving this problem.

Rule-based approach

We know which are the typical words and phrases that occur in a spam email. For example, words and phrases like "offer," "free," "extra cash," "you are a winner," etc. indicate spam email. A simple *rule* could be that if any of these words or phrases occur, the engine declares the email as spam. Slightly more complex rules could compute a score of the email based on the number or frequency of occurrences of such indicator words in the

---

[8] Philosophical note: there are varying perspectives of what AI is. We shall skip over the philosophical angles to this.

[9] You may know this AI engine by the name of *spam filter.*

email. Of course, as spammers get more creative, more such rules would need to be added to the engine by the developer. Also, as the complexity of patterns in the text that indicate spam increase over time, the complexity of the rules would increase correspondingly.

It can also be difficult to adapt the engine based on false positives. That is, if the engine declares an email to be spam but the user overrides and says that the email was not a spam, it can get tricky to adapt the rules accordingly unless the reason, the underlying pattern that caused this exception, is traced.

Note that this illustrative example of spam filter, and the solution we have taken is rather simplistic. In general, depending on the complexity of the problem, the rules in a rule-based AI system can be made increasingly complex and sophisticated.[10] Rule-based AI has been sufficient to power expert systems in industries for decades and to become so strong at chess that grandmasters eventually ceased competing against chess engines in the mid-2000s.

Data science approach

Now, consider a different data-driven scientific approach where we try to infer whether the new email is spam or not based on its resemblance to past spam or non-spam emails from our historical email dataset.

According to the data science process,[11] we begin with data capture, that is, by gathering observations (data) about emails, that is, we have a large body of emails that have been labeled as spam or non-spam. The data scientist then attempts to build a model based on this data. To do this, they would first perform the *data preparation* step to apply techniques to convert the email text into a format that is conducive to machine learning algorithms. They will then perform some *data visualization* to determine

---

[10] You may have heard of some techniques like minimax, alpha-beta pruning, etc., which are widely used in rule-based AI systems. There is a huge body of literature in this area that should not be overlooked.

[11] Refer to Figure 1-1.

the distribution or patterns in this data.[12] Accordingly, they would then execute *machine learning* – they would choose a suitable machine learning algorithm, which can take the prepared data to create a model that can classify the email as spam or non-spam. They will then evaluate the performance of this model; in this case, they might choose accuracy of spam detection as a measure to evaluate how good the model is. Based on the model performance, they would then continue to refine the model and overall approach; this typically entails iterations through the *data preparation* to *machine learning* steps.

Once a satisfactory model has been found, it can be deployed on an email server for spam detection – this is the inference step of the data science process. If there are false positives, that is, if the model says an email is spam and the user says that it is not, then this email and its label (non-spam) get added back to our data, that is, the body of mails and labels. The next time the machine learning step runs, it learns from this new information and builds a model that can classify a similar mail as non-spam in future without requiring any human intervention.

HYPE NOTES

AI has gone through various phases of decline and revival in the past several decades. After a decade of relative hype-stagnation in the mid- to late 2000s, the popularity of data science-based approach to AI that started around 2012 has propelled AI back into the hype-limelight.

Continuing recent innovations and successes in deep learning, particularly GANs and reinforcement learning in the past couple of years, are sustaining and fueling the AI hype. This time, we expect that AI is here to stay.

---

[12] Based on what they see, there may be iterations to data preparation before we proceed to the next step.

As we saw in the preceding example, machine learning techniques play a key role in data science. Over time, the term *machine learning*, or *ML*, has expanded its scope to subsume nearly all existing statistical and computational methods. You may have heard of decision trees, SVM (support vector machines), linear regression, and other such ML techniques, which we will cover in Chapter 16. Among all ML techniques, a subclass of techniques called deep learning has gained a lot of popularity and adoption, especially since around 2015, in solving complex problems such as object detection in images and natural language processing (NLP). Deep learning techniques are based on the concept of neural networks. Though the theory has a long history, the current revival started in the period of 2010–2012 when deeper networks, with more layers and complexity, could be trained successfully to solve problems in image processing problems such as object detection and image classification.[13]

Practically, there is a significant difference in approaches and skillset required to use deep learning techniques as compared to the other classical ML techniques. We shall elaborate upon these nuances in Chapters 3 and 20.

RULE-BASED VS. DATA SCIENCE

It is important to bear in mind that the term *data science* started gaining currency only in the last decade. Deep learning, while theoretically rather old, also started becoming tractable and useful only in the last decade.

But AI has been around for a long, long time. Expert systems controlled complex machinery, and computer programs became stronger than any grandmaster at chess, long before the term *data science* was popular. Thus, it is quite possible that your business may not really need data science – more traditional AI, for example, rule-based approaches, suffices in many cases.

---

[13] We shall cover more details of *computer vision* in Chapter 10.

Let us look at an example where one might feel the allure of data science, but rule-based systems may suffice. Consider a smart-city solution which integrates multiple devices, systems, and sensors to allow actionable policies. One common category of policies you may have encountered is that of parking policies – tiered parking rates based on time of day and day of the week are common. A smart-city platform may allow more complex policies that can dynamically increase or decrease the parking rate in a parking space based on the current occupancy, nearby traffic, and weather conditions, since all this information has been integrated into the smart-city platform. In this case, one might feel tempted to take an approach of creating a data science-based model to estimate parking demand and decide pricing accordingly. This has a couple of issues. First, we would need to collect a lot of historical data about parking in various traffic and weather conditions before we can even get started. Second, it may be a lot simpler and *sufficient* to define a set of rules based on which the parking rate should be varied. An example rule could be that if traffic in nearby lanes doubles, then hike the parking rate by 20%. An analyst could be given access to an application in which they can observe how the rules are performing and tweak them over time.

Note that a rule-based approach can often act as a stand-in, bootstrap mechanism until sufficient data is available to create data science-based predictive models. In the parking example just that we just saw, once we have enabled rule-based dynamic pricing and collected data for several months, data science can then be used to determine optimal pricing rules based on predictive models.

Conclusion

We covered the data science process around which the rest of the book is oriented. We also saw how the data science process effectively allows us to apply the scientific method to data using software, that is, to do data science.

We then clarified some of the terms related to data science and AI, to help determine which is most appropriate for the business problems at hand. The kinds of business problems determine the kinds of techniques that are best suited to solve those problems. Based on the kinds of techniques required, you can identify the appropriate technologies and the mix of skills needed in your team.

In the next chapter, we shall therefore begin looking into how data science fits into a business and how it benefits a business.

Further Reading

The gripping account of Eddington and Dyson's expeditions is given in Dyson, Eddington, and Davidson (1919). Thankfully, data collection for data science projects is a tad easier. At least, in this Internet and cloud-based data era, we seldom need to worry about situations such as "a strike of the steamship company" while collecting data.

Varied definitions of data science, and explanations of what data science is, abound in the literature. For more theoretical and historical background of data science, refer to Chapters 1, 2, and 8 of Braschler, Stadelmann, and Stockinger (2019).

References

Braschler, Martin, Thilo Stadelmann and Kurt Stockinger. *Applied Data Science, Lessons Learned for the Data-Driven Business*. Cham, Zug, Switzerland: Springer, 2019.

Dyson, F. W. , A. S. Eddington and C. Davidson. "A Determination of the Deflection of Light by the Sun's Gravitational Field, from Observations Made at the Total Eclipse of May 29, 1919." *Philosophical Transactions of The Royal Society*. London, 1920. 291-333.

CHAPTER 2

Data Science and Your Business

Having understood the data science process and what it entails, we now delve into the business-fitment considerations of data science.

We shall first cover the various kinds of benefits that data science can provide your business, including a few examples of each kind of benefit. Then we shall touch upon a few aspects to consider while ensuring that your business is ready to begin doing data science.

How Data Science Fits into a Business

Data science can be used in a business in a few different ways. Figure 2-1 illustrates this at a high level.

V. Raina and S. Krishnamurthy, *Building an Effective Data Science Practice*, https://doi.org/10.1007/978-1-4842-7419-4_2

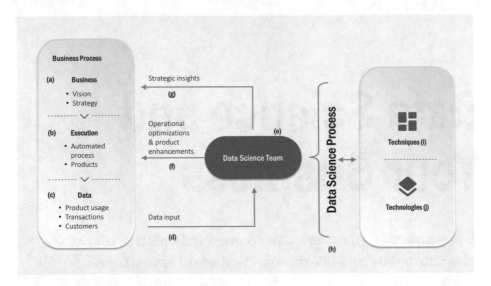

Figure 2-1. *Data science in a business*

Let us walk through this, beginning from the *business process* box. When the business strategy (a) is executed, either products are created, or certain operational processes are automated (b). An example of a product would be a cloud-hosted app your technology company may have created. An example of operational automation could be SCADA[1] systems or IoT infrastructure that you might have set up as part of digitalization of your enterprise.

In either of these cases, data is generated (c). For example, data can be about how customers are using your service online or about how the equipment on your shop floor is performing. All this data can be used (d) by a data science team[2] (e), to create models that help improve processes/ products through operational optimizations/product enhancements (f), and/or to provide strategic insights (g) to the business.

---

[1] Supervisory control and data acquisition (SCADA) is widely adopted by industries for monitoring and controlling devices.

[2] Part 4 of this book covers the skills, roles, and typical structure in a data science team.

To provide these varying kinds of benefits to the business, the data science team executes the data science process (h) using techniques (i) an technologies (j) curated for your business. Recall that we regard application of *the scientific method* to data using *software* as data science – the techniques used in the data science process realize the scientific method, while the technologies enable the required software. (We shall look at techniques and technologies in Part 3 of this book.)

Let us now delve deeper into the previously mentioned business benefits with some examples.

Operational Optimizations

The data science team can create predictive models indicating when certain activities might occur – these predictive models can be used for optimized scheduling of activities.

As an example, consider the case of predicting the inventory requirements at a gas station. Suppose we use data science to create models that can predict, based on past usage data, when each type of fuel would need a refill at each gas station in the neighborhood of the main terminal of the gas company. Knowing the refill needs well in advance allows the creation of an optimized plan of deliveries from the main terminal to the gas stations for future dates. Optimizations can be based on the type/amounts of fuels needed at the gas stations, the type of trucks available on the future dates, and the optimal route to complete the refills on those dates.

ROI NOTES

In this example of predicting inventory requirements at a gas station, the path from the predictive models to business RoI has been chalked out. So, embarking on data science would be a sound decision. You are also prepared with the knowledge that the predictive models yielded by data science are not the end; further sophisticated optimization algorithms would be needed on top of these models to start seeing RoI.

Product Enhancements

If you are building technology products, data science models can help add differentiating features to your product. One common example is that of recommender engines that suggest movies on Netflix or products on Amazon. Recommender engines often make recommendations based on the past choices of similar users. Voice-based technologies, chatbots, etc., are other examples which can be added to any product for improving customer interaction.

Suppose you have a technology solution for customer care. You could add a feature into your solution that could automatically detect during a voice call, whether the customer is disappointed or angry or having any negative sentiments. To achieve this, you might use a speech transcription service that converts the speech to text in real time. You would then feed this text to a data science-based sentiment analysis model which can classify the emotion of the customer. Once your product has access to customer sentiment in real time, it can provide various business benefits. It can act as real-time feedback loop to the team lead. Offline analytics can also determine which customer care executives faced difficult customers and how well they handled those situations. As creator of the product, you can provide these analytics as value-added services to your customer (the customer care company).

Similarly, an IoT solution often differentiates itself using data science-based predictive capabilities. For example, a cloud-based IoT solution for monitoring industrial energy or water consumption can provide value-added services to predict energy or water requirements based on models tailored to a particular customer. Predictive maintenance is another common use case – anomalies in, say, power readings of a particular device or equipment can indicate onset of potential failures. These anomalies are detected by models based on trends in past readings. Addressing such situations proactively help foresee and prevent outages during operations. So, if your IoT solution offers such capabilities, it would be more attractive to potential industrial customers.

Strategic Insights

Data-driven transformations to business strategy have been on the rise, especially since the big data revolution. Data science is playing an increasing role in strategy decisions and management consulting.

Consider the problem of identifying an optimal location in which to open a new store. Traditionally, this has been done based on demographic factors of customers and geographic factors such as proximity to transport hubs, shopping centers, and competitive stores. In the past few years, there has been a rapid rise of data about movement of people using their mobile app and location – referred to as *mobility* data. Given this increased visibility into the mobility of potential customers, it is now possible to create more sophisticated ML models that include mobility aspects into the decision-making along with geographic and demographic factors.[3] Such models can determine which among a set of candidate locations is likely to attract the largest number of visits.

---

[3] Refer to Karamshuk (2013) for a detailed example, where mobility factors were based on Foursquare check-in data.

Another traditional problem is that of identifying potential customer churn. In addition to identifying the customers who are likely to churn, we would also want to determine the possible causative factors. To do this, we would first create a model that can predict which customers will churn and can also rank the factors such as sales channel, discounts, product assortment, etc., that are significant. This would then help take strategic decisions that address these underlying causes.[4] For example, if you find that discounts are a significant factor, you can conduct simulated analysis based on the model to determine the extent to which higher discounts can reduce churn – this kind of analysis will help arrive at the optimal discounts such that churn will be reduced with minimal impacts to revenue.

Is Your Business Ready for Data Science?

Everyone seems to agree that data science is apparently *cool*. And it seems to be applicable for solving some of the problems in your business. What next? Hypothetically, if you had a data science team available at your behest *right now,* what would they be doing? Would they be sufficiently productive?

Even before embarking on a data science journey, the potential routes to business RoI need to be chalked out. The importance of this cannot be overemphasized.

---

[4] For an example model, refer to Jeremy Curuksu, "Developing a business strategy by combining machine learning with sensitivity analysis," `https://aws.amazon.com/blogs/machine-learning/developing-a-business-strategy-by-combining-machine-learning-with-sensitivity-analysis/`, November 13, 2019.

A Cautionary Tale

One example we have seen is a company that invested in having the ability to predict the yield of a chemical product based on the various control parameters and readings taken during the chemical process that runs for several days at a time. Smart folks used cutting-edge deep learning algorithms and were able to predict the yield of the product over time as the process ran. They achieved exceptional accuracy in these predictions and even built an application that would show the predicted trend of the yield, along with notifying key personnel when the actual yield varied significantly from the predictions.

Having achieved this milestone, they now wanted to go back and tune the control parameters to improve the yield. Since extremely complex neural networks were used, they had no explainability[5] for their predictions and had not really gained actionable insights into how the control parameters impact the yield. Thus, it turned out that all their investment thus far did not generate significant business value that was hoped for.

On the other hand, the examples we saw in the previous section, particularly those of operational optimization, are cases where the route to business RoI was outlined before embarking on data science. Once we know the business goals, we can attempt to start data science.

In the Beginning Was the Data

As we see from the data science process, the starting point for data science is, well, data. Rather an obvious point, but often the implications and the criticality of this are overlooked.

---

[5] We shall cover this crucial aspect in more detail over Chapters 16, 20, and 23.

Does your organization have the data that is required to undertake data science toward solving your problem? If not, you would first need to define a data strategy aimed toward collecting data that is oriented toward this goal. Data strategy is best defined by someone like a chief data scientist. If you hire a chief data scientist, they can help define the strategy, but until the strategy is executed and data is available, they will be relatively idle. Practically the best bet therefore is getting a consultant in this early stage.

And the Data Was with... Whom Exactly?

If you do have the necessary data, would the data be accessible to the data scientists once they join your organization? In large enterprises where data is split across multiple LoBs and tens, if not hundreds, of applications, the most common complaint of data scientists is that they do not have access to the required data. Creating a data sandbox for data science, and ensuring the necessary plumbing to route data into this sandbox, is often required before data science can begin. This requires defining a strategic roadmap of developing the data pipelines that is aligned with the business problems that data science is trying to solve.

HIRING NOTES

The complexity and extent of data sources may also dictate the initial hires of your data science team – there are some data scientists who will do the necessary data integration and cleansing[6] and others who expect properly curated data to be made available for them so they focus purely on the scientific analysis.[7]

---

[6] Also referred to as data wrangling, munging, and other colorful terms.

[7] We will look at the skills framework of a data science team in Chapter 21.

The Model Said "Here Am I, Send Me"

By now you have ensured that data is available and accessible through the necessary infrastructure. For a successful data science journey, one other aspect to ensure is that the organization processes are mature enough to deploy and consume the data science models that will eventually get created. You would need to coordinate with the engineering teams of the respective systems to ensure this readiness is achieved by the time the models are created.

Businesses often undertake data science and end up with data scientists complaining about the data or with models that do not see the light of day in production. Conducting business readiness analyses along the outlines in this section will help de-risk the data science practice early on.

Conclusion

Business considerations are paramount – even for something as cool as data science; and particularly for something as interdisciplinary as data science. Data science can require quite some investment and readiness from the business – if done right, the RoI can be quite good. But there are a few pitfalls as well, and a hasty decision to embark on data science is often identified rather late in hindsight.

In this chapter, we have covered the benefits that can accrue from data science, as well as the aspects to consider before plunging into data science. In the next chapter, we shall delve deeper into the two cultures of data science and how they relate to your business. As you head toward forming a data science team, these considerations will help identify the kind of skills and scientific *culture* that would be required of your team members to best align with your business' goals.

Further Reading

The business and operational aspects of data science introduced in this chapter will be covered in fuller detail in Part 4 of this book.

Applications of data science to business strategy and management consulting is covered in quite some depth in Curuksu (2018).

References

Curuksu, Jeremy David. *Data Driven, An Introduction to Management Consulting in the 21st Century*. New York, NY: Springer, 2018.

Karamshuk, Dmytro et. al. "Geo-Spotting: Mining Online Location-based Services for Optimal Retail Store Placement." *Proceedings of the 19th ACM SIGKDD international conference on Knowledge discovery and data mining*. Association for Computing Machinery, 2013. 793-801.

CHAPTER 3

Monks vs. Cowboys: Data Science Cultures

Having touched upon data science in the context of your business, it is now time to determine what *culture* of data science is best suited for your business. There are primarily two cultures of data science – the monastic culture (as defined and practiced by monks) and the wild-west culture (as iconized by cowboys).

In this chapter, we shall elaborate on how these two cultures practice data science and the business implications of the two cultures. This will help determine which culture you wish to predominantly inculcate. The predominant culture will drive not only the choice of techniques and tools but also your hiring strategy – monks and cowboys both tend to call themselves data scientists, and discerning who you need in your formative team can be crucial to achieving your business goals.

The Two Cultures of Data Science

Recall from our discussion of the scientific method in Chapter 1, that a model serves two purposes: explaining the observations and predicting future observations. For example, refer to Figure 1-2. In this case, the model uncovers the underlying truth that the salary of an employee starts

© Vineet Raina and Srinath Krishnamurthy 2022
V. Raina and S. Krishnamurthy, *Building an Effective Data Science Practice*,
https://doi.org/10.1007/978-1-4842-7419-4_3

from around 40K and gets raised by (approximately) 8K every year. Based on this understanding, we can predict the salary for future observations of experience as well. Thus, this model[1] fulfils both purposes.

So, given the two purposes – explaining the observations and predicting future observations – *the two cultures of data science* pivot around whether the focus is on both purposes or only on prediction. To clarify this further, let us revisit a few examples we saw in the earlier chapters, delving deeper into the problems being solved.

Recall the *cautionary tale* from Chapter 2, where we saw that the ability to predict the yield of a chemical was not sufficient to help tune the control parameters for optimal yield. In this case, one requires deeper insights into how the chemical process works in *nature,* that is, given the control parameters and initial mixture, how the reaction will proceed over time and the resulting yield. Merely predicting the yield is a relatively simpler problem than determining the interrelationships among all the control parameters themselves and their collective effect on the yield. In these kinds of cases, especially involving *natural* processes, it is often beneficial to focus on estimating the truth underlying the data, that is, the process that might have generated the data. This allows us to control certain parameters to influence the underlying process itself to a great degree. Once understood fully, the chemical process itself is largely unchanging – unless new parameters/chemicals are introduced, we can continue to use the same model forever.

Contrast this to the problem of predicting potential demand for a product at your stores. In this case, we may use the historical sales data and several other data sources such as trends from social media, events

---

[1] Recall as mentioned in Chapter 1 that this is a simplified example for illustrative purposes. More realistic models would incorporate additional factors, and a similar model (linear regression) would then determine relationship between salary and the combined effect of all the other factors.

that might happen around the store location, etc., to build a complex model for predicting demand. In this case, our primary goal is prediction so that we can plan for inventory accordingly.

It may be useful to know which factors affect the demand more than others; in some cases, such as social media factors, we may even attempt to drive trends. But this aspect of controlling the underlying factors is secondary and incidental – demand *prediction* is the goal. As the sales data, social trends, and nearby events keep changing, we are also okay to frequently update our models with the new data.

Compared to the chemical process example earlier, the models in the demand prediction case are looking at shorter-term, relatively contingent aspects, rather than at long-term truths underlying natural processes.

These two extreme examples highlight the hallmarks of the two cultures of data science. One culture focuses on fully understanding the underlying process out of which the observations are generated, and the other culture focuses primarily on being able to predict future observations accurately. Correspondingly, the choices of mathematical, statistical, and algorithmic techniques tend to differ among these two cultures.

We refer to the first culture, focusing on deciphering the underlying truths, as the **monastic culture**. We refer to the second culture, focusing on empirical goals with predictive accuracy, as the **wild-west culture**. In our experience, while expert data scientists *can* navigate both the monastic and the wild-west territories, they tend to innately have a default, predominant culture to them. We shall cover the cultural spectrum of data scientists in a later section of this chapter.

We believe that, ideally, the problem statement and the business goals should dictate which culture/approach is appropriate for the problem. For *some* businesses, it is possible that a hybrid approach is suitable.

Hybrid Cultures

For example, consider a weather company. Since the business is primarily reliant on the natural weather processes, it makes a lot of sense to invest effort in understanding the underlying weather systems in greater detail. This enables the business to technologically advance the field, creating better instruments and sources of gathering data as well as advanced weather models. For this aspect of their business, a monastic culture is appropriate.

The customer facing end of your business might not just be limited to predicting weather. Maybe you are offering advanced services for shipping companies such as routing algorithms based on your weather predictions and other data about oceans. Or maybe you are offering services to coastline industries to predict disruption using models that incorporate your weather models along with other data of the customer's industry. In these cases, the more specific models for your customers could be based on the wild-west culture, because understanding the underlying processes of your client's data is not too beneficial to your core business. It is also reasonable to frequently update these models that are tailored to your customers.

If, at this point, the two cultures seem a bit abstract, don't worry – we shall continue to add more details demarcating these two cultures throughout this book. The primary reason for introducing these two cultures so early in this book is that we believe adopting the culture appropriate to your business is one of the keys to increasing chances of success of your data science practice.

In the following sections, we elaborate on some of the factors pertaining to these two cultures and map these factors to your business' goals.

Cultural Differences

Table 3-1 summarizes the key differences between the two cultures. We shall continue to add to this table in Chapter 20.

Table 3-1. *Monastic vs. wild west: first edition*

Factor	Monastic culture	Wild-west culture
Mindset	Find the underlying, eternal truth (nature) which led to (caused) the observations	Find what works *now*. Can update frequently. Empiricism is the only eternal truth
Purposes	Estimation of *truth* behind the observations, which enables prediction and deeper, accurate causative[2] insights	Predictive accuracy is the primary goal Causation is often a casualty. Causative insights are either irrelevant, less accurate, or just good to have
Evaluation	How close to the truth is my estimation?	Am I getting the predictions as accurately as I wanted to?

In the next section, we shall look at how these cultural factors relate to your business.

---

[2] Note that we are referring to *causality* loosely and intuitively here. Data scientists never confidently derive causality; they only attempt to derive insights that are indicative of likely causation. In Chapter 20, we shall be more technically precise about this.

Data Science Culture and Your Business

Though we are yet to understand how monks and cowboys do their work, and how they *differ* in praxis, we do have a sufficient idea of what motivates them fundamentally. Based on this, we can already see outlines of how to identify which culture is more appropriate to your business problems. Table 3-2 summarizes these factors. It is important to note that these are not exhaustive or prescriptive – they are only indicative.

Table 3-2. *Which culture would be suited for your business?*

Factor	Monastic culture appropriate if	Wild-west culture appropriate if
Business goals	Advancing a natural science is a business strategy, for example, getting insights into weather systems[3]	Management, tactical decision-making, or product/operational enhancements are the strategic goals, for example, demand prediction[4]
Etiology (causation)	Etiology is crucial, for example, impact of control parameters in a chemical process[5]	Etiology is good to have or irrelevant, for example, demand prediction, Netflix recommendations, etc.

(continued)

---

[3] Another example: human speech production based on other health factors.

[4] Also refer to other examples in Chapter 2.

[5] Another example: clinical trials for a disease condition.

Table 3-2. (*continued*)

Factor	Monastic culture appropriate if	Wild-west culture appropriate if
Data homogeneity	Your data is from a specific population/environment so that a single, true, underlying (natural) process that generated the data can be determined, for example, a chemical process in your company[6]	You are in big data territory, with multiple data sources and varied population/environments, where a single underlying truth may not exist, for example, demand prediction using social media and historical sales

In some cases, even within one business, different problems may seem to require different cultures. When we look at the *extant* problems in a business cohesively, one *predominant* culture tends to emerge – often this predominant culture then suffices for *future* problems as well.

For the occasional problem that deviates significantly from the predominant culture, a pragmatic approach would be to get a consultant on board for that specific problem. For example, if you inculcate a wild-west culture and there is one problem that requires etiological insights (e.g., say biological causative factors are relevant to the context of your problem), you can get a consulting monk (e.g., biostatistician) to help.

---

[6] Clinical trials are the archetype of data homogeneity.

The Cultural Spectrum of Data Scientists

The *monks vs. cowboys* dichotomy of data scientists is better viewed as a spectrum of traits as shown in Figure 3-1.

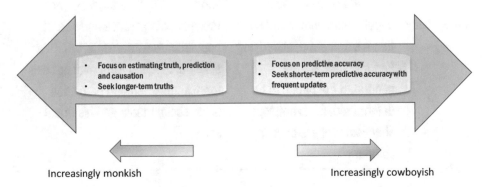

- Focus on estimating truth, prediction and causation
- Seek longer-term truths

- Focus on predictive accuracy
- Seek shorter-term predictive accuracy with frequent updates

Increasingly monkish   Increasingly cowboyish

Figure 3-1. *Data scientists – spectrum of traits*

While experts from either culture are usually flexible to adapt themselves as needed, it is often smoother if your team's formative members are closer to the culture that aligns with your business goals.

Theory and Experimentation in Data Science

Most scientific endeavors have two intermingled aspects – theory and experimentation. For example, in physics, proposing new candidate models such as Einstein's or Newton's models of gravitation[7] is the *theoretical* aspect. Conducting experiments to collect data – because there are not enough observations to either create a model or to validate a model – is the *experimental* aspect. Eddington and Dyson's expeditions are an example of experimentation.

---

[7] Seen in Chapter 1.

As in any other scientific field, data science too requires theory and experimentation. In case of data science, the theory consists of the numerous statistical techniques and algorithms used in the data science process that form the arsenal of a data scientist. Experimentation consists of writing software code to apply these techniques iteratively to arrive at candidate models.

Both monks and cowboys use statistical techniques and algorithms – their *default* choices in praxis typically differ though, depending on where they fall within the earlier spectrum. Correspondingly, the preferred methodologies of theory and experimentation also vary between the two cultures. Intuitively, the monastic culture tends to lean more toward formal statistical methods and experimentation driven by human insights. The wild-west culture, on the other hand, tends to lean toward increasingly complex algorithms and automation,[8] as shown in Figure 3-2. We shall cover these variations with concrete examples and summarize the cultural aspects with more technical details in Chapter 20.

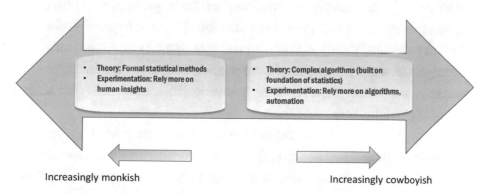

Figure 3-2. *Theory and experimentation in the two cultures*

---

[8] Automation can be at various levels, from automated feature extraction (e.g., from images using CNNs) to automating model choices (e.g., AutoML). We shall cover these in Part 3.

Note that, as mentioned in the previous section, this figure only illustrates the traits at the extremes. Data scientists typically cover the entire earlier spectrum, but lean toward one end of the spectrum to varying extents.

These aspects indirectly influence the infrastructural and engineering needs of the data science team.

Data Engineering

The engineering requirements are often driven by the data science culture. This is primarily related to the *data homogeneity* factor discussed previously.

If your data scientists are primarily monkish, they may prefer homogenous data because it's more amenable to discovering an underlying "truth." With heterogeneous data, it is less likely that there will be a single underlying truth to be discovered. Thus, they might typically work on data that is relatively contained and homogenous. This often implies that more data engineering effort may be spent to provide clean, relevant subsets of the data. Such dataset sizes typically are amenable to analysis on a single machine.[9] Monks often tend to analyze a single homogenous dataset for several weeks crafting their models as they obtain increasing insights about the truth.

Cowboys, on the other hand, do not have a specific preference for homogenous data. They often work with heterogeneous data obtained from multiple sources, characteristic of big data. At the very extreme, they would run deep learning on multiple GPUs during the machine learning step. Given the heterogeneous nature of their data, they also iterate more rapidly over multiple variations, starting from the data preparation step.

---

[9] As big as needed, often on the cloud. But still, typically a single machine rather than a cluster.

In this case, more data engineering effort is spent in efficient access to big data for all the steps in the data science process, including for data preparation, data visualization, and machine learning.

It is important to note that these are just a few observations based on our experience – we have seen deviations from these typical trends. Eventually, it all depends on the specific approach being taken by the data scientists for the problem at hand.

Conclusion

The two cultures in data science have been introduced – the undercurrent of differences between these cultures will appear throughout this book. This discussion will continue in Chapter 20, where we will summarize further differences, including technical aspects.

We also touched upon how the business goals can outline the appropriate culture – to establish the appropriate culture, the data science team needs to be formed accordingly of monks or cowboys. In Chapter 22, we shall revisit the defining characteristics of monks and cowboys, particularly with respect to their skills and background – this will help outline the team formation aspects based on the desired culture.

Summary of Part 1

With this, we conclude Part 1 of this book. We covered the data science process in Chapter 1 and how data science relates to your business in Chapter 2. In this chapter, we saw more details of the scientific approach, especially the two cultures within data science. The key takeaway is that business goals should determine how the data science practice is bootstrapped – this part of the book has broadly covered these formative factors.

We are now ready to delve deeper into the classes of problems that are solved using data science. We shall cover these in Part 2.

PART II

Classes of Problems

In Part 1, you read about what data science is and how it promises to be useful for businesses in general. You will now naturally be curious to learn more about the concrete problems data science can solve and understand how these problems relate to the problems in your business/organization.

A good way to learn about the data science problems is to first understand the classes of problems. Many individual problems can be mapped to one of these classes and require similar treatment though each problem has its own unique set of challenges to be addressed. This part of the book talks about the classes of problems that are solved using data science and contains one chapter for each class that walks through a concrete problem from that class – the chapter first establishes a business motive and then transforms that motive to a concrete data science problem and shows how you could solve it by choosing the appropriate techniques for each step of the *data science process*. The techniques we have chosen for each problem are just some examples meant only to give an overview of the thought process that goes into solving such a problem. Based on the exact nature of the problem that you might want to solve, you will have to yourself design the steps of the data science process by choosing from the plethora of techniques that are covered in more detail later in Part 3. We will also cover the libraries/tools that help you apply these techniques in Part 3.

You might relate to some of the business problems covered in these chapters in the context of your business, which might provide you some hints about what business problems you could target. These chapters should also equip you with the skill of converting those business problems into data science problems.

TERMINOLOGY CHAOS: CLASSIFICATION AND REGRESSION

The meaning of terms like *classification* and *regression* depends on the context – they can refer either to classes of problems or to categories of machine learning algorithms.

The titles of the first two chapters in this part ("Classification" and "Regression") refer to classes of problems and ***not*** to categories of machine learning algorithms. Hence, these two chapters talk about classification and regression *problems*. (The same holds for the other chapter titles in this part, including "Clustering," etc.)

Note that machine learning algorithms and their categories (including classification and regression *algorithms*) are discussed in detail later in Part 3 (Chapter 16).

CHAPTER 4

Classification

Let's begin with a common class of problems called *classification* problems. A classification problem requires you to infer/predict the class/category to which a new observation belongs based on values of some observed attributes. For example, infer whether a mail is "Spam" or "Regular" based on the body of the mail, sender's email address, etc.; infer whether a digital payment transaction is "Fraud" or "Non-Fraud" based on the details of the transaction like the location of the transaction, the amount and mode of payment, etc.

Let's say an automobile company has launched a new car and the marketing team has executed an effective advertising strategy leading to a steady stream of inquiries from interested customers. Data science can help identify interested customers who are likely to eventually buy the car so that the sales team can focus on such customers leading to improved sales. This is a classification problem since the goal here is to infer whether an interested customer belongs to the class of customers who buy the car or to the class who don't. Let's look at the detailed steps of the data science process that you could follow to achieve this goal. This being the first end-to-end problem we are discussing, we will discuss its steps in more detail compared to problems covered in the following chapters. We will also use this first problem to introduce some new terms that we will use throughout the book.

© Vineet Raina and Srinath Krishnamurthy 2022
V. Raina and S. Krishnamurthy, *Building an Effective Data Science Practice*,
https://doi.org/10.1007/978-1-4842-7419-4_4

Data Capture

The goal is to predict which customers would eventually buy the car. The source of all magic in data science is **data**. You could use the past data containing details of interested customers of previous similar cars if it is available. If that data is not available, you would define a strategy to capture the relevant details of a first few interested customers. This data would then be used in the later steps of the data science process to build models that can predict which interested customers coming in future are likely to buy the car based on the trends seen in the initial customers. So, as part of your data capture strategy, you might direct the sales team to capture the *Gender, Age, Occupation, and Annual Income*[1] of each initial customer along with the *Outcome* for that customer indicating whether the customer purchased the car or not. You believe that it should be possible to predict with reasonable accuracy the *Outcome* of an interested customer based on the values of the other four variables. The variables based on which you make the predictions (*Gender, Age,* etc., in this case) are referred to as *features,* and the variable whose value you try to predict (*Outcome* in this case) is referred to as the *target*. Note that the values of the *target* variable here just like in all *classification* problems are classes (Purchased, Not Purchased, etc.). A snapshot of the data collected is shown in Figure 4-1. Assume that, in this case, the sales team manually enters these details in an excel file. We will discuss how you can capture data programmatically and the tools/libraries that help you do this in Part 3.

---

[1] Annual income reported in USD.

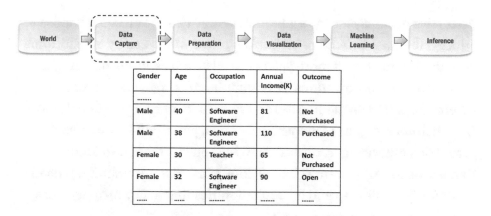

Gender	Age	Occupation	Annual Income(K)	Outcome
....	....	....	....	....
Male	40	Software Engineer	81	Not Purchased
Male	38	Software Engineer	110	Purchased
Female	30	Teacher	65	Not Purchased
Female	32	Software Engineer	90	Open
....	....	....	....	....

Figure 4-1. *Snapshot of data collected in the data capture step*

Data Preparation

After you have captured the data, you need to prepare the data in various ways for building effective models. The data we have captured in the previous step has some rows where *Outcome* is *open* which indicates an ongoing inquiry. These are customers who had initiated inquiry and were in active discussions with sales team when the data was captured. Since we do not know whether these customers will eventually buy the car or not, the data of such customers is not relevant for building our predictive model. As part of preparing the data, we will remove the observations for such customers. If you look at the snapshot of data prepared by the *data preparation* step in Figure 4-2, you will notice that the data preparation step has removed observations of such customers.

While working on classification problems, you might also run into the scenario where the classes in the *target* variable are not equally represented. For example, you might have many more customers whose *Outcome* is *Not Purchased* compared to those whose *Outcome* is *Purchased*. This is referred to as *class imbalance* and might lead to low predictive accuracy for the underrepresented class.[2] You could choose to address the *class imbalance* in the *data preparation* step by transforming your dataset to make it more balanced.[3] Also, the captured data might have erroneous observations. For example, you might encounter rows where age is "0" which indicates an error while entering the details for that customer. As part of preparing the data, you should remove such erroneous observations/rows; otherwise, you risk creating a model that learns incorrect trends. We will look at a few more techniques used commonly in this step and the tools/libraries that help you apply these techniques to your data in Part 3.

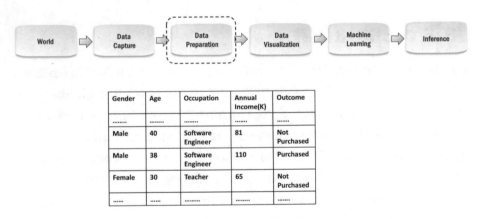

Gender	Age	Occupation	Annual Income(K)	Outcome
....	....	....	....	....
Male	40	Software Engineer	81	Not Purchased
Male	38	Software Engineer	110	Purchased
Female	30	Teacher	65	Not Purchased
....	....	....	....	....

Figure 4-2. *Snapshot of data prepared by the data preparation step*

---

[2] We recommend an in-depth study of the class imbalance problem.

[3] There are a few simple techniques commonly used for modifying datasets to make them more balanced. We recommend familiarizing yourself with these.

Data Visualization

In this step, you can analyze your *prepared data* using powerful visualizations to get insights into the trends. These insights are useful in various ways and can help you build effective models in the *machine learning* step. Figure 4-3 shows a visualization created in this step based on our prepared data. The visualization here is a stacked bar chart that stacks the number of customers who didn't purchase the car on top of the customers who purchased the car for every income segment. Overall height of each bar depicts the total interested customers for the corresponding segment, and the green portion in each bar indicates the interested customers who actually purchased the car in that segment. We can see that we have had more interested customers in the past for higher-income segments. Also, the percentage of interested customers who purchased the car seems to be higher in the higher-income segments. This means that *Annual Income* seems to have an impact on whether a customer will eventually buy the car, that is, *Annual Income* seems to impact the *Outcome*. This insight should make you feel more confident about your decision of using *Annual Income* for building models that predict the *Outcome*. You could visualize other features as well, and once you feel confident about your choice of features, you are ready for the next step, *machine learning*.

As mentioned earlier, since this is a *classification* problem, the values in the *target* variable are classes (*Purchased, Not Purchased*) which we have stacked in this visualization. The visualizations would be different if the *target* variable contained continuous values (e.g., salary) as in the case of regression problems which are discussed in the next chapter. Data visualization is a vast subject in itself, and the art of designing the right visualizations for your problem can help you easily uncover trends which would otherwise be difficult to identify. We will look at a few more popular visualizations and the tool/libraries you can use to create these visualizations in Part 3.

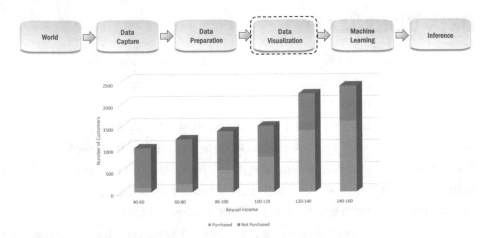

Figure 4-3. *Data visualization for our classification problem*

Machine Learning

Since the values in our *target* variable are classes (*Purchased, Not Purchased*), we will use one of the *classification* machine learning algorithms in this step. *Classification* machine learning algorithms learn from the past observations to infer the class for a new observation. We choose a decision tree algorithm here for simplicity since we haven't yet introduced the more complex algorithms which are discussed later in Part 3 of the book. The corresponding tools/libraries that implement such algorithms are also discussed in Part 3.

The *decision tree* algorithm builds a *decision tree* model based on our prepared data. Figure 4-4 shows a partial view of our *decision tree* model that focuses on the portions relevant to this discussion and omits other details. Note that the decision tree has learned that females below 35 years of age do not buy the car irrespective of their occupation or income. On the other hand, males above 35 years of age with income above 100K buy the car irrespective of their occupation. This model is now capable of predicting which interested customers in the future are likely to buy the car.

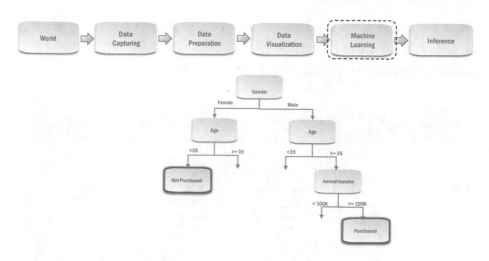

Figure 4-4. *Partial view of the decision tree model created by the machine learning step*

Inference

Now that all the hard work has been done, it is time to reap the benefits. You can now deploy the model you just created in production environment and request application developers to create an app which a sales executive can use for predicting whether a new customer will purchase the car. The sales executive will fill the details (Gender, Age, Occupation, Annual Income) of a new interested customer in the app which will pass on these details to your deployed model for prediction. The model will traverse the tree based on the details to do the prediction. Figure 4-5 shows how the deployed *decision tree* model traverses the tree based on the details of a new customer to predict the *Outcome*. The new customer here is a female of age 30, so the model will go left[4] at *Gender* node and then go left again at *Age* node and predict *Not Purchased* indicating that the customer is not likely to buy the car. The app will receive this predicted *Outcome* and show it on the

---

[4] Reader's left.

executive's screen. We will look at a few common approaches for deploying models and using them for inference/prediction in the production environment and the related tools/libraries in Part 3.

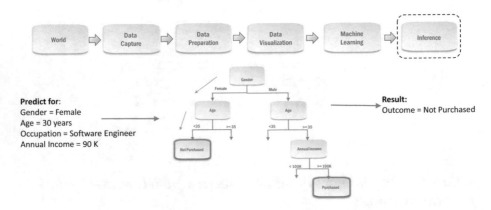

Figure 4-5. *Traversal of decision tree model during inference*

Data Engineering

Data engineering takes care of storage and access of data throughout the *data science process* as shown in Figure 4-6. In this example, we assumed that data was stored in a spreadsheet in the data capture step and later read into an appropriate data structure in the later steps. So we didn't require heavy *data engineering* for our scenario, but *data engineering* becomes important for ensuring efficient storage and fast access when you are dealing with large amounts of data. We will look at a few techniques for efficient storage and access of data and related tools/libraries in Part 3. We will skip the data engineering section for other problems in the following chapters unless a problem requires unique treatment from the point of view of data engineering.

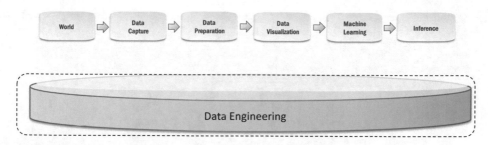

Figure 4-6. *Data engineering for our classification problem*

Conclusion

Classification problems are among the most common types of problems that data scientists work on. So if you are setting up a data science practice, it is highly likely that you or your team will end up working on one. In this chapter, we looked at what classification problems are and discussed a concrete scenario to demonstrate how such problems are tackled.

CHAPTER 5

Regression

A *regression* problem requires you to infer/predict a quantity corresponding to a new observation based on the values of some observed attributes. The problems we briefly discussed in Chapter 1 which aimed at predicting the salary of a person based on their experience and predicting the amount of rainfall based on the temperature, pressure, etc., were both examples of *regression* problems.

Let's say you are an insurance company that offers health insurance policies and want to optimize the insurance premium for maximizing profits. While you may want to offer an affordable premium to attract customers, you would charge higher premium for customers who arc likely to claim high amounts in order to reduce your losses. You can build models that predict the amount that a customer is likely to claim and use that as one of the factors for deciding the final premium for that customer. This is a regression problem since we want to predict a quantity *Claim Amount*. Let's look at the possible techniques you could use in the different steps of the data science process for this problem.

© Vineet Raina and Srinath Krishnamurthy 2022
V. Raina and S. Krishnamurthy, *Building an Effective Data Science Practice*,
https://doi.org/10.1007/978-1-4842-7419-4_5

Data Capture

You would begin by looking at the stored policy records of past users and their claim details. Let's look at the factors that can affect the amount that a customer claims. Older people are more likely to need medical care and hence might claim higher amounts. People with higher BMI could claim higher amounts because they are at higher risk of having heart disease. Similarly, smokers might claim higher amounts because of the adverse effects it has on health. There are many other factors like gender, profession, etc., on which the amount a person will claim depends. You might pull all such relevant details (*Age, Smoking Status*, etc.) that can act as *features* for our model along with the *Claim Amount* which is our *target* from the policy records into another location for easy access in subsequent steps of the data science process. For simplicity, we will only focus on *Age, Smoking Status,* and *Gender* as features. Note that the target variable here just like in all *regression* problems is continuous valued. We will assume that each customer has only one yearly policy and the *Claim Amount* is the total amount that was claimed in the corresponding year by that customer. A snapshot of the data extracted from policy records is shown in Figure 5-1. Each row here corresponds to one user and their policy.[1]

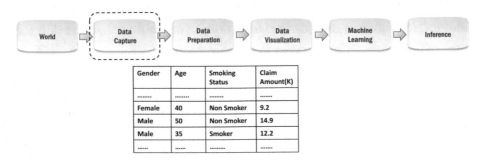

Gender	Age	Smoking Status	Claim Amount(K)
....	....	....	....
Female	40	Non Smoker	9.2
Male	50	Non Smoker	14.9
Male	35	Smoker	12.2
....	....	....	....

Figure 5-1. *Data extracted from policy records*

---

[1] Claim amount measured in USD.

Data Preparation

Since this is a regression problem, you will need to choose a *regression* machine learning algorithm in your machine learning step later. As is often the case, let's say you decide to use the *linear regression* algorithm in your initial experiments. Linear regression tries to create a linear equation that explains how the value of the target variable can be calculated from the values of features. The example from Chapter 1 where the machine learning step came up with the equation "Salary (K) = 8 × Experience (yrs) + 40" is an example of linear regression. It is obvious that such an equation will work only for *numeric* features, that is, features whose values are numbers. In our captured data, *Age* is a numeric feature, but we also have features like *Gender* that are *categorical*, that is, they contain categories or classes (e.g., Male/Female).

So as part of preparing our data, we will need to convert our categorical features (*Gender, Smoking Status*) to numeric features. Each of these features has just two possible values so you can easily encode one value as *0* and the other value as *1*. Hence, for Gender, you could encode *Male* as *1* and *Female* as *0*. For Smoking Status, you could encode *Smoker* as *1* and *Non Smoker* as *0*. Figure 5-2 shows a partial snapshot of the prepared data after the encoding.

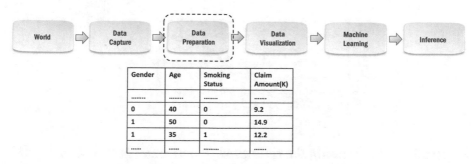

Gender	Age	Smoking Status	Claim Amount(K)
....	....	....	....
0	40	0	9.2
1	50	0	14.9
1	35	1	12.2
......	......	....	....

Figure 5-2. *Prepared data with encoded categorical features*

Data Visualization

Let us now explore our target variable and its relationships with the features visually. Since this is a regression problem, the target variable contains continuous values, and hence, we design visualizations that would be useful in such a scenario. Let us focus on visualizing the relationship of the target *Claim Amount* with *Age*. You could generate a scatter plot that displays each customer/policy as a marker whose x coordinate is based on the customer's *Age* and y coordinate is based on their *Claim Amount*. You can simplify the exploration by restricting it to just one segment of customers at a time – let's look at customers who are females and nonsmokers. If you look at Figure 5-3, you will notice that Claim Amount has a linear relationship with Age. Let's say you notice a linear relationship of Claim Amount with Age for other segments (male smokers, male nonsmokers, etc.) as well. This makes this scenario suitable for trying out the linear regression algorithm which could figure out this linear relationship. So now you have a convincing reason to use linear regression in the machine learning step.

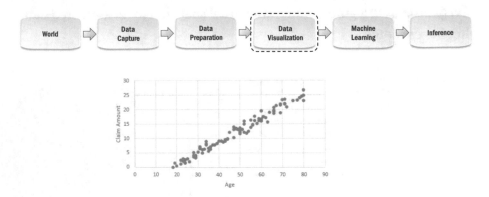

Figure 5-3. *Visualizing the relationship between claim amount and age*

Machine Learning

Since our *target* variable contains continuous values, we will use one of the *regression* machine learning algorithms in this step. *Regression* machine learning algorithms learn from the past observations to predict a quantity corresponding to a new observation. We have already discussed various reasons for using the linear regression algorithm to build our predictive model for this case.

The *linear regression* algorithm builds a *linear regression* model based on the prepared data which, as discussed earlier, is a linear equation that explains how the target variable value can be calculated from the values of features. Figure 5-4 shows the linear equation created by the linear regression algorithm for this problem. Based on this equation, we can tell that Claim Amount increases by 0.4K with every year of Age. We can also tell that for males (Gender = 1), Claim Amount is higher by 2.1K as compared to females. And smokers (Smoking Status =1) tend to claim 2.9K more than nonsmokers. This model is now capable of predicting the Claim Amount for a new customer based on their age, gender, and smoking status.

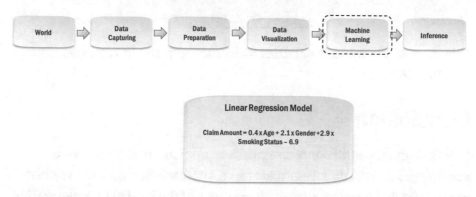

Figure 5-4. *Linear regression model created by the machine learning step*

Inference

The linear regression model we just created can be deployed and used for predicting the Claim Amount for a new customer. The model will simply use the equation to calculate the Claim Amount using the Age, Gender, and Smoking Status. Figure 5-5 shows how the deployed linear regression model calculates the Claim Amount using the equation for two new customers. The model predicts that the second customer who is a male smoker is likely to claim a higher amount than the first customer despite being the younger one. So you will recommend that the second customer should be charged a higher premium.

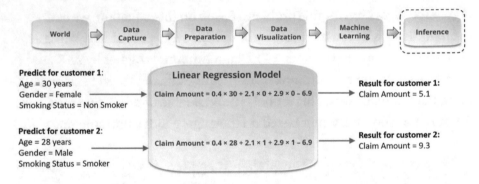

Figure 5-5. *Prediction of claim amount using the linear equation during inference*

Conclusion

In this chapter, we introduced regression problems and discussed a specific problem in detail as an example. We discussed the data science process for this problem to give an overview of the kind of techniques that could be used for this class of problems. As mentioned earlier, each new problem will require you to decide the techniques best suited for solving it.

CHAPTER 6

Natural Language Processing

AI, as discussed in Chapter 1, refers to computers behaving intelligently like humans. One aspect of human intelligence is the capability of understanding and speaking languages. The subfield of AI that focuses on making computers seemingly intelligent in understanding and generating languages just like humans is called *natural language processing*. We will henceforth refer to this subfield by the popular acronym *NLP*. Teaching computers how to understand and speak natural languages offers a plethora of benefits. Humans can do mathematical calculations, but when computers learn to do them, they can perform much more complex calculations much faster than humans would. Similarly, when computers learn human languages, they can process much more language data which opens up myriad possibilities.

© Vineet Raina and Srinath Krishnamurthy 2022
V. Raina and S. Krishnamurthy, *Building an Effective Data Science Practice*,
https://doi.org/10.1007/978-1-4842-7419-4_6

As just discussed, NLP involves making computers *understand* and *generate* human languages. The former is called *natural language understanding* or *NLU*, and the latter is called *natural language generation* or *NLG*. Let's look at a few common NLP problems:

- **Sentiment analysis** refers to finding the overall sentiment of a piece of text. For example, finding whether a review from a customer is positive or negative. Performing sentiment analysis on all reviews available on different platforms for a product your company makes can give you an overall idea of how the product is being received by customers.

- **Document classification** refers to assigning documents to classes or categories. Sentiment analysis can be considered as a special case of document classification where the classes are positive, negative, or neutral.

- **Autocomplete** refers to predicting the rest of the text based on the first few characters typed. For example, predicting the text of your query as you begin typing in the search box of a search engine can save you from the pain of typing the entire text on the small keyboard of your phone.

- **Language translation** refers to translating the text in one language to a different language.

- **Intent classification** refers to assigning an intent (from a given set of intents) to a piece of text. For example, chatbots could use intent classification to figure out if the intent for the text typed by user is *Purchase* or *Install* or some other intent and then send back details relevant to the intent.

- **Text summarization** refers to automatic creation of summary for a large piece of text.

Just like its parent field *AI*, there are two approaches to NLP: rule-based approach and data science approach. Let's look at a document classification problem in detail and see how you can solve it using the data science approach. Let's say your company has a personal assistant product that helps the user manage their to-do list, emails, meetings, devices, etc., based on voice commands from them. Let's say the user of this personal assistant is an engineer who receives emails related to product development, research work, trainings, etc. They may find it useful to create a folder for each such category and organize their emails by moving each email to its relevant folder. You could add an interesting feature to the assistant that automatically moves the user's emails to their correct folders. For example, if the user has received an email requesting them to complete an online training, the assistant could figure out, based on the text in the email, that the email belongs to the category "Trainings" and hence move it to the folder "Trainings". This problem falls under *document classification* since the goal here is to assign each document (email in this case) to a category. Let's take a look at how data science can help you achieve this goal by choosing the appropriate techniques in each step.

Data Capture

The assistant silently observes the user in the initial period as they move the emails to the appropriate folders. This initial manual movement of emails captures the necessary data using which the assistant will learn how to automatically determine the right folder for each email in the future based on the email text without asking the user. Figure 6-1 shows the folders and some sample emails that have been moved into these folders by the user.

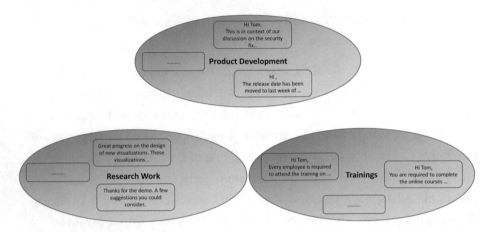

Figure 6-1. *Snapshot of emails and the containing folders*

Data Preparation

The solution to this problem is different from the ones we discussed so far, as all the steps of the data science process are automated inside the assistant, instead of a data scientist performing each step. As part of the data preparation, the assistant could strip the *greeting* (e.g., *Hi Tom,*) and *closing* (e.g., *Regards, Rich*) from each email and tag the remaining email body with its *Category* which is the name of the folder containing that email. Figure 6-2 shows a snapshot of the consolidated data which has the stripped email bodies tagged with their categories. The idea is that the assistant will use this data to build a model that learns how to infer the category of an email by looking at the important words in the email body.

Email_Body	Category
This is in context of our discussion on the security fix...	Product Development
The release date has been moved to last week of ...	Product Development
Great progress on the design of new visualizations. These visualizations...	Research Work
Thanks for the demo. A few suggestions you could consider..	Research Work
Every employee is required to attend the training on ...	Trainings
You are required to complete the online courses ...	Trainings
....	....
....	....

Figure 6-2. *Prepared data containing email bodies and their categories*

Next, the assistant preprocesses each email body by removing punctuation, converting it to lowercase, extracting individual words, and removing stop words like "a", "in", "the", etc., which might not be useful for inferring the category of an email. Figure 6-3 shows the prepared data after these preprocessing steps.

Email_Words	Category
'context', 'discussion', 'security', 'fix', …	Product Development
'release', 'date', 'moved', 'last', 'week',…	Product Development
'great', 'progress', 'design', 'new', 'visualizations', 'visualizations',…	Research Work
'thanks', 'demo', 'suggestions', 'could', 'consider',…	Research Work
'every', 'employee', 'required', 'attend', 'training',…	Trainings
'required', 'complete', 'online', 'courses',…	Trainings
………………	………………
………………	………………

Figure 6-3. *Prepared data after removal of punctuation, conversion to lowercase, tokenization, and removal of stop words*

As mentioned previously, the assistant is attempting to learn how to infer the category by looking at the occurrence of important words in the email body. The different inflected forms of words might not give any additional clue about the category of an email. For example, it does not matter whether an email contains the word "course" or "courses", both indicate that the email might belong to the category "Trainings." Hence, the assistant could perform lemmatization on the email words which will convert the inflected forms of words back into their base forms. So "course" and "courses" in all emails will become "course" which is the base word. Converting multiple inflected forms to their base words across all emails will also reduce the vocabulary (total set of unique words) that the assistant has to deal with. Figure 6-4 shows the prepared data after lemmatization – the column *Email_Base_Words* contains the base forms of email words. To keep things simple, we have intentionally avoided a detailed handling of *parts of speech*[1] during lemmatization. On real projects, you might want to take into account the part of speech to which each word belongs when performing lemmatization.

Email_ Base_Words	Category
'context', 'discussion', 'security', 'fix',...	Product Development
'release', 'date', 'move', 'last', 'week',...	Product Development
'great', 'progress', 'design', 'new', 'visualization', 'visualization',...	Research Work
'thank', 'demo', 'suggestion', 'could', 'consider',...	Research Work
'every', 'employee', 'require', 'attend', 'train',...	Trainings
'require', 'complete', 'online', 'course',...	Trainings
....	....
....	....

Figure 6-4. *Prepared data after lemmatization*

The assistant will create a model that learns to infer the *Category* of an email. Hence, *Category* in the prepared data is the target variable for the model. But the model will also need features based on whose values it will do the prediction. So, the assistant will use some mechanism to extract features from the *Email_Base_Words*. Let's assume the assistant uses the *bag-of-words* technique to achieve this – we will look at a more advanced technique used for this purpose in Chapter 14. Bag-of-words will determine the vocabulary which is the total set of unique base words across all emails and then create one feature for every base word in the vocabulary. The value of a feature for an email is the number of times the corresponding base word occurred in that email. Figure 6-5 shows a

---

[1] For example, verb, noun, etc.

partial view of the features extracted using the bag-of-words technique; the figure also shows the target variable *Category*. You can see that there is one feature corresponding to each base word in our vocabulary. The value of the feature *fix* for the first email is "1" because the base word *fix* appeared once in the list of base words for this email. The value of this feature for the second email is "0" as the second email does not contain the word *fix*. Similarly, the value of feature *visualization* is "2" for the third email as the list of base words for this email contains the word "visualization" twice. Now that the features and target are available, the assistant can move on to the next steps of the data science process. Since there is no data scientist actively involved here who can look at visualizations and draw insights from them, the assistant will move directly to the machine learning step.

context	...	security	fix	release	...	...	design	...	visualization	...	demo	suggestion	...	...	attend	train	...	...	course	...	...	Category
1	...	1	1	0	...	...	0	...	0	...	0	0	...	...	0	0	...	...	0	...	...	Product Development
0	...	0	0	1	...	...	0	...	0	...	0	0	...	...	0	0	...	...	0	...	...	Product Development
0	...	0	0	0	...	...	1	...	2	...	0	0	...	...	0	0	...	...	0	...	...	Research Work
0	...	0	0	0	...	...	0	...	0	...	1	1	...	...	0	0	...	...	0	...	...	Research Work
0	...	0	0	0	...	...	0	...	0	...	0	0	...	...	1	1	...	...	0	...	...	Trainings
0	...	0	0	0	...	...	0	...	0	...	0	0	...	...	0	0	...	...	1	...	...	Trainings
...	...	...	...	...	...	...	...	...	...	...	...	...	...	...	...	...	...	...	...	...	...	....
...	...	...	...	...	...	...	...	...	...	...	...	...	...	...	...	...	...	...	...	...	....

Figure 6-5. *The features and target after application of bag-of-words technique*

Machine Learning

The assistant will now give this prepared data to a machine learning algorithm which can learn how to infer the *Category* to which an email belongs based on the values of the features. This problem is now reduced to a plain classification problem, so we won't go into too much detail as we have already discussed such classification problems in an earlier chapter. The assistant could try different available classification machine learning algorithms including deep learning algorithms. We will talk about deep learning in Chapter 16. The assistant will also need a mechanism to evaluate how well the models produced by different algorithms are able to infer the categories of emails. Based on the performance evaluation, it can decide which model has the best performance and whether that performance is good enough for it to start inferring the categories of new emails and accordingly moving them to their right folders. We will look at this crucial aspect of evaluating model performance later in Chapter 16. Once the assistant has zeroed in on a model that looks promising, it will switch to the inference mode.

Inference

The assistant till now was just observing and learning; now it becomes active and tries to route new emails to their correct folders. It will use the model that it has created to infer the category of each new incoming email and move it to the folder corresponding to that category. But the model, as discussed in the previous section, can only infer the category based on the values of the features. This means that the assistant will need to extract the feature values from each new email and then pass them to the model for inference. To do this, it will follow the same preprocessing steps described in the data preparation section earlier. Figure 6-6 shows a new incoming email and the preprocessing it goes through before inference. The greeting and closing are removed first, followed by removal of punctuation, conversion to lowercase, extraction of words, and removal of stop words. This is followed by lemmatization, and finally, the bag-of-words is applied on the list of base words to generate the feature values which are passed on to the model. Note that the values of features *fix* and *release* are both "1" as the list of base words for this email has one occurrence of both words. The model then infers based on the feature values that the category of the email is *Product Development,* so the assistant moves the email to the folder *Product Development.*

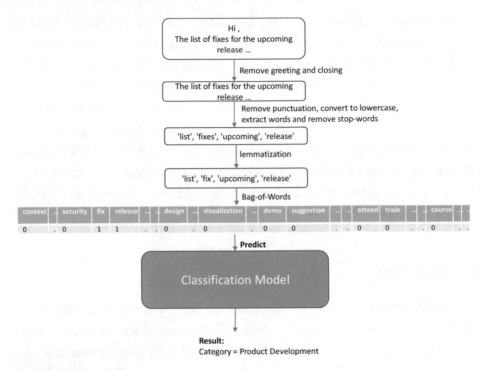

Figure 6-6. *Inference using the model with the features extracted from the new email*

It may happen that the model infers the category for an email incorrectly and the assistant ends up putting the email in the wrong folder. When the user reads the email, they will move it to the right folder which acts as feedback for the assistant. The next time the assistant repeats the entire process of using the emails and their folders to build a model, the new model will automatically learn from the new emails and their folders. When the assistant starts using the new model, the emails that might have got incorrectly classified earlier might now get correctly classified. So, over time, the assistant keeps getting better at moving the emails to the correct folders.

Conclusion

NLP is a popular subfield of AI that is advancing at a fast pace. We saw the two aspects of NLP and briefly looked at a few common NLP problems. We discussed the data science approach to NLP and walked through the steps for making a personal assistant product capable of moving emails to the appropriate folders. This involved a discussion of some common text preprocessing steps used in NLP. The steps also covered how text is transformed into numeric features that are used by the ML models.

CHAPTER 7

Clustering

We tend to determine, almost instinctively, when two objects are similar or dissimilar to each other. For example, when we see all the myriad objects in nature, we tend to divide them into two groups: one that is able to ingest food and convert it to energy, is able to reproduce etc. and the second group of objects that do not show these characteristics. Once we discern two such apparently distinct groups, we give them a name – *living* and *nonliving* things. While this may seem like a simplistic example, similar groupings based on biological characteristics, evolution, etc., lead to various biological taxonomies.[1]

The same tendency is seen when a company such as a retail store is interested in grouping its customers based on their demographics, purchase patterns, and other personal details.

These are a couple of examples of a fundamental aspect of our human "intelligence" – our innate tendency and ability to create groups of *similar* objects/observations, that is, create groups such that an observation is more similar to other observations in its group, than it is to observations in other groups. We refer to such groups of observations as *clusters*. And we refer to the class of problems that involve identifying clusters given a set of observations as *clustering*.

---

[1] For example, see https://tree.opentreeoflife.org/

V. Raina and S. Krishnamurthy, *Building an Effective Data Science Practice*,
https://doi.org/10.1007/978-1-4842-7419-4_7

For clustering, we first decide which characteristics/attributes of the observations to focus on. Once the clusters are created based on these attributes, we analyze the clusters to understand what exactly the similarities within each cluster are; this then results in a name and a useful description for each cluster. Finally, such insights about these clusters lead to certain business benefits – such as determining the appropriate marketing campaigns for targeted customers segments (clusters) of a retail store.

In this chapter, we shall look at an end-to-end example of clustering customers based on their purchase patterns. This will illustrate how clustering problems are solved using the data science process to yield insights from the data.

Data Capture

Let us suppose we have data about customer transactions at a store, containing details of the various products purchased by a customer as shown in Figure 7-1.

Trans_id	Trans_date	Customer	Product	Quantity
...	...	...	...	...
2	02-Apr-2021	Alice	Potato Chips	2
2	02-Apr-2021	Alice	Chocolates	1
...	...	...	...	...
9	13-Apr-2021	Alice	Potato Chips	2
9	13-Apr-2021	Alice	Fruits	1
...	...	...	...	...
3	02-Apr-2021	Chandler	Chocolates	3
3	02-Apr-2021	Chandler	Cakes	2
...	...	...	...	...
8	22-Apr-2021	Chandler	Chocolates	2
8	22-Apr-2021	Chandler	Cakes	3
...	...	...	...	...

Figure 7-1. *Customer transactions*

Each row captures the quantity of a product purchased by a customer.[2] Note that a customer typically purchases multiple products in a single transaction – in this case, the corresponding rows have the same value of *Trans_id*.

Given this data, we are interested in finding common behavioral (purchase) patterns across our customers.

---

[2] In real systems, Customer, Product, and Trans_id would be UUIDs (universally unique identifiers) rather than such simple names/numbers. Also, products would have a complex hierarchy of categories, and a transaction would capture the SKU. Finally, the timestamp of transaction would be captured rather than the Trans_date. We are glossing over these details for simplicity.

Data Preparation

In this case, let us suppose we are interested only in recent trends and patterns. So, we shall first filter the data to focus only on the transactions in the last month, say April. We can filter the rows based on *Trans_date* to achieve this.

Then, we shall aggregate and pivot this data of recent transactions to obtain the structure shown in Figure 7-2.

Customer	Potato Chips	Plain Donuts	Fruits	Fresh Fruit Juices	Chocolates	Cakes
Alice	4	4	1	2	3	3
Bob	15	12	9	9	9	6
Chandler	2	4	1	3	5	5
Dilbert	12	8	20	16	8	4
Einstein	2	2	4	5	1	1

Figure 7-2.   *Total quantity of each product per customer*

Note that we have aggregated the product quantity per customer for the entire month of April, for example, Alice has bought four items of Potato Chips overall in April.

Handling Missing Values

For clustering, it is important to consider how any missing values in the observations will be handled. Handling missing values can be rather nuanced for clustering. Some techniques follow an iterative approach, where clusters are formed based on only available values, and then the clusters are used to infer missing values. Deep understanding of the domain is typically needed to ensure that if any value is inferred to replace a missing value, it does not adversely impact the clustering.

In our case, we do not have any missing values – if a customer did not purchase a particular product, we would simply have a value of zero in the preceding table.

Normalization

It is possible that some attributes have rather different ranges of values than others. For instance, some products may be purchased more frequently than other products (e.g., socks may be purchased much more frequently than an electronic item). In such cases, we can normalize the values so that the quantities of all products would fall in similar ranges. This helps ensure that products that sell more do not bias the clustering heavily.

In our example, we believe the products do not have such variation. So we can proceed with the previous data.

Data Visualization

A data visualization technique that is especially applicable to clustering is *dendrograms*. This is typically used in a second iteration after the machine learning step. So we shall look at it in a subsection of the machine learning step.

Machine Learning

We shall use a technique called agglomerative clustering.[3] The idea of this is very simple, and it works as follows:

1. Begin with single-observation clusters, that is, create as many clusters as there are observations, and assign an observation to each cluster.

2. Merge the two clusters that are most *similar* to each other into a single bigger cluster.

    a. Perform this step iteratively until a single cluster remains containing all observations.

    b. Keep track of the various merge operations – these result in a hierarchy of clusters.

When the preceding steps are completed, we will have a hierarchy of clusters that can be visualized in a plot as shown in Figure 7-3.

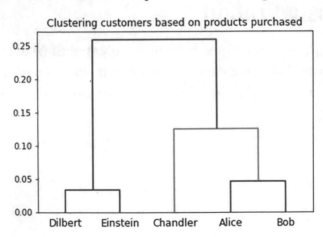

Figure 7-3. *Dendrogram: hierarchy of clusters*

---

[3] Also known as bottom-up hierarchical clustering.

We shall analyze this plot in detail in the following "Data Visualization Iteration" section. But before that, let's pause to understand what exactly is meant by "similar" in the previous steps – how do we quantify the similarity of observations?

Similarity of Observations

There are several ways to define the similarity of two observations – refer to Figure 7-4 for a couple of them.

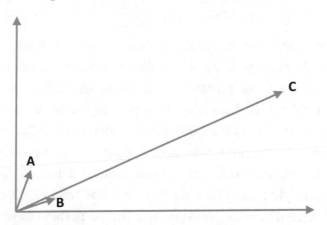

Figure 7-4. *Motivation of similarity measures*

Refer to the three points A, B, and C and their corresponding vectors. Now, let us compare two notions of similarity:

1.   Distance between the points: If we look at the pairwise distance between the points, we see that A and B are closest to each other. Thus, if this measure – the Euclidean distance – were taken as a similarity measure, then B would be more similar to A, than to C.

2. Angle between the vectors: If we look at the angles between the pair of vectors, we see that B and C are "closest" to each other. Thus, if this measure were taken as a similarity measure, then B would be more similar to C, than to A. The cosine of the angle, referred to as *cosine similarity*, is a common measure, as its value falls neatly between -1 (highly dissimilar) and 1 (extremely similar). Note that cosine similarity judges only the direction, and *not* the magnitude, of the vectors.

To summarize, if observations are represented as points in n-dimensional space,[4] then Euclidean distance would measure how close two observations are to each other, while cosine similarity would measure the extent to which two observations are pointing in the same direction.

We thus see that there can be multiple notions of "similarity" – the domain dictates which is the most appropriate. For example, if some of the attributes represented actual locations on land, Euclidean distance can be used – this might be applicable if, say, you have readings from multiple sensors at different locations and you want to group them based on their readings as well as their location.

In our particular case, we are interested in the *preferences* of a customer, that is, which kinds of products they prefer more than others. If we choose Euclidean distance, then customers who buy smaller quantities would tend to get clustered together regardless of their *preferences* – just like A and B are regarded more similar in the preceding example. We need a measure that is not affected by the *absolute* quantities of products purchased, but only affected by the *relative* quantities of various products

---

[4] Where the coordinates of a point in different dimensions are based on the values of different features of the corresponding observation.

indicating *preferences* – this depends purely on the "directions" of the vectors and not their magnitudes.[5] Thus, we decide to use *cosine similarity* as a similarity measure in our case. We shall see the effect of this on our clusters in the following section.

The choice of the similarity measure is the most crucial factor in clustering. As we see, this can be heavily dependent on the domain understanding. Thus, the similarity measure is best decided by working closely with a data analyst/domain expert.

ADVANCED NOTE: LINKAGE

Recall that in step 2 of agglomerative clustering, we need to merge the two *clusters* that are most similar. When the two clusters have multiple observations, in order to merge them, we also need a mechanism to quantify the similarity of two *clusters* – this is referred to as *linkage*.

Three types of linkage typically used are *single*, *complete*, and *average* linkage.[6] They vary in regard to which observation(s) from each cluster are chosen to represent the overall similarity of the two clusters. Typically, models are evaluated with various linkage mechanisms to arrive at the variant that is most useful. More details of linkage are beyond our scope here.

In our example, we have used *average linkage*.

---

[5] For example, suppose the horizontal and vertical axes in Figure 7-4 represented the (normalized) values of purchases of products P1 and P2, respectively. Then A clearly prefers P2 over P1, while both B and C slightly prefer P1 over P2. This is indicated by the direction of the corresponding vectors.

[6] Other linkages exist, such as centroid and Ward.

Having created an agglomerative clustering model, let us now analyze the dendrogram in Figure 7-3 in more detail. In regard to the data science process, this can be regarded as an iteration back to the data visualization step.

Data Visualization Iteration

Let us now walk through the dendrogram of Figure 7-3 in more detail.

The x axis contains the initial single-observation clusters labeled using the Customer.

Each horizontal bar represents a cluster formed by merging two clusters, for example, the red horizontal bar represents the cluster formed by merging the two initial single-observation clusters containing Alice and Bob. Similarly, the green horizontal bar represents the cluster formed by merging the Chandler cluster with the red cluster (containing Alice and Bob).

We can now read the dendrogram moving from the bottom toward the top to see the order in which the clusters were formed. When we move from the bottom toward the top, the sequence in which we encounter the horizontal lines indicates the order in which the clusters were formed. Thus, the clusters were formed in the order:

1. Magenta cluster by merging the clusters of Dilbert and Einstein: to begin with these two customers were the most similar to each other.

2. Red cluster by merging the clusters of Alice and Bob.

3. Green cluster by merging the cluster of Chandler and the red cluster: Chandler is more similar to Alice/Bob than to Dilbert/Einstein.

4. Blue cluster by merging the magenta and green clusters.

The y axis represents the dissimilarity, that is, lower values indicate higher similarity. In our case, since we used cosine similarity, the *dissimilarity* is computed as (1 – cosine_similarity), which is also referred to as the *cosine distance*. Thus, we can see from the plot that the cosine distance between the clusters of Dilbert and Einstein is around 0.03 (height of the magenta horizontal line), while the cosine distance between the magenta and the green clusters is around 0.26 (height of the blue horizontal line).

Having understood how to read the dendrogram, let us now see how to interpret the dendrogram and what insights can be inferred from it.

ADVANCED NOTE: ROLE OF THE SIMILARITY MEASURE

Note the role that the similarity measure played in clustering – even though Dilbert has bought many more products than Einstein, they are deemed similar because we had used cosine similarity, and they both have a similar direction, that is, similar *preferences*. It seems, for example, that they both prefer fruit/juices to chocolates/cakes.

If we had used Euclidean distance, Einstein would instead have been clustered with Alice/Chandler first, because they have purchased fewer quantity of products and would be closer together in terms of points in a Euclidean space.

Inference

In the earlier chapters, we saw examples where we predicted some value for new observations in the inference step. In case of clustering, we instead infer some insights based on the clusters created – this is also referred to as *knowledge discovery.*[7]

Interpreting the Dendrogram

One of the advantages of using agglomerative clustering is that we can analyze the hierarchy to determine what kinds of clusters are most meaningful in the context of the business. Refer to Figure 7-5 to see how this can be done in our current example.

In the dendrogram, the number of clusters increases as we move from the top toward the bottom. If we draw a horizontal line anywhere, then the number of vertical lines that it intersects determines the number of clusters. Two such horizontal lines are shown in Figure 7-5, and they represent two possible mechanisms to identify clusters, that we have called L1 and L2.

1. L1 results in two clusters: one cluster containing Dilbert and Einstein and the second cluster containing Chandler, Alice, and Bob.

2. L2 results in three clusters: one cluster containing Dilbert and Einstein, the second containing only Chandler, and the third containing Alice and Bob.

---

[7] Clustering problems are rather common in KDD/data mining projects – see Chapter 23.

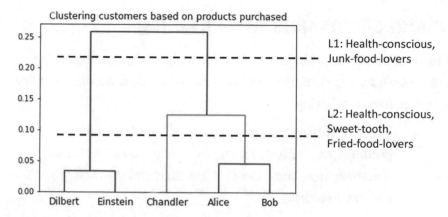

Figure 7-5. *Identifying meaningful clusters from the dendrogram*

A data analyst might investigate the observations in each of the clusters and determine that, as shown in Figure 7-5,

- In case of L1, the two clusters represent customers who prefer healthy and junk foods, respectively.[8]

- In case of L2, the three clusters represent customers who prefer healthy, sweet, and fried foods, respectively.

The domain understanding and business context would then determine which among L1 and L2 is chosen. For example:

- If the sweet-tooth cluster has very few customers and engaging/targeting them will be costly, then it may be useful to have just two clusters. Thus, L1 would be chosen.

- If the sweet-tooth cluster happens to be a focus area for the business, then L2 might be chosen.

---

[8] Note that this is merely an *illustrative* example that we hope will be intuitive to most readers – we are not considering the "are chocolates junk food?" kind of debates here.

Actionable Insights for Marketing

There can be different kinds of actionable insights depending on the business context. Assuming you have chosen L2, the following are a few examples from marketing:

- Suppose you are planning to stock a couple of new products, say butter cookies and energy bars. You know that these new butter cookies are fried and the energy bars are healthy.

  - You would likely advertise the butter cookies to the fried food-lovers cluster.[9] As the cookies are also somewhat sweet, you might also advertise it to the sweet-tooth cluster.

  - You would likely advertise the energy bars to the health-conscious cluster. If you know that the energy bars also happen to be quite sweet, for example, containing natural sugars, you would also advertise it to the sweet-tooth cluster.

- Suppose that soon after creating these clusters using L2, you have stocked a new product. Even without deeply analyzing the content/nature of the product, who might like it, etc., you could use the clusters to make recommendations. For example, if you find Dilbert purchasing the new product, you could then recommend it to Einstein (e.g., using discount coupons). Similarly, if you find Bob purchasing the new product, you could recommend it to Alice as well. We shall revisit recommendations in Chapter 9.

---

[9] We refer to this kind of marketing practice as cross-selling.

Conclusion

Clustering problems are encountered frequently in any business that has captured a lot of data and is aiming to derive some insights from it. Solving clustering problems typically leads to new knowledge about the customer, process, domain, etc., and is one of the common ways to conduct *knowledge discovery from data* – more commonly referred to as KDD. We shall look at KDD projects again in Chapter 23.

In this chapter, we looked at one end-to-end example of a clustering problem. The thought process and techniques used for clustering are often applicable in other areas – we shall see an example of this in Chapter 9, "Recommendations."

Further Reading

James et al. (2013) have an excellent introductory coverage to clustering problems and the typical challenges. It also covers more details of various techniques for clustering, including agglomerative clustering.

Reference

James, Gareth, et al. *An Introduction to Statistical Learning*. New York: Springer, 2013.

CHAPTER 8

Anomaly Detection

Often, we tend to have an intrinsic notion of whether an observation is unexpected or abnormal. Sensors that seem to behave erratically or give readings that are rarely seen; an unheard-of combination of symptoms/ test readings, or a rare pattern in a medical image such as a CT scan; and network traffic in an IT system that is unusual, these are a few cases that tend to raise attention. Detecting any abnormal occurrences in the data is referred to as anomaly detection.

Broadly, there are three categories of anomaly detection based on the kind of data you have:

- Labeled data: If you know which observations in your data are normal vs. abnormal, and the goal is to predict which new observations are abnormal, then it is similar to classification with the two target classes as *normal* and *anomaly*. Since you regard some observations as abnormal, it is likely that you have a lot more normal observations than abnormal ones. So, you would need to handle class imbalance appropriately. Since this can be solved using classification techniques, we shall not cover this further in this chapter.

© Vineet Raina and Srinath Krishnamurthy 2022
V. Raina and S. Krishnamurthy, *Building an Effective Data Science Practice*,
https://doi.org/10.1007/978-1-4842-7419-4_8

- Unlabeled data: If you do not know which observations are normal vs. abnormal, you would need to train a model to determine abnormal observations in the existing data first. Then you may apply the same model on new observations as well to detect anomalies. An implicit assumption in this case is that the percentage of abnormal observations is relatively small.

- Pure data: You have data that you *know* does not contain any abnormal observations. In this case, you would need to train a model that learns what normal observations are. You can then determine if any new observations are not regarded as normal by the model, that is, if any new observations are *novel* with respect to the model. A novel observation can potentially indicate an anomaly. This subcategory of anomaly detection is often referred to as ***novelty detection***.

In this chapter on anomaly detection, we shall first cover examples of anomaly detection using unlabeled data and pure data. We shall then look at an end-to-end example of the steps in the data science process for an anomaly detection problem with both variants of unlabeled data and pure data. We shall then summarize slightly more formally the notion of an anomaly and how the choice of ML algorithm affects this notion. Finally, we will look at a few examples of complex anomalies including the notions of collective and contextual anomalies.

Anomaly Detection Using Unlabeled Data

- You have data from patients, some of them having a particular disease that you are interested in studying, say, breast cancer. The percentage of people with cancer in the population is rather small, so you would want to regard this as an anomaly detection problem, that is, to identify patients that are anomalous, which would potentially indicate breast cancer. In this case, the features may consist of the patients' relevant medical information in addition to medical images.

- You have audit data of remote logins from the thousands of users in an enterprise. Based on the login patterns, you want to deduce if any intrusion attacks have occurred, for example, potentially by a user account being hacked. In this case, the features may consist of the number of IP addresses the user logs in from during a day, the geographic locations of remote logins, month, day of the week, and other such factors. Our goal is to detect if any unusual patterns have occurred, for example, a user who typically logs in from, say, four to six distinct IP addresses during a day, suddenly logged in from more than ten IP addresses during one day.

- You have data about various measurements of a part manufactured in your industrial plant. Based on the prior analysis of your industrial process, you know that typically 2% of the parts manufactured turn out to be defective in some manner. You are interested in automatically determining which parts are defective on an ongoing basis by applying anomaly detection techniques to the measurements of each of the parts. (A more complex variation of this is to be able to detect these defective parts based on multiple images of each of the parts.)

Novelty Detection Using Pure Data

- As part of a video surveillance system, you have videos of normal situations. And you need to raise an alarm in case any abnormal images or actions are seen. For example, normal situations on a railway carriage would involve folks calmly walking or sitting. If we train a model using these videos, the model can then detect anomalous situations (images or videos) such as someone waving a gun, harassment, or crowd panic.

- Your company creates pipes that go into forming long stretches of pipelines that carry oil or gas. The pipelines often stretch into remote areas with no supervision and are liable to tampering. The pipes contain sensors that monitor vibrations, and the goal is to detect if any unusual vibrations occur, for example, due to some drilling into the pipe. In this case, you would capture a lot of data about normal vibration values, but due to practical constraints, you may not have data about someone breaking into pipes in different ways. In this case, your data – that of normal vibration values – can be regarded as pure data, and your goal is to train a model that can capture the normal behavior correctly. And when vibration values are seen that are very unlike the normal behavior, we can call them as an anomaly, potentially indicating tampering or fault in the pipe.

Data Science Process for Anomaly Detection

In this section, we shall look at an example dataset (*HeartDisease*) and cover the steps in data science process in the context of anomaly detection.

The World and Data Capture

The data[1] contains readings from a cohort of patients, of certain tests related to cardiac function, some symptoms and preexisting conditions, and patient metadata such as age and sex. Given this information, our goal is to find which patients are anomalies – an anomaly might indicate, say, presence of an underlying heart condition.

The kind of data captured would dictate further analysis. For example, if we were to have a cohort of healthy[2] patients only, then we need to use techniques that work on pure data. On the other hand, if our cohort potentially contains patients with heart disease as well, and their percentage is relatively small, then this is a case of anomaly detection with unlabeled data. At this point, it also makes sense to check the World (with the help of an analyst – in this case, possibly a diagnostician or clinician) as to whether there is a known prevalence of heart disease in the population we are looking at. This can help us determine the threshold for anomaly scores later.

---

[1] www.dbs.ifi.lmu.de/research/outlier-evaluation/DAMI/semantic/ HeartDisease/

[2] Healthy, in this context, implies not having a heart disease.

Data Preparation

The usual data preparation aspects such as handling missing values, etc., would apply here. Also, a quick look at the range of the values of the various features indicates that some features such as sex are categorical, while others are numeric. The numeric features also have varying ranges.

Usually, for algorithms that work on numeric features, it can be useful to *normalize* them such that all the values fall between 0 and 1. In this case, let us also prepare a normalized dataset. (In some cases, we might do this only after an initial exploratory visual analysis of the data.)

Data Visualization

Typically, we would first like to see if any of the values of individual features are outliers. This can be seen, for example, with box plots. Also, we can try to see if certain combinations of feature values are rather rare, for example, with scatter plots.

Note that we are using the term *outlier* here in the sense that a point in a plot is a "visual" outlier. An outlier in a plot may or may not indicate anomalous observations; visually eyeballing outliers is often just a starting point for the analysis.

For example, this kind of analysis might indicate which features are more likely to identify anomalies and help gain more intuition about the data.

Box Plots

Let us first look at a box plot of one of the features, *SerumCholestoral*, in Figure 8-1.

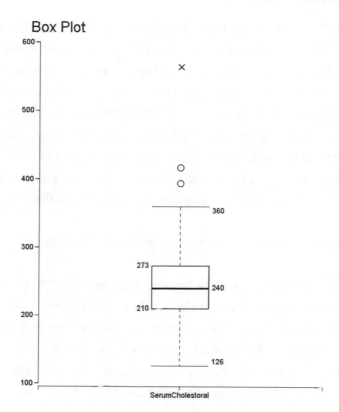

Figure 8-1. *Box plot of SerumCholestoral*

This plot indicates that most of the observations tend to fall between 126 and 360 (with half of the observations falling between 210 and 273). We can regard values outside this range of 126–360 as outliers. With the library we have used for plotting, it indicates extreme outliers using crosses and mild outliers using circles. In this case, we see there are three outliers, of which one is an extreme outlier.

Let's take a closer look at what the different visual elements in this box plot represent at a high level. The lower edge of the box represents the *first quartile (Q1)* and indicates that 25% of the observations fall below this value (210). The upper edge of the box represents the *third quartile (Q3)* and indicates that 75% of the observations fall below this value (273). The thick horizontal line inside the box represents the median and indicates that 50% of the observations fall below this value (240). The distance between the third quartile and first quartile is known as *interquartile range* (i.e., IQR = Q3 − Q1). The upper whisker extends up to the largest observation that falls within a distance of 1.5 times the IQR measured from Q3 (so the upper whisker extends up to 360). The lower whisker extends up to the smallest observation that falls within a distance of 1.5 times the IQR measured from Q1 (so the lower whisker extends up to 126). And as you can see in Figure 8-1, the observations beyond the two whiskers are drawn as outliers. Note that, in this case, there are no outliers below the lower whisker.

A box plot is a quick way to get intuition about the values of a single feature.

You can jot down some of the observations that look interesting, for example, if they are outliers in the box plots of multiple features, etc., for further discussion with a domain expert or business analyst. In this case, the domain expert could be a diagnostician/cardiologist.

This analysis only used the numeric features. We can further include categorical features in the analysis, using conditional box plots.

Conditional Box Plots

Box plots that are created for each value of a categorical feature are referred to as conditional (or grouped) box plots. For example, Figure 8-2 shows a conditional box plot of *SerumCholestoral* across values of *Sex* (say, Male/Female is represented as 0/1).

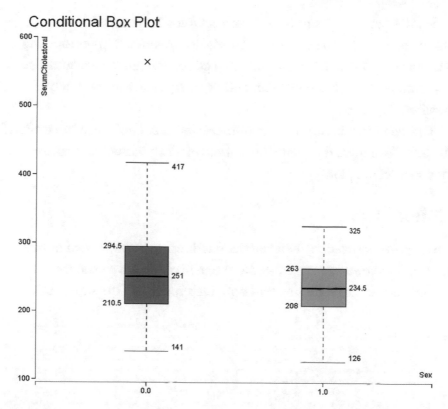

Figure 8-2. *Conditional box plot – SerumCholestoral across values of Sex*

If we compare this against the earlier box plot of *SerumCholestoral* in Figure 8-1, we can see how the outliers are affected by sex of the patient. For example, we saw three outliers in the *SerumCholestoral* box plot, but here, we see only one. This is because the normal range for *Sex=0* is much larger, from 141 to 417. Thus, two of the outliers we earlier thought could be anomalies in Figure 8-1 now seem to be normal *within males* in Figure 8-2. Also, we see that within females, it seems there are no anomalies in the context of *SerumCholestoral*.

So, the *Sex* of a person would impact which *SerumCholestoral* values are regarded to be normal. This is how relationships among the features are important for anomaly detection. Similarly, we would also look at conditional box plots using other categorical features such as *ChestPainType,* etc.

The relationships among the numeric features could also be similarly relevant. To analyze the relationship between two numerical features, we can use a scatter plot.

Scatter Plots

Scatter plots are used to visualize the relationship between two numeric features, as shown in Figure 8-3. Note that here, we have used the normalized feature values so that both features are on the same scale.

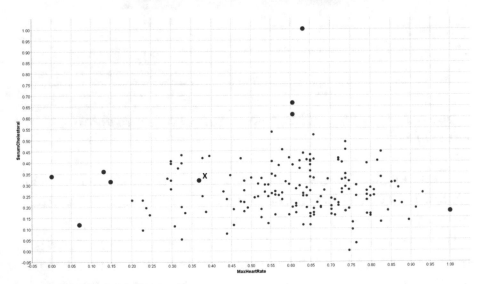

Figure 8-3. *Scatter plot of SerumCholestoral vs. MaxHeartRate*

We have highlighted, with bigger dots, a few points that indicate potentially anomalous observations because they seem somewhat isolated in the plot. Note also point X, which looks somewhat more isolated than its neighbors. By looking at the two features independently, we might have noticed the other potentially anomalous observations, but our attention would not have been drawn to an observation like X.

We can plot multiple scatter plots to determine which *pairs* of features are potentially indicating some anomalies.

Using techniques such as box and scatter plots, we can get some intuition into which features are possibly relevant to indicating anomalies. After exploring some of the visualizations, we typically get a sense of how anomalies depend on multiple features. Potentially, it is also possible that an observation may not be an anomaly w.r.t. just one or two features, but the combination of values of all the features could be an anomaly.

Once we go beyond two or three features, it is not possible for us to "visualize" the data to arrive at this type of insight. But our intuition so far does show that we can hope to detect some anomalies based on the relative location of the observations in an n-dimensional space. Let us now turn to machine learning to aid us in extending our visual intuition to an n-dimensional space using multiple features.

Machine Learning

When we use box and scatter plots, we are effectively eyeballing the distance between the observations, that is, observations that are *seen* to be far away are regarded as anomalies. There are several algorithms that work on detecting anomalies based on the distances between the observations in a similar way, by extending the notion to multiple features.

We shall use the local outlier factor (LOF) algorithm. Our choice here is due to the following reasons. First, it is intuitive and highly resonates with what we tend to visually sense as outliers. Second, it is one of the few algorithms that can reasonably be used in both cases – unlabeled data or pure data. Finally, in the case of a healthcare example like this, we may be interested in finding patients who are different from "similar" patients, rather than patients who are different w.r.t. the entire cohort. This naturally leads us to find "local" anomalies, that is, observations which are anomalous w.r.t. similar observations, but not necessarily w.r.t. the overall dataset. LOF finds observations that are relatively isolated compared to their neighbors and is thus able to detect local anomalies.

We shall use the term "local density" of an observation to refer to the density of the neighbors around that observation, that is, if the neighbors are densely packed around an observation, the local density of that observation is high.[3] LOF works on the intuition that if an observation has a *local density* that is lower than the local density of its neighbors, then the observation is more anomalous than its neighbors. Figure 8-4 provides a quick intuition of this using a *toy* example.

---

[3] The number of neighbors to be considered in calculating the local density is a parameter that has to be tuned empirically.

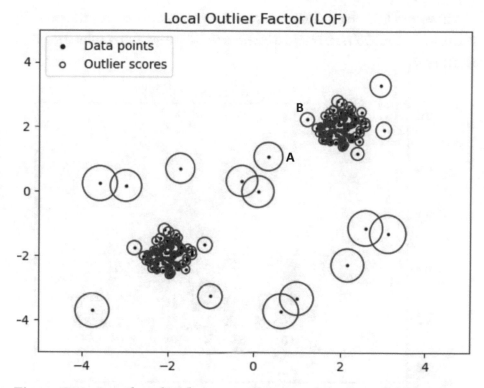

Figure 8-4. *Local outlier factor: a toy example with two features*[4]

As we see from this figure, the points that are relatively isolated compared to their neighbors get a higher outlier (anomaly) score. The anomaly score, in this case, is effectively a function of the deviation of the local density of an observation as compared to its neighbors. For example, the local density of point A is similar to the local density of its two closest neighbors, so A gets a score similar to its two closest neighbors. On the other hand, the local density of point B is less than the local density of its closest neighbors, due to which B gets a higher score than its neighbors.

---

[4]https://scikit-learn.org/stable/auto_examples/neighbors/plot_lof_outlier_detection.html

If we run LOF on our HeartDisease dataset, but using only the two features *SerumCholestoral* and *MaxHeartRate,* we get the results shown in Figure 8-5.

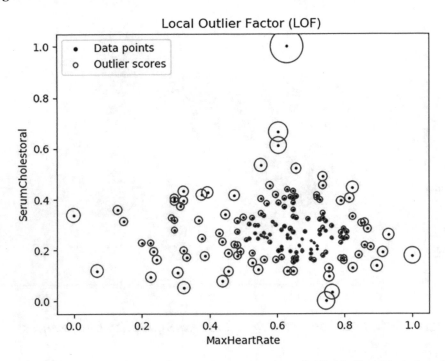

Figure 8-5. *LOF using only two features: SerumCholestoral and MaxHeartRate*

We can extend this to run the LOF algorithm using multiple features in our normalized HeartDisease dataset to obtain anomaly scores for all the observations and rank them by the anomaly scores. When we ran LOF using seven selected features, including *SerumCholestoral, MaxHeartRate,* and *Sex,* we obtained anomaly scores as shown in Figure 8-6.

D id	D ▼ anomaly_score
2	1.81
200	1.418
177	1.403
104	1.317
123	1.31
235	1.285
188	1.271
148	1.249
4	1.231
120	1.222
173	1.214
185	1.207
36	1.184
53	1.182
12	1.178
5	1.173

Figure 8-6. *Anomaly scores using LOF on HeartDisease dataset*

These anomaly scores can now be used for inference.

Inference

Now that a model has generated anomaly scores for the observations in the machine learning step, we can proceed to determine anomalies. In order to do so, we would first set an appropriate threshold for the anomaly scores. For example, if we kept a threshold of 1.3, we would call the first five observations as anomalies. This is where the insights of the analyst are useful in deciding an appropriate threshold. The analyst can also determine if the relative anomaly scores seem appropriate, for example, checking that a normal observation isn't getting a high anomaly score. Based on the inputs from the analyst, we can perform further iterations by modifying the parameters[5] and features used in the LOF algorithm.

---

[5] Such parameters to an ML algorithm, such as the number of neighbors to be considered in calculating local density, are referred to as *hyperparameters*. We shall look at hyperparameters in Chapter 16.

NOVELTY DETECTION USING LOF

Note that the LOF algorithm could be used with pure data for novelty detection as well. In this case, each new observation is independently tested for novelty. The local density of the new observation is compared to the local density of its neighbors (in the pure data) to determine its anomaly score. If the new observation's local density is significantly lower than the local densities of its neighbors, it can be regarded as a novel observation.

Anatomy of an Anomaly

Having seen an example of anomaly detection, let us delve slightly more formally into what exactly we mean when we say, "this observation is an anomaly." We rarely mean that an observation is abnormal in itself – we typically mean that it feels abnormal in relation to *other* observations that we have seen.

This intuition is reflected in the *anomaly score* generated by most anomaly detection techniques. The anomaly scores can be used to determine relative anomalousness as we saw in the HeartDisease example earlier. For example, a business analyst could rank the observations based on their anomaly score and determine an appropriate threshold – observations whose scores exceed this threshold can be flagged as an anomaly. In cases where we need deeper insight into the anomalous behavior, this approach of including a business analyst in the loop can be quite beneficial. For example, an analyst can tailor the false-alarm[6] rate according to the domain requirements:

---

[6] False alarm, that is, when the algorithm incorrectly flags a normal observation as an anomaly.

- A medical diagnosis use case would suggest that more false alarms are better rather than risk a disease go undetected. So, the analyst may choose a conservatively low threshold.

- In an IoT use case, where data points are in the millions from a multitude of sensors, false alarms can make the analysis overwhelming. If anomalies do not indicate a critical failure, but a tolerable failure or merely an observation of interest, then a higher threshold may be chosen to reduce false alarms at the risk of overlooking an occasional failure.

In addition to this, the various anomaly detection techniques impose their specific notions and interpretations to what an anomaly is. For example:

- In techniques based on nearest neighbors, observations are regarded as points in an n-dimensional space. Then, each observation is compared to its neighbors in some way to arrive at an anomaly score, that is, the anomalousness of an observation is determined by its location and the location of its nearest neighbors in an n-dimensional space. (LOF is an example of this category of techniques.)

- In techniques based on probability density functions, such as kernel density estimation, observations that are extremely unlikely, probabilistically, to occur are regarded as anomalies.

- In techniques based on clustering, such as k-means, observations are grouped together into clusters based on their similarities. Points that do not belong to any cluster,[7] or are far away from the cluster center, or belong to very sparse clusters, can then be regarded as anomalies.

Determining which of these notions is most appropriate to the problem at hand can also be a factor in choosing a corresponding technique.

Complex Anomalies

Anomalies do not necessarily occur in isolation. Often it is a particular group of observations that is anomalous, or an anomaly depends on additional contextual information. We shall look a few examples of each of these cases.

Collective Anomalies

Several common anomalies occur as a group of observations, such that each observation in itself isn't abnormal, but the occurrence of the entire group is abnormal. For example, if on a computer, a buffer overflow, remote session initiation, and data transfer events all occur together, it is an anomaly potentially indicating a hack. But individually, each of those three events can occur during normal operations.[8]

---

[7] More precisely, points that belong to a cluster containing only that one point.
[8] A buffer overflow by itself can be due to a bug in an application.

Other typical examples of collective anomalies are

- A sequence of readings from a sensor that seems abnormal. For example, in the pipeline example we saw earlier, suppose we expect that an occasional single reading could be unusual, that is, it is not an anomaly. But a somewhat sustained sequence of unusual readings is anomalous (and would indicate tampering). In this case, the sequence of readings is a collective anomaly.

- A sequence of logs or events can indicate an intrusion attack either on a software or the network. In some complex systems, a sequence of logs can also potentially indicate buggy behavior that can lead to undesired user experience. In these cases, NLP can be combined with anomaly detection techniques to flag the abnormality.

Contextual Anomalies

In many cases, anomalies depend on the context within which the data is observed. Common contexts are time and location of an observation.

For example, an individual might typically spend at most $500 on any day, except for a vacation season like Christmas when they might spend up to $2000. Now, if they spend, say, $2000 in December, it is normal. But if in July they spend even $1000, it could be regarded as anomalous.

Similarly, the geographic context of location (captured as, say, latitude/longitude), nearby events/attractions, and other such information can play an important role.

In some cases, it can be useful to craft a summarized context to reduce the complexity and make the analysis tractable. For example, in credit card fraud detection, one approach could be to treat each individual as a context because the spending patterns would vary significantly from one individual to another. But this would require a large number of models and increased complexity. A more tractable approach would be to build *profiles* from customer *segments* and use the profile as a context.

Incorporating an appropriate context is crucial to improve the accuracy of anomaly detection. Particularly in the big data era, when there is easy availability of contextual data on the Internet, such as on social media, you can try to assimilate further context into your analysis for more relevance and accuracy.

Time Series

A sequence of observations seen over time, in a temporal sequence, is referred to as time series data. Examples include sensor readings, financial transactions, or ECG readings. Here, *time* is a context for a *sequence* of observations that we are analyzing for anomalies. Given its importance and widespread applicability, we cover a couple of additional examples of this special case.

It may be inappropriate to ignore the time information and treat such data as simply a sequence. Incorporating time information into the analysis can uncover anomalies that depend on the periodicity of the data. For example:

- In an ECG, a specific reading or a collection of readings could be in a normal range, but still be inconsistent with the regular and periodic form that is typically expected. Such an inconsistency in the periodicity of the readings may indicate arrhythmia.

- An individual's transactions may have certain periodicity, for example, overseas transactions occurring at regular intervals, say, every quarter. If we then see multiple overseas transactions within a quarter, it will indicate an anomaly.

- Consider the example we saw at the start of this section, of detecting intrusion attacks based on login patterns such as number of distinct IP addresses a remote user logs in from. In this case, time often plays an important factor, for example, the login patterns on weekends or holidays could vary from those on weekdays. Also, an individual may have a specific pattern that needs to be accounted for, for example, someone who travels regularly on Thursdays and Fridays for official purposes may have a different pattern on those two days.

Conclusion

In this chapter, we covered the various nuances and types of anomaly detection problems. We also looked at one example to get a feel of both human ways (e.g., box plots) and algorithmic, slightly mysterious, ways to determine anomalies.

Anomaly detection is one of the areas where the role of the domain expert (or business analyst) can be significant – to try to make sense of when a model flags an anomaly or misses one. The importance of this would vary depending on the criticality and impact of an anomaly in your business setting.

Further Reading

There are numerous survey papers for anomaly detection. One of the classics is Chandola, Banerjee, and Kumar (2009). Though anomaly detection techniques have evolved a lot since then, the conceptual framework of classifying types of data, problems/applications, and techniques is still largely applicable.

For more details and up-to-date coverage of the field, refer to Mehrotra, Mohan, and Huang (2017). It covers applications of anomaly detection in various domains, followed by the approaches and algorithms used for anomaly detection.

References

Chandola, Varun, Arindam Banerjee and Vipin Kumar. "Anomaly detection: A survey." *ACM Computing Surveys, Volume 41, Issue 3* July 2009.

Mehrotra, Kishan G., Chilukuri K. Mohan and HuaMing Huang. *Anomaly Detection Principles and Algorithms.* Cham, Switzerland: Springer, 2017.

CHAPTER 9

Recommendations

Once upon a time, you may have had a close friend recommending a book, song, or movie to you – since the friend knew your "tastes," you would typically check out their recommendations.

In the online world today, websites and mobile apps (and the companies that build them) have collected data about all their visitors and customers at a granular level of possibly each click that has happened on the website/app. This data includes every book/song/movie/product they have purchased/rejected and liked/disliked.

Based on this data, if a company is able to determine a user's "taste," it can then masquerade as their friend and recommend stuff that they might be interested in. This not only acts as an excellent mechanism to cross-sell/upsell and thus increase sales for a company but also adds tremendous value for the user given the breadth of inventory these companies would carry (think of Amazon.com, Netflix, etc.) and thus increases customer engagement.

In this chapter, we shall look at an end-to-end example of how individual "taste" is estimated from data of past customer purchases, ratings, etc., and how recommendations are made to improve the user experience.

© Vineet Raina and Srinath Krishnamurthy 2022
V. Raina and S. Krishnamurthy, *Building an Effective Data Science Practice*,
https://doi.org/10.1007/978-1-4842-7419-4_9

Data Capture

In this section, we shall first look at the generic notion of items/ interactions and some common variations in regard to how this data would be captured. Then we look at the example data used in this chapter for determining recommendations.

Items and Interactions

We use the term "item" to denote anything that a user has an "interaction" with – the interactions and items could be, for example:

- Viewing a movie on an online streaming platform; movies are the items.

- Purchasing products from an ecommerce website; products are the items.

- Liking/dating another individual on a dating platform; other users are the items.

Our goal is to be able to recommend items to a user that they would most probably like, based on the data of their past interactions with several items. For the rest of this chapter, we shall focus on the example of users viewing movies – but similar concepts apply to other kinds of interactions/ items as well.

Quantifying an Interaction

When a user interacts with an item, how do we capture the nature and quality of the interaction? Broadly, there are two ways to capture the feedback of a user regarding an item:

- Implicit feedback: We determine whether the user liked the item *implicitly*, for example, if they viewed the entire movie in one sitting and then searched for similar movies, etc., they probably like it. If they left a movie midway and never came back to it, they probably disliked it.

- Explicit feedback: We ask the user for feedback explicitly. Asking the user to rate the movie using stars or thumbs up/down, etc., is an example of this.

All this information is eventually captured in some quantitative form – it could be, for example, a 0/1 simply indicating whether the user watched a movie, a rating on a scale of 1–5, or a complex rating score computed using a combination of these mechanisms.

Example Data

In our current example, we shall refer to the sample data shown in Figure 9-1.

User	Movie	Rating
Alice	Titanic	4
Alice	Terminator	1
Alice	Hot Shots	3
...		
Chandler	Titanic	2
Chandler	Terminator	1
Chandler	Hot Shots	5
...		

Figure 9-1. *Movies rated by users, one row per user-movie pair*

In our data, we are representing the user feedback given to various movies on a rating scale of 1–5 captured as explicit feedback. A lower score indicates the user did not like the movie, while a higher score indicates that the user liked the movie, for example:

Alice loved *Titanic* and disliked *Terminator*, while Chandler didn't like either.

Given this data, our goal is to recommend movies to a user that they have not yet seen. Our aim is to only recommend movies that they would probably like, that is, movies which we predict that they would rate highly.

Data Preparation

We shall pivot the data to obtain the structure shown in Figure 9-2.

User	Titanic	You've got mail	Terminator	Terminator 2	Hot Shots	Scary Movie	My best friend's wedding	Men in Black
Alice	4	4	1	2	3	3	4	
Bob	5	4	3	3	3	2		3
Chandler	2	4	1	3	5	5	3	5
Dilbert	3	2	5	4	2	1	1	
Einstein	2	2	4	5	1	1		4

Figure 9-2. *Movies rated by users, one row per user, one column per movie*

There are two primary kinds of preparatory steps typically required in such problems: normalization and handling missing values.

Normalization

Users vary not only in their tastes/preferences but also in regard to how they provide feedback. Two common variations in how users provide feedback are

1. Some users tend to give high or low ratings in general. For example, if one user usually tends to give high ratings, then a rating of 3 might mean that they did not like the movie at all.

2. Users with a similar average rating can differ in the range of ratings. For example, consider two users who give an average rating of around 3. Of these, suppose one user mostly gives a score of 3 to nearly all movies, while another user always rates movies as only 1 or 5. Now, if the first user gives an occasional 5, it is more significant/appreciative than a 5 given by the second user.

To adjust for these inherent personal scales, it can be important to *normalize* the data. Techniques such as *mean centering*[1] (for point 1) or *Z-score normalization*[2] (for point 2) modify the ratings to account for any inherent personal scale a user might be scoring with.

While such normalization can help improve recommendations, they can also be misleading or inappropriate within the context of some domains. For example, suppose a user researches a movie in a lot of detail (e.g., reads reviews, looks at the director, cast, etc.) before viewing it. This user might typically give only high scores not because they have a tendency to give high scores, but because they only view movies

---

[1] Subtracts the mean of a user's ratings from each of their ratings.
[2] Divides the mean-centered ratings by the standard deviation of a user's ratings.

that they will probably like. In this case, adjusting their score using the aforementioned techniques could be inappropriate.[3]

In our current illustrative example, we shall not apply any normalization.

Handling Missing Values

In practice, the data could have numerous missing values, particularly if most users rate only a small number of items even after interacting with them. For example, users might often watch movies but not rate them. There are ways to fill in missing ratings; refer to Xue et al. (2005) for an example.

In our current example though, we shall regard a missing entry to mean that the user has not watched that movie. For example, Alice has not watched *Men in Black*. Our goal will be to find out if we should recommend that movie to the user. However, for our analysis at this stage, we shall consider only those movies that have been rated by all the users, that is, we shall exclude *My Best Friend's Wedding* and *Men in Black*.

Data Visualization

Systems that provide recommendations to a user are typically automated end-to-end. Thus, we are not covering data visualization for such recommender systems.

---

[3] See Ning, Desrosiers, and Karypis (2015) for a more detailed coverage of these aspects.

Machine Learning

The high-level approach we shall take is to, given a user A

1. Find users who are "similar" to A.

2. For movies that A has not yet seen, predict how A would rate those movies based on ratings given to those movies by these "similar users."

3. Recommend the movies that are predicted to get a high rating by A (i.e., movies that A would probably like).

We shall look at step 1 in the following section; steps 2 and 3 are covered in the *inference* section.

Clustering-Based Approach

We first cluster the users based on the ratings they gave to the movies – this will enable us to find users similar to a given user (step 1). Conceptually, this is like what we saw in Chapter 7. We shall thus reuse the agglomerative clustering[4] technique that we saw in Chapter 7 to yield a hierarchy of clusters as shown in Figure 9-3.

---

[4] We have done clustering based on Euclidean distance in this case. Refer to Chapter 7 for details.

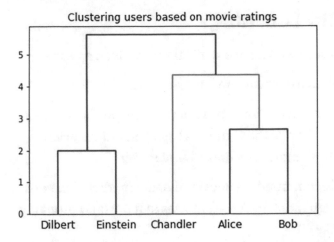

Figure 9-3. *Clusters of users based on how they rated the movies*

Let us suppose we decide to form three clusters – the first cluster containing Dilbert and Einstein, the second cluster containing Chandler alone, and the third cluster containing Alice and Bob. (In an automated system at scale, the choice of number of clusters depends on the ML techniques used; if we use agglomerative clustering, this choice might be automated based on the relative heights of the vertical lines in the dendrogram – details of this are beyond our scope here.)

Inference

Once clusters are formed, we can then predict how user A would rate a movie based on ratings given to it by other users in their cluster.[5] For example, we could calculate a simple average of the ratings that other users in their cluster have given to a movie; or we could calculate a weighted average based on how similar another user is to A.

---

[5] In practice, we could also include users from other similar clusters – refer to Xue et al. (2005) for more details.

In our simplistic example, we can thus fill the table with predicted ratings shown in red in Figure 9-4.

User	Titanic	You've got mail	Terminator	Terminator 2	Hot Shots	Scary Movie	My best friend's wedding	Men in Black
Alice	4	4	1	2	3	3	4	3
Bob	5	4	3	3	3	2	4	3
Chandler	2	4	1	3	5	5	3	5
Dilbert	3	3	5	4	2	1	1	4
Einstein	2	2	4	5	1	1	1	4

Figure 9-4. *Predicted ratings are indicated in red*

The entries with high predicted ratings would then lead to the following recommendations by the system[6]:

- *My Best Friend's Wedding* would be recommended to Bob.

- *Men in Black* would be recommended to Dilbert.

End-to-End Automation

As users watch and rate movies, our data will continue to grow. The clustering algorithm can be automated to run periodically to form clusters of users. When recommendations are to be shown to a user, we would then run the inference step.

How frequently the clusters are updated would depend on the domain and use case. In our case, we can update the clusters every few days.

---

[6] Note that, unlike in Chapter 7, here, we are not interested in understanding what the clusters represent, etc.

ML TECHNIQUES AND CLASSES OF PROBLEMS

In this chapter, we used the "agglomerative clustering" *ML technique* to solve a "recommendations" *problem*. We had used the same "agglomerative clustering" *ML technique* to solve a "clustering" *problem* in Chapter 7. In general, an *ML technique* could be applied to multiple *classes of problems*.

Conclusion

Recommender systems are now a vital part of several online services – websites and mobile apps. In this chapter, we covered an end-to-end example of building a recommender system using a clustering technique we first saw in Chapter 7.

The techniques to build recommender systems are continuing to evolve rapidly – see the "Further Reading" section for some new developments.

Further Reading

Our clustering-based approach to recommendation in this chapter is inspired by Xue et al. (2005).[7]

One of the earliest recommender systems at Internet scale was at Amazon.com to recommend products online. For a brief history of recommender systems and some recent developments using deep learning techniques, refer to Hardesty (2019).

---

[7] Note that for conceptual simplicity, we've used agglomerative clustering with Euclidean distance; the paper actually used k-means clustering with Pearson correlation as the similarity measure.

If you are looking to include a recommender system into your applications, you may consider getting started with a cloud service such as Amazon Personalize.

References

Hardesty, Larry. *The history of Amazon's recommendation algorithm.* 22 11 2019. <`www.amazon.science/the-history-of-amazons-recommendation-algorithm`>.

Ning, Xia, Christian Desrosiers and George Karypis. "A Comprehensive Survey of Neighborhood-Based Recommendation Methods." *Recommender Systems Handbook.* Ed. Francesco Ricci, Lior Rokach and Bracha Shapira. New York: Springer, 2015.

Xue, Gui-Rong and Lin, Chenxi and Yang, Qiang and Xi, WenSi and Zeng, Hua-Jun and Yu, Yong and Chen, Zheng. "Scalable Collaborative Filtering Using Cluster-Based Smoothing." *Proceedings of the 28th Annual International ACM SIGIR Conference on Research and Development in Information Retrieval.* Salvador, Brazil: Association for Computing Machinery, 2005. 114–121.

CHAPTER 10

Computer Vision

The term *computer vision* fundamentally refers to the ability of a software algorithm to process visual information such as images and videos, similar to how humans process visual information. Under the overarching field of *artificial intelligence*, the field of computer vision is one of the more complex, higher levels of "intelligence." The tremendous successes of deep learning approaches to computer vision resuscitated neural networks, data science, and AI in general, starting from 2012.

In this section, we cover various problems that fall in the category of computer vision. We begin by looking at various types of problems that involve processing images and then move on to problems that involve processing videos. We shall then have a brief look at some public datasets and competitions that have propelled this field into the limelight in the past decade. Finally, we shall wrap up with a brief example of how the data science approach can be used to solve computer vision problems.

Processing Images

As humans, when we perceive a scene or an image visually, we draw various conclusions:

- We categorize the overall scene: We feel we're looking at an office, a residence, a hospital, or a scenic valley. In this case, we are categorizing the entire scene (image) rather than focusing on individual aspects

© Vineet Raina and Srinath Krishnamurthy 2022
V. Raina and S. Krishnamurthy, *Building an Effective Data Science Practice*,
https://doi.org/10.1007/978-1-4842-7419-4_10

(such as people, rooms, beds, trees, etc.) within the scene. This can be regarded as *image classification*, that is, assigning a target class to each image (scene) as a whole.

- We segregate multiple objects that we see in a scene. For example, in a room, we may see multiple persons, furniture, and so forth. In a natural setting, we may see mountains, trees, birds or animals, and other people. This is referred to as object detection or object recognition.

When we try to automate these perceptions using software, the following subclasses of problems arise.

Image Classification/Regression

The ability to assign an overall target class or numeric value to an image has several applications. For example:

- Classification: Detecting cancer grade from biopsy images, determining existence of cancer from a CT scan, automating the annotation of images,[1] and so forth.

- Regression: Determining the age of a person from an image of their face. This is useful, for example, to prevent kids from accessing certain entertainment avenues/websites or determining whether a buyer at a vending machine is underage or not.

We shall look at an end-to-end example of detecting cancer grade from biopsy images later in this chapter.

---

[1] That is, determining the label of an image such as tree, bird, cat, etc.

Object Detection

When we look at any scene, we not only detect the objects such as persons, vehicles, etc. but also their locations – in our human perception, we typically detect the type of objects and their locations simultaneously.

Figure 10-1 shows an example of detecting objects such as persons and airplanes in an image.

Figure 10-1. *Object detection example[2]*

Note that the location of objects can be represented in a few different ways: as bounding boxes or as a polygon boundary around the object, or as precise pixels of the entire object. Different techniques and frameworks support these mechanisms to varying extents.

---

[2] This example is taken from the documentation of the open source Mask-RCNN library at https://github.com/matterport/Mask_RCNN

Object detection is one of the most extensively researched, and rapidly evolving, fields since 2012. Various frameworks such as Mask-RCNN, YOLO, and others offer varying trade-offs between accuracy and performance latency.

Object detection has numerous applications, for example, in intrusion detection systems to locate presence of unexpected objects (people), monitoring traffic density by detecting vehicles and their types as part of an automated traffic lights control system, detection of tumors in medical images, and so forth.

Datasets, Competitions, and Architectures

The successful application of convolutional neural networks (CNN) in 2012 to win the annual ImageNet Large-Scale Visual Recognition Challenge (ILSVRC) ushered in a new age of AI and revolutionized the deep learning landscape.

Apart from the ImageNet dataset on which ILSVRC was based, Pascal VOC (Visual Object Classes), MS COCO (Common Objects in Context), and Open Images are a few datasets that have been crucial in advancing the field of computer vision. In object detection, various challenges arise from the location of the objects, their orientation, varying sizes, and so forth. MS COCO and Open Images contain a richer set of images in more realistic settings and are the latest standards for evaluating performance of image classification and object detection models.

Deep learning approaches,[3] especially based on CNNs, have emerged as the most successful in competitions based on these datasets. We shall cover neural networks in Chapter 16; for now, it may suffice to mention that neural networks are organized into multiple layers and connections between the layers. This design choice of the layers and interlayer

---

[3] Briefly introduced in Chapter 1.

connections in a neural network is referred to as its *architecture*. Popular neural network *architectures,* especially those that perform the best on the previous datasets, find widespread use in various computer vision problems in nearly any domain. Typically, when you set out to solve a computer vision problem that involves processing images, you would first look up the latest literature to identify a state-of-the-art architecture for image classification or a framework for object detection as reported against these standard datasets.

At the time of writing, the EfficientNet family of architectures is one of the better performing architectures for image classification. YOLO is one of the popular frameworks for object detection.

We shall look at CNNs in Chapter 16, which is the basis for all these modern techniques for processing images.

Processing Videos

As humans, when we perceive a scene visually over time, or when we watch a recorded video, we draw various conclusions:

- We categorize the overall activity, for example, if a person is dancing, or if a video footage is of a sporting activity, etc. This is referred to as video classification.

- We track various objects over time, for example, the various players in a team sport, the cars in a car chase in a movie clip, etc. This is referred to as object tracking.

We shall look at a few common applications in the industry that process recorded videos to derive insights such as these.

Video Classification

The problem here is to classify an entire video, for example, to determine the kind of activity happening in the video or to determine the genre of a video. These can be used, for example, in

- Entertainment or education purposes, because automatically tagging videos with the type of activity or genre can enable faster, accurate search and retrieval of relevant content.

- Surveillance systems to detect, for example, crowd panic or similar abnormal situations

These are challenging problems, and the techniques are an active area of research.

Object Tracking

This is the most commonly encountered kind of problem in video analysis and finds applications in varied domains. Examples include

- Tracking movement of pedestrians, vehicles, objects, etc., in a surveillance system or a crowd/traffic monitoring system. This can be a part of a bigger smart city ecosystem including traffic control systems.

- Tracking equipment on a shop floor, for example, as part of assembly lines and workshops.

This, too, is an active area of research – while initial adoptions have been in surveillance systems and smart city use cases, we anticipate increasing adoption soon in the shop floor in manufacturing industries as well.

Data Science Process for Computer Vision

In this section, we shall cover the steps in the data science process for an example of detecting the grade of cancer from a biopsy image.

The World and Data Capture

The data consists of images of prostate tissue biopsies and their ISUP grades as determined by experts. To understand how experts arrive at the ISUP grade, Figure 10-2 shows a sample image and an illustration of the grading process.

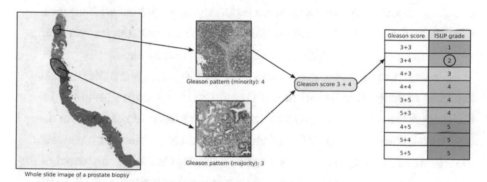

Figure 10-2. *ISUP grading methodology[4]*

As we see, there are certain localized patterns that indicate the presence of cancer, based on how benign glands, and the various cancer cells, look like. A single image may contain several such local "markers" of cancer which need to be combined together in the final evaluation of

---

[4] This figure is sourced from www.kaggle.com/c/prostate-cancer-grade-assessment/overview; our example is based on this Kaggle competition.

an ISUP grade. If there is no cancer, we regard it as ISUP grade 0 in this case. What is relevant to our coverage in this section is that each image is assigned an ISUP grade which is based ultimately on certain localized patterns. References to more details can be found in the *"Further Reading"* section.

Data Preparation

One of the challenges that we see from the biopsy image is that there is a large amount of background whitespace that does not contain any useful information. Also, the image is typically longer in one direction than another – most image classification techniques work best with square images and can tolerate some variation in the aspect ratio, but probably won't work well with the kinds of variations in our images.

Since in our case, we are interested more in localized patterns that indicate cancerous cells rather than a pattern in the entire image, one technique is to slice the image up into smaller tiles and reassemble the tiles into a square image. While doing so, we pick the tiles with the least background whitespace, that is, the most tissue, thus covering most of the tissue regions. By taking this approach, we resolve both the challenges. Figure 10-3 shows an example of this.[5]

---

[5] Refer to www.kaggle.com/iafoss/panda-16x128x128-tiles; this novel data preparation technique turned out to be crucial to solving this problem.

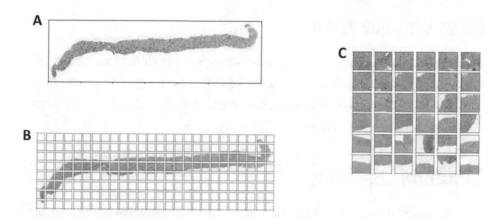

Figure 10-3. *Data preparation: tiling example. "A" is the original image. "B" shows the tiles created. "C" is the transformed image formed by reassembling 36 tiles from "B" into a square image with maximal tissue*

But how to break the image into tiles, that is, what size should the tiles be? Very small tiles will ensure that nearly no background whitespace is present, and most of the tissue region is retained. But it can lead to breaking up the localized patterns into multiple tiles making it difficult to detect the patterns. On the other hand, large tiles would retain most of the relevant patterns, but may result in incorporating a lot of background whitespace. These variations are initially eyeballed using visual analysis like in the previous figure.

In some cases, images may contain other marks, for example, pen marks drawn by a pathologist. It would be better to remove this noise in the images[6] – this also falls in data preparation – and visualize (some of) the cleaned images to validate the cleansing process.

---

[6] The field of image processing that deals with filters, cleaning, filling, etc., in images is referred to as *morphology*. Data scientists may need to gain some expertise in morphological techniques for improving the accuracy in computer vision solutions.

Data Visualization

After preparing the data, you might typically want to design visualizations for gaining insights such as variation of tissue coverage based on the size and number of selected tiles, etc. But we will skip directly to the machine learning step for conciseness.

Machine Learning

Our prepared data now has the transformed square images with maximum tissue region and the ISUP grade. We shall train a neural network using this prepared data to predict ISUP grade directly from a transformed square image.[7] From the literature, we see that the EfficientNet family of models, described in Tan and Le (2019), is apparently state of the art. The EfficientNet family of models has architectures called B0, B1 ... up to B7. EfficientNet-B0 is the simplest architecture with the least complexity and is typically used to create a first baseline model. So, let us use an EfficientNet-B0 model for our problem.[8] We shall look at CNNs, on which EfficientNet is based, in more detail in Chapter 16.

If the model doesn't perform well, we may need to go back to improving the data preparation methodologies, for example, using the tiling approach with varying tile sizes to determine which data preparation results in the best model. But how to determine whether a model is performing well? In other words, how do we evaluate the performance of a model in this case?

---

[7] Without determining the intermediate Gleason score that we saw in Figure 10-2.

[8] We're acting as cowboys here – treating an EfficientNet model as a black box, interested only in predictive accuracy rather than understanding which regions are possibly cancerous and led to the final grade, etc.

Model Performance Evaluation

In many cases, such as the example in Chapter 4, the performance of a model while predicting classes is determined based on how many observations are correctly classified by the model – in other words, a prediction is treated either as right or wrong; there is no gray area in between.

In the case of a problem like cancer grade detection, if an image of cancer grade 4 is predicted as 5, it is incorrect but still closer to the truth than, say, a prediction of 1 or 2. In this case, the grades are not really distinct categories but are *ordered* in the sense of how serious the cancer is.[9] Thus, we are interested in how close the model's predictions are to the truth, rather than merely right or wrong. In a case like this, a more appropriate metric would be something like the *weighted kappa* – we shall look at model performance evaluation in more detail in Chapter 16. Meanwhile, this brief note is to highlight that when we use a term like "model performance," it does not necessarily imply simply whether the prediction is right or wrong – the precise choice of metric depends on the problem at hand.

While an appropriate metric is chosen to begin with, the metric is also often crafted or refined over multiple iterations of the data science process.

Once we have a model that performs reasonably well, we can use it for predicting ISUP grade from a biopsy image.

---

[9] A variable like ISUP grade, whose values are an ordered set of categories, is referred to as an ordinal. When the target variable is an ordinal, the problem is referred to as ordinal regression, which is slightly different from both classification and regression that we saw earlier. (Ordinals are discussed further in Chapter 14.)

ADVANCED NOTE: ENSEMBLES

During multiple iterations and experiments, we may have several models that we have trained. In practice, rather than use the best of these models, it is often better to use an *ensemble* of models.

An ensemble model basically takes the predictions from all its constituent underlying models and aggregates them to give the final result. As a crude example, the ensemble might simply return the majority result, for example, if a majority of the models is predicting an ISUP grade of 3, then the final result is 3.

There are various methods to aggregate the results of multiple models, ranging from simple majority voting to advanced ML techniques for aggregation. The details are out of our scope here – the key takeaway is that multiple experiments and iterations are especially useful in computer vision problems, where ensembles have demonstrated high predictive power and generalizability in practice.

Inference

During inference, we will need to run the exact data preparation steps that we used during training. For example, prior to creating our final model in the machine learning step, we would have used certain values for the size and number of selected tiles and transformed the image into a square image as explained in the data preparation section. Those exact transformations, with the same values for the size and number of selected tiles, should be applied to the new images during inference as well.

ADVANCED NOTE: TEST-TIME AUGMENTATION

One common technique applied during inference for computer vision problems is that of test-time augmentation (TTA). TTA is intended to increase robustness against variations in the orientation or positioning of the image.

To understand TTA, it is necessary to understand a detail about how the model inference works. When we train an EfficientNet-B0 model using the prepared data (transformed square images) and the target feature as ISUP grade, the model actually learns to predict, given a new image, the *probabilities* of the image belonging to each of the ISUP grades. We then infer that the ISUP grade with the highest probability is the predicted grade.

Now for TTA, we can create an augmented image by, for example, shifting the original image slightly to the right. Then the model is used to infer the probabilities of the ISUP grades from both the original image and the augmented image. By averaging the probabilities of each ISUP grade across the original and augmented images, we obtain the final probabilities of the ISUP grades. We then predict the ISUP grade with the highest probability as our final result.

Data Engineering

In our dataset, each individual image can be quite large, and the overall dataset size can be in the order of hundreds of gigabytes. Typically, if you have a team of data scientists working collaboratively on large datasets, a shared file system will be useful. This way, as data scientists perform the various data preparation steps we saw earlier, the modified images will also be accessible to the entire team.

Also, for training models such as CNN-based models, you would need to use powerful GPUs because the computations are rather intensive and complex. While it is possible to setup an on-premises infrastructure of this sort, it is increasingly common and cost-effective to use cloud services such as AWS[10] for such deep learning experimentation. For example, AWS Elastic File System (EFS) can be used as a shared file system, and GPU machines of varying sizes can be used to train models.

Conclusion

In this chapter, we covered the various subclasses of problems that fall under the ambit of computer vision. We also looked at an end-to-end example of detecting prostate cancer grade from biopsy images.

Further Reading

Refer to Liu, Ouyang, and Wang (2020) for a survey of object detection techniques based on deep learning.

Chollet (2018) has an excellent chapter that introduces technical details of *deep learning for computer vision*.

Lu et al. (2019) cover a wide range of topics in medical imaging.

Refer to Prostate cANcer graDe Assessment (PANDA) Challenge for more details of the prostate cancer grading process.

---

[10] Amazon Web Services, https://aws.amazon.com/

References

Chollet, Francois. *Deep Learning with Python*. NY, USA: Manning, 2018.

Liu, L., W. Ouyang and X. Wang. "Deep Learning for Generic Object Detection: A Survey." *International Journal of Computer Vision 128* (2020): 261–318.

Lu, Le, et al. *Deep Learning and Convolutional Neural Networks for Medical Imaging and Clinical Informatics*. Cham, Switzerland: Springer, 2019.

Prostate cANcer graDe Assessment (PANDA) Challenge. www.kaggle. com/c/prostate-cancer-grade-assessment/overview/additional-resources. n.d.

Tan, Minxing and Quoc V. Le. "EfficientNet: Rethinking Model Scaling for Convolutional Neural Networks." *Proceedings of the 36th International Conference on Machine Learning*. Long Beach, California, 2019.

CHAPTER 11

Sequential Decision-Making

One of the more advanced manifestations of "intelligence" is the ability to voluntarily take decisions that knowingly accept losses in the short-term with a view to gaining a desired outcome in the longer run. The "desired outcome" can take various forms – maximizing profits/rewards (e.g., in an investment strategy), maximizing the chances to realize a targeted goal (e.g., winning in a competition such as chess), or saving patients with life-threatening diseases.

The common thread to these is the ability to take a sequence of decisions – buy/sell, or the move to make, or the test/treatment to recommend. And these decisions are to be taken dynamically in an environment which is itself ever changing and influenced by the decisions taken as well.

Reinforcement learning (RL) is a branch of ML that deals with this aspect of automating sequential decision-making to maximize long-term rewards, often at the *seeming* cost of short-term losses. While *sequential decision-making* is a class of problems, RL is currently the de facto framework within which these kinds of problems are formulated and solved. In the rest of this chapter, we shall thus cover reinforcement learning.

© Vineet Raina and Srinath Krishnamurthy 2022
V. Raina and S. Krishnamurthy, *Building an Effective Data Science Practice*,
https://doi.org/10.1007/978-1-4842-7419-4_11

The intuition behind RL is very similar to how a child learns good behavior based on the rewards or punishments they receive from their parents – parental appreciation *reinforces* the adherence to good behavior, while parental punishment *reinforces* the avoidance of bad behavior.

RL has extended the horizons of AI in recent times[1] by creating the strongest AI engines at games such as chess and Go. Let us consider the example of chess: long before the RL-based AlphaZero chess engine came along in 2017, we had strong chess engines during the 2000s that were already regarded to be stronger than the best human chess players. Those chess engines were typically able to sacrifice pieces if it led to a quick victory, for example, by a quick attack on the opponent's king; in chess parlance, as in real life, these are referred to as "tactical" decisions or sacrifices. Chess engines were thus widely regarded as tactical monsters that could nevertheless struggle to find or appreciate certain "strategic" sacrifices made by human grandmasters for long-term gains – until, in late 2017, AlphaZero came along. AlphaZero not only seemed to appreciate and validate a lot of the strategic sacrifices that human grandmasters would make but also expanded the creative horizon by making more nuanced and daring strategic sacrifices that surprised many human grandmasters as well.

In real life outside of sporting/gaming competitions though, such as in investment or healthcare, such sequential decisions are inherently high-risk activities; we would still rather trust an investment banker or a doctor's credentials than a complex algorithm to make decisions for us. Thus, RL is an active area of research, particularly with a focus on mechanisms to reduce risk. At this point, we feel that RL is far from replacing the decision-makers in a company – so, in this book, we shall only offer brief coverage of the fundamental concepts of RL, just enough to enable you to determine if you have any use cases for which RL might be a good fit. For more detailed coverage of RL, we'll point to references in the *"Further Reading"* section.

---

[1] RL has been around for a long time, with the theory originating in the late 1950s. But RL combined with deep learning (deep RL) has led to the recent popularity of RL since 2017. In this book, we simply use the term RL to refer to the overall field.

The RL Setting

As an illustrative example for this chapter, let us consider a diagnostic expert Dr. House, whose only goal is to save his patient's life by diagnosing and treating the patient's mysterious ailment in time before they succumb to the illness. Unfortunately, this one-pointed focus causes him to violate legal, ethical, or professional rules and conventions when required, if it enables him to improve the chances of saving his patient's life. This can often result in drastic measures such as subjecting the patient to extreme pain and suffering temporarily, or violating hospital policies/legalese, if it offers slightly improved odds of diagnosing the patient faster than traditional tests for which there isn't sufficient time.

Each case that House handles begins with a patient exhibiting intriguing symptoms. After House takes several *sequential decisions* that each recommend further tests resulting in new observations, a case is concluded when the root cause of the patient's symptoms is determined in time or when the patient dies. House, being the expert that he is, the latter outcome has been rather rare.

Let us see how an AI engine, Dr. Nestor,[2] can be trained to diagnose like House. While we would like Nestor to learn the diagnostic skills of House, we also want to temper it with some aversion to illegal actions. In the process of looking at how Nestor can be trained to achieve this, we shall cover the basic variations of RL and some of the challenges.

---

[2] The name is a nod to the robot Nestor-10 in Asimov's *Little Lost Robot* which is not fed with the constraint to prevent harm to humans.

Basic Knowledge and Rules

To begin with, Nestor is fed all the basic medical knowledge, such as known diseases, symptoms, and actions that can be taken such as recommending medications and tests. We are then ready to train the agent to take appropriate decisions in an environment using this knowledge.

Training Nestor

The agent can be trained in a few different ways depending on the kind of data and domain. In our current example, we will be structuring the training into multiple phases. Note that, depending on the details of the problem being solved, there can be numerous variations in regard to the kinds of phases used – the phases we cover are oriented toward our illustrative example of Nestor.

In this section, we shall first understand how Nestor interacts with its environment while attempting to solve a single case; this interaction with the environment is common for all the training phases that follow.

Episode

We provide an intuitive notion of what an episode is, based on Figure 11-1 which shows what happens within each *episode* – this forms the basic framework for RL.

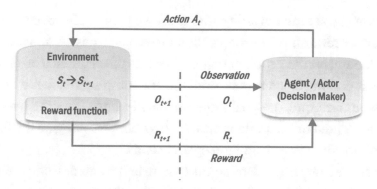

Figure 11-1. *An episode in RL*

In our illustrative example, each episode corresponds to a patient's case:

- The agent (Nestor) receives an initial observation, O_0, from its environmental state S_0. An observation could be the set of symptoms, medical history, etc., of the patient.

- On obtaining observation O_t, the agent (Nestor) takes an action A_t – this could be recommending a test or medication that will obtain further information.

- Based on the action taken, the environment (state of the patient) changes; new symptoms are uncovered resulting in the next observation O_{t+1}. And the agent (Nestor) is given a reward R_{t+1}. We will look at examples of rewards later.

As you can see, an episode consists of a sequence of <action, observation, reward>. How long a sequence constitutes an "episode" would depend on the problem being solved, as the sequence of <action, observation, reward> continues until the environment reaches a final state. In our example, the final state is reached when either the patient is diagnosed/cured or the patient dies. At this point, Nestor gets the final observation[3] and reward, and the episode ends.

There are a few important points to note in how an episode unfolds. Firstly, each episode (handling of a single patient case) is independent from the previous one.

Next, rewards are crucial in how Nestor "learns" what are good decisions/actions. Suppose we specify a *reward function* that assigns a reward of

- -0.2 for any illegal interim action, that is, such actions are penalized slightly.

- 0 for all other interim actions, that is, the immediate change in the environment (e.g., new symptoms uncovered or any changes in the patient's condition) due to an action is considered irrelevant.

- +1 if patient gets diagnosed/cured, -1 if patient dies, that is, the final outcome of the episode is the most significant factor.

At the end of each episode, Nestor "learns" based on the ***total*** reward it got for all its actions. For example, it knows that a sequence of decisions that led to a total reward of 1 is better than a sequence of decisions that led to a total reward of 0.6, etc.

Having understood how Nestor interacts with its environment, let us now look at the phases of training.

---

[3] Final observation is that the patient gets diagnosed/cured or dies.

Training Phases

In this section, we shall look at the phases that could go into one possible way of training Nestor.

Past Cases

In our current example, we shall first use the past case files of House during the episodes, because we want Nestor to diagnose like House would.

To execute the previous framework on *past* case files of House, the setup can be such that the agent mimics the action of the expert (House), and the environment/observation is updated to reflect what actually occurred in the case as a result of the action. The mechanism of assigning rewards to each action, and learning based on the total reward at the end of an episode, is the same as mentioned in the previous section. In this way, the basic framework explained earlier unfolds, and the agent learns from the past case files and their handling by the expert.

Ongoing New Cases, with Imitation

After an initial phase of training from the past case files, we can allow the agent to be trained using ongoing cases as well. Again here, the agent can mimic the action of the expert, House, and be fed the resulting state/observation and reward. Based on the outcome of the episode and the total reward accumulated, the agent learns to imitate the expert.

Supervised *Exploration*

Now, we allow the agent to take its decisions independently, rather than imitate the expert. In this case, we shall continue to supervise the agent, that is, the action recommended by the agent isn't executed in the real world unless approved by a supervising expert diagnostician. The framework can be slightly modified so that if an utterly nonsensical[4] action is suggested, the agent gets a severe rebuke immediately (e.g., a reward of -1) and the episode (for the agent) is terminated. Also, if, for a particular episode, the actions recommended by the agent are entirely nonsensical, we can fall back to allow the agent to imitate the expert for that episode (as in the previous section). Apart from these minor modifications, the rest of the framework continues in the same way, that is, rewards are assigned similarly, and the agent learns similarly at the end of each episode.

Once Nestor has been trained and is found to be taking reasonable decisions, it can be *exploited* to take decisions on new cases. (Our kid AI engine is now a teenager.)

Supervised *Exploitation*

When being exploited, the environment-agent interaction shown in Figure 11-1 and the supervisory setup in the previous section still apply, with one important difference. In the earlier supervised exploration phase, Nestor was trying to learn as much as possible about which decisions are better – so it could often take new random decisions to see what reward it gets. In the exploitation phase, Nestor will instead only take decisions that it expects will result in maximum overall reward for the entire episode. The agent can now be considered as assisting an expert by suggesting novel approaches which the expert carefully evaluates – Nestor is now a part of the expert's "team" of doctors, effectively.

---

[4] Nonsensical, that is, incorrect, inappropriate, or impossible to execute.

Having seen an example of training and using an agent, let us now look at a few variations, particularly in regard to the data used for training.

Data in the RL Setting

We shall cover a couple of variations, especially in regard to how the data is obtained and correspondingly how an agent is trained. There are several other variations related to how reward is specified, actions are taken, or how the environment is modeled – these can be found in the references.

As we have repeatedly seen, data science begins with data. In the previous example, we required data about real patient cases, the actions taken during the diagnoses, and the outcomes. We obtained them from past case files and ongoing cases.

Depending on the specific use case/domain, you may need real data generated by human actions, or simulated data may be appropriate. In some cases, we can combine both the approaches as well. We shall look at these variations briefly.

Data of Experts' Decisions

In many cases, existing data that includes decisions taken by experts is used. In the first two phases of training Nestor in the previous section, we used past and ongoing case files of House. This is an example of training an RL agent using data of experts' decisions.

In a similar manner, the initial version of AlphaGo was trained on past Go games played by experts.[5] If we have past data, the only reason to not use it is if we want the agent to be entirely free from any human bias/limitations.

---

[5] It "learned" further by playing thousands of matches with human players.

Simulated Data

In addition to learning from human games, the initial version of AlphaGo also learned from data simulated by self-play, that is, playing games against itself. This version of AlphaGo was strong enough to defeat Lee Sedol, the Go World Champion.

The next version of AlphaGo – called AlphaGo Zero – was trained solely by *self-play*, that is, the engine played games against itself starting from random play without any use of human data. This way, the engine would not be limited by the human understanding of the game. AlphaGo Zero defeated AlphaGo by 100 games to 0.

Motivated by these successes, the latest AlphaZero system was created, which generalized the AlphaGo Zero approach into a single algorithm that learns games such as chess, Go, and shogi. See Silver et al. (2018) for more details. It is this version we referred to at the beginning of this chapter.

Similarly, in simulations for areas such as self-driving cars,[6] the agent can try arbitrary random trajectories of the car that may result in crashes until it learns to drive properly. This is one of the more popular environments for developers to learn about RL.

Challenges in RL

Having covered some basic concepts around RL, in this section, we look at a few common, practical challenges in RL.

---

[6] For example, see Amazon DeepRacer.

Availability of Data

Reinforcement learning requires a *lot* of data. For games such as chess and Go, in addition to the historical archive of grandmaster games, simulations can be used to generate an arbitrary amount of data, which is one of the reasons those were the first areas to be "solved." For realistic applications where the risk of using simulations is very high, and which therefore rely on expert imitation and/or supervision, the availability of sufficient data is a primary challenge.

Information in Observations

Even if we manage to get a large amount of data, the other challenge in realistic situations is ensuring that each observation has sufficient *information*. As Figure 11-1 shows, an *observation* is only a subset of the overall *state* of the *environment*. In other words, an observation may not capture sufficient information from the environment. Often, data that humans "observe" are not available in an automated way, for example, for automating diagnosis/treatment, many aspects seen by an expert doctor when they size up a patient may not be captured as "readings" in the patient records. Humans also tend to have an intuition that lead them to gather more information (i.e., expand the scope of an observation) in some cases. House, for example, has been known to break into a patient's house to get more information or to regard an apparent personality trait such as bravery or altruism as symptoms. The notion of when to expand the scope of observations needed is one of the keys to decision-making and is a challenge to automate.

Exploration vs. Exploitation

Finally, one of the fundamental challenges is the exploration vs. exploitation trade-off. For an AI engine to continue to "learn," it needs to occasionally take slightly random decisions to *see* what happens – maybe a new random decision might be better than its previous "learnings." We have referred to these attempts by an agent to learn as exploration; on the other hand, when an agent is taking decisions aimed at achieving an optimal outcome, we refer to it as exploitation.

In our illustrative example, we had looked at *supervised* exploration and exploitation – generally speaking, both exploration and exploitation could be supervised or unsupervised. The ultimate vision is an unsupervised agent that can determine by itself when exploration can be done and when it can continue with exploitation.

There is increasing research into the exploration vs. exploitation trade-off – one of the common intuitive ways is to exponentially increase the frequency of exploitation (and decrease the frequency of exploration). A mechanism like this, with appropriately tuned exponential decay, is likely going to be the way RL will be adopted in real use cases in the near future.

Data Science Process for RL

As mentioned earlier, the phases of training an RL agent can vary widely depending on the specifics of the problem; nevertheless, we can usually try to map the various steps in the life cycle of an RL agent to the steps of our data science process.

In the case of our illustrative example covered in "The RL Setting" section

- Collecting data of past case files of House and making it available to the agent can be regarded as data capture. Likewise, when ongoing cases and the expert's actions are used to train the agent, collecting this data can also be regarded as data capture.

- Various transformations that might be required to convert data from the format of medical records and device readings to that of state/observations that an agent can understand – this can be regarded as data preparation.

- Monitoring how an agent is progressing during training (exploration) can be regarded as data visualization iterations.

- The training phases, based on past or ongoing cases, can be regarded as machine learning iterations.

- The (supervised) exploitation phase can be regarded as inference.

In the extreme vision of an entirely unsupervised agent, all aspects of the environment-agent interaction, as well as the details of how the agent learns from the rewards, are implemented as part of an end-to-end automated software system, that is, we can regard that all the steps of the data science process are entirely automated. This has been achieved to a significant extent in case of games like chess and Go, but in other real-world domains, this is one of the most complex, challenging, and ambitious visions – not only of data science but of AI in general.

Conclusion

In this chapter, we only touched upon some of the fundamentals of modern deep reinforcement learning and covered a basic setting for RL. Numerous variations abound regarding the way rewards are determined, how actions are taken based on the observations, and so forth. We shall point to some of the relevant literature in the next section.

The reader may have realized that Dr. House in our illustrative example is based on the eponymous TV series. The semi-fictional narrative in this chapter is indicative of the notion that classical science fiction, somewhat reminiscent of a few of Asimov's works, is increasingly becoming a reality, especially when machines can take decisions that can seem "intuitive" like humans.

Our take is that, apart from gaming systems, we are far from letting AI agents loose in the field to take sequential decisions for maximizing overall reward. Initial adoption will likely be along the lines of augmenting human experts to improve decision-making based on novel, alternative decision paths suggested by the agent. There is increasing research in this regard, even in fields such as healthcare.

Further Reading

For a detailed introduction to RL, including intuitive and some mathematical details, refer to Sutton and Barto (2018).

For the milestone publication of AlphaZero, refer to Silver et al. (2018) and its supplementary material.

Amazon DeepRacer is one of the more popular web services to begin to start learning RL principles with a hands-on approach.

For a general survey of reinforcement learning in healthcare – it doesn't get more real than in healthcare! – refer to Yu, Liu, and Nemati (2020). It provides a good overview in general of the extant jargon and variations in the field of RL, followed by applications in healthcare including diagnosis and dynamic treatment regimes, and the significant challenges. An example of a real-world application in the field of dynamic treatment recommendation is Wang et al. (2018).

References

Silver, David et al. "A general reinforcement learning algorithm that masters chess, shogi, and Go through self-play." *Science 362* 7 December 2018: 1140–1144.

Sutton, Richard S. and Andrew G. Barto. *Reinforcement Learning - an Introduction, 2nd edition.* Cambridge, Massachusetts: The MIT Press, 2018.

Wang, Lu, et al. "Supervised Reinforcement Learning with Recurrent Neural Network for Dynamic Treatment Recommendation." *Proceedings of ACM Conference (Conference'17).* New York, NY, USA: ACM, 2018.

Yu, Chao, Jiming Liu and Shamim Nemati. *Reinforcement Learning in Healthcare: A Survey. https://arxiv.org/abs/1908.08796.* 2020.

PART III

Techniques and Technologies

In Part 2, we looked at a few data science problems and how they are solved by choosing the appropriate techniques in the different steps of the data science process. The skill of choosing the right techniques depends on a good conceptual understanding of the host of techniques available for each step of the data science process. In this part, we cover the various techniques used in different steps of the data science process and the technologies (libraries, tools, services, etc.) that you can use to apply these techniques. This part forms the technical meat of the book.

In Chapter 12, we first cover an overview of the techniques and technologies involved in all the steps of the data science process. In Chapters 13–17, we look at each step of the data science process in more detail – one chapter per step of data science process covering the techniques/technologies for that step. Then, in Chapter 18, we cover other important tools and services that cut across multiple steps in the data science process.

In Chapter 19, we look at a reference architecture which brings together these technologies to enable an operational data science team.

Having thus grasped the concepts behind the techniques, in Chapter 20, we wrap up the discussion about monks vs. cowboys that we started in Chapter 3. We fill in the differences in their praxis, particularly regarding how the culture determines the preferred choices of techniques and technologies.

CHAPTER 12

Techniques and Technologies: An Overview

In this chapter, we provide a very high-level overview of the various techniques and technologies used for data science. This brief overview is intended to establish the framework for specifics covered in Chapters 13–19.

Figure 12-1 and Figure 12-2 show some of the techniques and technologies, respectively, used in each step of the data science process.

© Vineet Raina and Srinath Krishnamurthy 2022
V. Raina and S. Krishnamurthy, *Building an Effective Data Science Practice*,
https://doi.org/10.1007/978-1-4842-7419-4_12

Data Capture	Data Preparation	Data Visualization	Machine Learning	Inference
Data Sources	**Data cleansing, transformations**	**Axis-based visualizations**	**Supervised**	Model conversion
• Web-scraping	• Standardization	• Scatter plot	• Linear regression	Model packaging
• APIs	• Missing values	• Histogram	• Logistic regression	
• IoT protocols	• One-hot encoding	• Box plot	• Decision tree	Model inference
		• KDE plot	• Random forest, Gradient boosting	
Ingestion	**Feature extraction**		• SVM	Model monitoring
• ETL scripts	• PCA	**Non-Axis visualizations**		• AB testing
• Workflow orchestration	• Signal processing (from audio & images)	• Tree-map	**Unsupervised**	
• Event stream processing		• Pie chart	• K-Means	
		• Word cloud	• Agglomerative clustering	
Data Storage	**NLP**	**Layouts**	• Local Outlier Factor	
• Data Lake	• Stemming	• Overlay	**Neural networks**	
• Compressed columnar storage formats	• Lemmatization	• Data Lattice	• CNN	
	• tf-idf		• RNN	
• Data Warehouse		**Interactive visualizations**	• Architectures e.g., EfficientNet	
• File systems		• Drill-down	**Time series**	
		• Time-based animation	• ARIMA	
			• SARIMA	
			Model performance and tuning	
			• Grid search	
			• Cross-validation	
			• F1, ROC curves	
			• Cohen's kappa	

Figure 12-1. *Some techniques used in each step of the data science process*

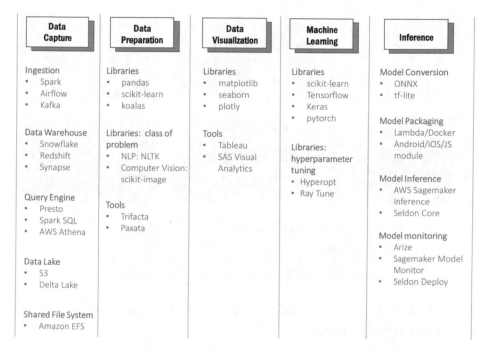

Figure 12-2. *Some technologies used in each step of the data science process*[1]

We shall be covering a few of these techniques and technologies in more detail from Chapter 13 to Chapter 17 – one chapter per step of the data science process. While doing so, we shall also cover the data engineering aspects of each step in the corresponding chapter itself.

There are several tools and services that cut across multiple steps of the data science process. Some of these are shown in Figure 12-3 and are covered in more detail in Chapter 18.

---

[1] Some of the technologies depicted within one step might be useful in other steps as well. We have included them within the step where we find them most useful.

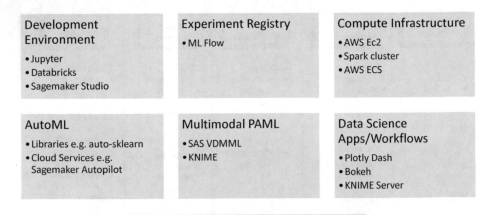

Development Environment
- Jupyter
- Databricks
- Sagemaker Studio

Experiment Registry
- ML Flow

Compute Infrastructure
- AWS Ec2
- Spark cluster
- AWS ECS

AutoML
- Libraries e.g. auto-sklearn
- Cloud Services e.g. Sagemaker Autopilot

Multimodal PAML
- SAS VDMML
- KNIME

Data Science Apps/Workflows
- Plotly Dash
- Bokeh
- KNIME Server

AI Services & Libraries
- Time series forecasting: Prophet, Amazon Forecast
- NLP: Amazon Comprehend, Azure Text Analytics
- Computer Vision: Open CV, Amazon Rekognition

Figure 12-3. *Some tools and services that cut across multiple steps of the data science process*

Thus, by the end of Chapter 18, we would have covered the various technologies used for data science. Then in Chapter 19, we shall look at how these technologies come together in a *reference architecture* to enable the operations of a data science team.

Note that the three figures in this chapter are intended to capture some of the key representative terms and concepts in the field of data science at the time of writing. We find them useful also as a framework for categorizing the overall field, that is, whenever a new technique or technology is encountered, we find it useful to place them within an appropriate category in one of these figures. This helps capture the primary capability of a technique/technology and enables communication with other team members and stakeholders about it. Placing a technique or technology in an appropriate category can also be useful to determine, compare, and evaluate alternatives.

CHAPTER 13

Data Capture

In this chapter, we shall cover the typical techniques and technologies used in the data capture step of the data science process.

For data capture, the very first activity is to identify what data is relevant and which are the sources of the relevant data. Once these are determined, the further activities in the data capture step, and the relevant components, are shown in Figure 13-1.

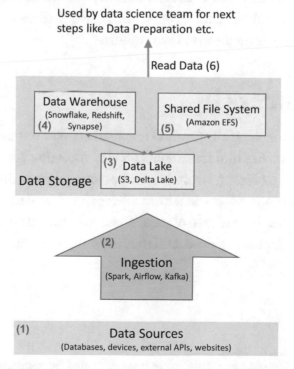

Figure 13-1. *Activities and components in data capture*

© Vineet Raina and Srinath Krishnamurthy 2022
V. Raina and S. Krishnamurthy, *Building an Effective Data Science Practice*,
https://doi.org/10.1007/978-1-4842-7419-4_13

As seen in the figure, we broadly segregate the components involved in data capture into three groups: *data sources, ingestion,* and *data storage.* It is important to note that the specific data science problem you are targeting might require only one data source, and the relevant data might already be readily available in, say, a CSV, excel file, or database.[1] In such cases, a data scientist can directly use this data. But more commonly in a mature organization, there would be multiple data sources relevant to the data science problems you are planning to solve – the earlier diagram depicts this more extensive scenario.

In the first few sections of this chapter, we shall cover Figure 13-1 starting from the bottom and moving upward in the numeric sequence indicated in the boxes/arrows. While doing so, we shall discuss both the techniques and the technologies involved in each area. We shall then touch upon a few factors to consider while choosing between open source and paid tools for data capture. Finally, we shall mention the data engineering aspects involved in data capture.

Data Sources (1)

In an organization, typically the data is spread across multiple sources. If your organization has multiple applications or tools that generate data, then these internal systems would typically store data into **databases**. If your organization collects data from **devices**, such as data from IoT systems, these too are a source of data. These are typically the primary sources of data for data science, and they are unique to your business.

---

[1] In some cases, the data could also have been collected by manual entries in an excel file by personnel.

In some cases, you may source data from **external APIs**. Examples of external APIs are

- Social media websites that expose APIs, such as Twitter.

- Web services that provide some information about common environmental factors such as weather, geolocation, etc.

- Third-party tools that you have deployed that expose APIs, for example, if you have installed a local weather station on your premises, it could expose APIs for querying the data.

In a few rare cases, you may want to extract some information from **websites** directly. This is referred to as web scraping and requires some knowledge of the layout of a source web page. It is not a recommended approach, because whenever the structure of a website changes, you would need to modify the way you extract information – thus, maintenance and reliability tend to be an issue with this approach. But this approach is followed in rare cases – for example, if you are building an information system based on publicly available information from multiple websites that do not expose an API.

A data scientist could theoretically query these disparate sources to obtain the data they need for analysis. But a significantly more effective approach would be to collate this data into a single, centralized sandbox, that is, *data storage*, from which the data science team can perform their analysis. This requires *ingesting* the data from these multiple data sources, which we shall look at next.

Ingestion (2)

Various ETL[2] and workflow libraries/tools can be used to merge, transform, and ingest data into the central data storage from multiple data sources – we are referring to this broadly as **ingestion**. Spark, Airflow, and Kafka are commonly used – often together – and represent three common categories of tools:

- ETL scripts: Spark is representative of big data ETL scripts and batch jobs required to merge multiple data sources, cleaning and transforming the data.

- Workflow orchestration: Airflow is representative of tools that orchestrate complex workflows spanning across multiple scripts/jobs.

- Event stream processing: Kafka is representative of *event stream processing*. As real-time data arrives from the data sources into Kafka, listeners are triggered, which in turn can trigger ETL scripts or workflows.

If your company has traditional enterprise data integration tools such as Informatica, they can also be used for these purposes as appropriate.

The goal of ingestion is to have the data available in reasonably organized form in the centralized data storage.

Data Storage

The data storage contains all the ingested data and is used by the rest of the data science team for the other steps in the data science process, beginning with data preparation.

---

[2] Extract, transform, and load: refers to *extracting* data from one or more sources, *transforming* the data, and finally *loading* it into a destination system.

The data storage can consist of one or more of the following: data lake (3), data warehouse (4), and shared file system (5). We shall look at each of these in the following subsections.

Data Lake (3)

A data lake is typically where all your data assets would get collected. In addition to the data ingested from data sources, data is also often moved from/to the data lake to/from other forms of storage covered in the following subsections.

Low storage cost is one of the primary hallmarks of a data lake. Amazon S3 (or its equivalent on Azure and other cloud providers) has been the technology of choice for data lakes in the past few years.[3]

A data lake can be used for storing data such as images, videos, audio, etc. It can also be used to store tabular data in formats such as CSV, JSON, Parquet, or ORC.

For tabular data, data lakes have traditionally had a couple of limitations:

1.   Data lakes do not support efficient updates of individual records. This often led to issues[4] in a data processing pipeline.

2.   SQL is a common mechanism for querying tabular data for complex analysis and for updating records. But data lakes do not support SQL natively.

---

[3] Before S3, HDFS (Hadoop Distributed File System) was a popular choice.

[4] When engineers have to handle row-level updates themselves without support for atomicity, etc., from the storage technology, it often leads to issues related to data inconsistency, duplication, etc.

Recent technologies such as Delta Lake support an SQL layer on top of a data lake that allows efficient updates of records as well. This simplifies data processing pipelines significantly.

Since Delta Lake is built on top of data lake technologies, we categorize it also as a data lake.

Data Warehouse (4)

The primary purpose of data warehouses is to enable rapid execution of complex analytical queries using SQL. This enables data scientists and data analysts to perform rapid exploratory data analysis using visualization tools/libraries or SQL. While data warehouses have been around since the 1980s, the most significant developments in the past decade have been the ability to store semi-structured and unstructured data, such as JSON, together with the traditional tabular form.

Often while beginning a new series of experiments, a data scientist/engineer will load the relevant data for analysis from the data lake into the data warehouse.

Advanced BI tools are commonly used for the data visualization step (see Chapter 15). These BI tools typically require a data warehouse to execute multiple SQL queries concurrently and efficiently.

Modern cloud data warehouses also support querying tabular data stored in data lakes using SQL. For example, if you have tabular data stored in Parquet format in Amazon S3, it can be queried from Amazon Redshift.[5]

Data warehouses also support efficient updates of individual records using SQL. This is one of the additional benefits of a data warehouse compared to tabular data stored in a data lake.

Snowflake, Amazon Redshift, and Azure Synapse are examples of modern data warehouses.

---

[5] Using Redshift Spectrum.

ADVANCED NOTE: DECOUPLED COMPUTE AND STORAGE

Around 2015, cloud data warehouses began to be architected to offer decoupled storage and compute to enable scaling as per the needs of a data science team. For example, a data scientist or data engineer could quickly spin up a compute cluster of an appropriate size to perform analysis and shut it down when not required. In case of traditional data warehouses, on the other hand, you typically had to keep a cluster up all the time since storage and compute were on the same cluster.

All the three examples of data warehouses we mentioned support decoupled storage and compute scaling.

TERMINOLOGY CHAOS: LAKEHOUSE

A term that is recently in the limelight is *lakehouse*. A lakehouse's vision is to combine the best of both worlds – data lakes (low cost) and data warehouses (performant SQL, with the ability to update records) – with decoupled storage and compute.

We feel that the term "lakehouse" is useful to describe the vision, rather than to categorize the tools. For example, Delta Lake, which we categorize as a data lake, can also be characterized as a lakehouse. The modern cloud data warehouses we cited all have capabilities that enable them to also be characterized as lakehouses.

In any case, we would suggest that you choose the right technology, that is, data lake and/or data warehouse, for your team and organization – *without* getting distracted by the notion of *lakehouse*.

Shared File Systems (5)

If your team is working with images, video, audio, etc., and deep learning frameworks that require GPUs, then a shared file system such as Amazon EFS can be considered to enable efficient access to the data for machine learning from multiple machines or clusters.

As various transformations happen in the data preparation step, the outputs of data preparation – such as transformed images, etc. – can also be written back to EFS. This enables seamless collaboration across the data scientists and data engineers in your team, for example, if one data scientist develops a new data preparation mechanism, the resulting transformed data can be stored in EFS and be immediately available to the other team members for further analysis.

Read Data (6)

The data in data storage is accessed by the data science team for the further steps of the data science process, beginning with data preparation, etc. In this section, we shall cover how the data is typically accessed.

If you are using only a data warehouse, then your team would use SQL to read the data for analysis.

If you are using a data lake, then the data stored is typically read by the data science team using programmatic APIs or SQL. We shall cover these two variations of reading data from data lakes in the rest of this section.

Programmatic Access

Tabular data stored in a data lake in a format such as CSV, JSON, or Parquet can be read using programmatic APIs in a language such as Python, R, Scala, etc. Examples include

- The Python library *pandas*

- The Spark library in Scala or PySpark in Python

Apart from tabular data, other kinds of data such as images, etc., can be accessed using the programmatic APIs provided by the data lake. For example, AWS provides libraries in programming languages such as Python to access data stored in S3.

SQL Query Engine

When it comes to big data, it is rather common for an organization to store tabular data in a data lake (e.g., in AWS S3) without having a data warehouse. To support querying such tabular data in a data lake using SQL, a common approach is to use an SQL query engine.

Presto, Spark SQL, and AWS Athena are examples of SQL query engines. These are often used for ad hoc queries by an analyst, data engineer, or data scientist.

Open Source vs. Paid

For ingestion, the libraries and frameworks we have mentioned are open source. There are some paid services that make it easier to manage and scale the infrastructure – AWS, for example, offers managed services for Spark, Airflow, and Kafka.[6]

---

[6] AWS also provides paid services of its own, for example, AWS Kinesis is an alternative to Kafka.

For data lakes and data warehouses, paid tools and services on the cloud are typically preferred these days as they offer a flexible pricing model and elastic scaling.[7] They are often more cost-effective than deploying an open source warehouse (such as PostgreSQL) and managing it in your own infrastructure.

Data Engineering

Within the data capture step, a domain expert or the chief data scientist typically determines which data is to be captured and the appropriate data sources.

The further activities mentioned in this chapter – of ingesting the data into the data storage and enabling efficient access to it – primarily fall within the ambit of data engineering. The various tools mentioned in this chapter are also typically owned by data engineering.

Conclusion

In this chapter, we covered the various components and activities involved in the data capture step of the data science process, including some of the technologies used. We also touched upon some aspects around opting for an open source vs. a paid tool.

---

[7] Elastic scaling refers to the capability of automatically or easily scaling the infrastructure to meet the demands.

CHAPTER 14

Data Preparation

This chapter is dedicated to the *data preparation* step of the data science process. The *captured* data is typically explored to understand it better.[1] Such exploration may reveal that the captured data is in a form which cannot be directly used to build models – we saw one such case in Chapter 6 where the data captured for predicting the category of an email consisted of just emails and their folders. This data had to go through a lot of preparation before it could be used for building models. In some other cases, it may seem that the data could be given to ML algorithms directly, but preparing the data in various ways might result in more effective models. We saw such a case in one of the examples we discussed in Chapter 1, where the captured data contained the timestamps and sale amounts for transactions at the checkout counter of a store. In this case, we felt that sale amount might have some trends based on what day of the week it is, what month it is, etc. Hence, we transformed the data so that it contains the hour, day, month, etc., along with the corresponding aggregated sale amount hoping that it will enable ML algorithms to find such trends. Hence, preparing the data in such ways might result in better models.

---

[1] This may also involve looking at statistics like mean, median, standard deviation, etc.

© Vineet Raina and Srinath Krishnamurthy 2022
V. Raina and S. Krishnamurthy, *Building an Effective Data Science Practice*,
https://doi.org/10.1007/978-1-4842-7419-4_14

In this chapter, we will revisit a few data preparation tasks that we performed in the chapters of Part 2 related to classes of problems. We used a few techniques to perform these tasks in those chapters; now we will discuss a few other techniques that can be used for those tasks. The idea is to understand that many techniques are available for each data preparation task and a good understanding of the techniques can help you decide which one is most appropriate for your problem.

Handling Missing Values

A task that we discussed in earlier chapters and you will very likely end up doing in the data preparation step is handling the missing values in your data. You could do this in several ways like simply removing the observations that have any missing values or fill the missing values in intelligent ways. Let's say your data has daily sale amounts, but the amounts are unknown for some days and hence are *missing* in the data. If you choose to simply fill these missing amounts by 0, it will cause the ML algorithm to incorrectly think that there was no sale on those days and thus possibly disturb any sale trends present in the data. For example, if the sale amounts in the data for Sundays are always high, filling the missing sale amount for a particular Sunday with 0 will disturb the trend of high sales on Sundays. So you could instead fill the missing sale amount for this Sunday with the average of sale amounts for all other Sundays because you believe that sale on this Sunday might have been similar to the sales on other Sundays. Doing so will fill the missing sale amount for this Sunday with a high value (average of other Sundays) causing the sale trend to remain intact. You could even go to the extent of building machine learning models just to predict the missing values.

Feature Scaling

Another task that we have discussed earlier, and you will likely be doing in the data preparation step, is transforming your features so that they have the same scale.[2] To do this, you could perform a *min-max scaling* that transforms the feature values so that they range from 0 to 1 – smallest feature value is thus transformed to 0 and largest to 1. The other common approach to achieve this is a technique called *standardization*. This approach transforms each feature value by subtracting the mean from it and dividing the difference by the standard deviation. You can see that this approach does not restrict the transformed values to a specific range.

Text Preprocessing

Let's revisit the text preprocessing tasks from the NLP problem in Chapter 6, where the goal was to build a model that could infer/predict the category of an email based on the text in the email. For achieving this goal, the personal assistant stripped the greeting and closing from each email body in the data and preprocessed the remaining email body by removing punctuation, converting it to lowercase, extracting individual words, and removing stop words which it thought were not useful for inferring the category of an email. As the next step, the assistant used a technique called *lemmatization* on the words in all emails to convert the inflected forms of words to their base forms because it thought that the inflected forms might not give any additional clue about the category of an email. Lemmatization also reduced the vocabulary that the assistant had to deal with. The assistant then extracted features from the lists of base words of all emails using the *bag-of-words* technique.

---

[2] There are various reasons why you might want to do this (c.f. Chapters 7 and 8).

In this section, we will discuss another technique that you can use to reduce words to their base forms which is known as *stemming*. We will also see a different technique known as TF-IDF that can be used for extracting features from lists of base words.

Stemming

Lemmatization performs a sophisticated analysis on each word considering its part of speech and accordingly maps the word to its correct base form. Stemming on the other hand adopts a more crude approach which applies rules that simply cut off portions of words to arrive at their base forms. For example, if you perform stemming[3] on the word "*working,*" the suffix "*ing*" will be chopped off and you will get "*work*" as the base word. This crude approach adopted by stemming obviously works faster than lemmatization which performs a detailed analysis.

However, stemming could sometimes give you a result that is not a valid word. For example, performing stemming on the word "*dries*" might simply remove the suffix "*es*" and return "*dri*" as the base word which is not a valid word. Let's look at another word, "*worse.*" If you pass this word "*worse*" along with its part of speech "*adjective*" to lemmatization operation, it will be able to figure out with its detailed analysis that the base word is "*bad.*" On the other hand, there is no way that the approach of cutting off portions of words adopted by stemming can produce the result "bad" from the original word "worse." To summarize, stemming and lemmatization have their strengths and weaknesses, and you need to decide which one is suited for you as per your requirements.

---

[3] For example, using Porter Stemmer.

TF-IDF

We used the *bag-of-words* technique in Chapter 6 to extract features from the lists of base words of all emails. This technique determined the vocabulary (total set of unique base words across all emails) and then created one feature for every base word in the vocabulary. It then calculated the value of a feature for an email by counting the number of times the corresponding base word occurred in that email. Figure 14-1 shows a partial view of the features extracted from the lists of base words of all emails using the bag-of-words technique – the figure also shows the target variable *Category*. Note that there is a feature for every unique base word. You can see that the value of feature *visualization* for the third email is 2 because the base word *visualization* was present twice in the list of base words of this email.

context	...	security	fix	release	...	...	design	...	visualization	...	...	Category
1	...	1	1	0	...	...	0	...	0	...	...	Product Development
0	...	0	0	1	...	...	0	...	0	...	...	Product Development
0	...	0	0	0	...	...	1	...	2	...	...	Research Work
0	...	0	0	0	...	...	0	...	0	...	...	Research Work
0	...	0	0	0	...	...	0	...	0	...	...	Trainings
0	...	0	0	0	...	...	0	...	0	...	...	Trainings
...	...	...	...	...	...	...	...	...	...	...	...	....
...	...	...	...	...	...	...	...	...	...	...	...	....

Figure 14-1. *Features and target variable for emails*

So you can see that the *bag-of-words* technique uses a very basic approach of counting the number of occurrences of a base word to calculate the value of a feature. There are several enhancements you can make to this approach of calculating features which could lead to more effective features. And more effective features could result in more effective models which is crucial for success in data science. Let's look at a few such enhancements.

Let's say there was an email in our data which was very long and contained the word *visualization* many times. The *bag-of-words* technique would simply count the occurrences and give a high value for the feature *visualization* for this email. The ML algorithm would think that the feature *visualization* has a much higher value for this email compared to the third email in the previous figure. But this is probably true only because this email is much longer than the third email. So it will be a good idea to make adjustments for the email size while calculating feature values. You can do this by simply dividing the original value of the feature for an email by the size of the list of base words for that email. The modified value of the feature is a more effective representative of how frequently the base word occurs in the email. We refer to this modified feature value as *term frequency (TF)*.

However, this modified feature calculation process still has limitations. The frequent occurrence of a base word in an email may not be of special significance if that word is in general a very common word and thus occurs frequently in other emails too. But our modified feature calculation process does not consider this aspect, so it gives a high feature value if a base word occurs frequently in an email even if it is a very common word. So we could modify our feature value calculation process further by scaling down the feature value considerably if the corresponding base word is a very common word. To do this, we can multiply the feature value calculated previously by a value which is called *inverse document frequency (IDF)*. IDF is equal to the logarithm of the quotient obtained by dividing the number of emails by the number of emails containing the corresponding base word. So if a base word is a very common word that appears in most emails, the quotient will be close to 1 and its logarithm will be close to 0. In other words, IDF is close to 0 if the corresponding base word is extremely common. Hence, the feature value corresponding to a very common base word gets scaled down considerably due to multiplication with IDF value just as we wanted.[4] This modified method of calculating feature values is known as TF-IDF and the final calculated feature values are known as *TF-IDF* values. These final feature values could then be used for machine learning.

Converting Categorical Variables into Numeric Variables

Converting categorical variables into numeric variables is another data preparation task that we have seen earlier (Chapter 5) and is also quite common. In Chapter 5, each categorical variable we wanted to convert had just two possible values, and we simply encoded one value as *0* and the other value as *1*. For example, you might remember that the value of Gender variable for each observation was either *Male* or *Female*. And to convert this variable into a numeric variable, we simply encoded *Male* as *1* and *Female* as *0*. However, you may need to adopt other approaches/ techniques as demanded by the situation.

Let's say the observations in your data correspond to patients, and one of the variables indicates the level of fatigue experienced by the patients. For each patient, this variable can take one these five possible values: *Very Low, Low, Moderate, High, and Very High*. The value *Low* indicates a higher level of fatigue than the value *Very Low*, the value *Moderate* indicates a

---

[4] On similar lines, you can figure out what effect this operation will have for a rare base word.

higher level of fatigue than the value *Low,* and so on. Thus, these possible values have a natural order. Such a categorical variable whose possible values have a natural *order* is called an *ordinal* variable. It will be ideal to preserve this order while converting such a variable into a numeric variable. For example, since the value *Low* indicates a higher level of fatigue than the value *Very Low,* you should encode *Low* using a higher number compared to the number you use to encode *Very Low,* and so on. So you could simply encode *Very Low* as 0, *Low* as 1, *Moderate* as 2, *High* as 3, and *Very High* as 4. Thus, for all patients whose level of fatigue was originally *Very Low*, the encoded value of the variable will be *0*. Similarly, for patients whose level of fatigue was *Low*, the encoded value will be *1,* and so on.

Let's look at a different kind of categorical variable now. Figure 14-2 shows a partial view of the data where each observation corresponds to a movie. The variable *Length* indicates the length of the movie in minutes, variable *Rating* indicates the average rating given by users, and *Genre* indicates what type of movie it is. For each movie, the categorical variable *Genre* can take one of the three possible values: *Action, Comedy*, and *Horror*. These possible values are just names of movie genres and do not have a natural order. Such a categorical variable whose possible values are just *names* that do not have a natural order is called a *nominal* variable. To convert this variable into a numeric variable, you could obviously encode *Action* as *0, Comedy* as *1,* and *Horror* as *2* as shown in Figure 14-3. But this approach could be misleading in some cases. Let's say you were trying to identify clusters of movies based on Euclidean distance between movies (we discussed clustering in Chapter 7). If the encoded data in Figure 14-3 is used for clustering[5] and distances are calculated based on the three variables, the third movie seen in the table will seem closer to the second movie than to the first movie. This is because the length and rating of the third movie is equal to the length and rating of the other two movies, but the encoded genre of the third movie is closer to the encoded

---

[5] We have avoided feature scaling for simplicity of discussion.

genre of the second movie than to the encoded genre of the first movie. However, this interpretation is not correct because you can see in the original data (Figure 14-2) that the genre of the third movie is simply different from the genres of the other two movies – it is not closer to one and farther from the other. So we will discuss a different technique to convert the categorical variable *genre* into numeric form.

Length	Rating	Genre
....	....	....
125	8.1	Action
125	8.1	Comedy
125	8.1	Horror
....	....	....

Figure 14-2. *Movie data*

Length	Rating	Genre
....	....	....
125	8.1	0
125	8.1	1
125	8.1	2
....	....	...

Figure 14-3. *Movie data with encoded genre*

We will replace the variable *Genre* in Figure 14-2 with three new variables corresponding to the three possible values of *Genre* variable. Figure 14-4 shows the movie data with these three new variables. You can see that there is a variable for each genre. If a movie belongs to a particular genre, the value of the variable corresponding to that genre is 1, and the value of other two variables is 0. For example, the first movie seen in this figure belongs to the genre *Action,* so the value of variable *Action* is 1, the value of variable *Comedy* is 0, and the value of variable *Horror* is 0. This is the general idea behind the popular technique known as *one-hot encoding.* So we can see how the data and the nature of problem being solved affect our choice of the technique for converting categorical variables into numeric variables.

Length	Rating	Action	Comedy	Horror
....	....	....	....	....
125	8.1	1	0	0
125	8.1	0	1	0
125	8.1	0	0	1
....	....	....	....	....

Figure 14-4. *Movie data with one-hot encoding of genre*

Transforming Images

As we discussed in the beginning of the chapter, preparing the data in various ways can result in more effective models. For computer vision problems, a common task that is carried out in data preparation is transforming original images to produce new images, with the aim of building effective models. The exact techniques you use to transform the images depend on the effect you want the transformations to have for creating better models. We talked about transforming images in Chapter 10 where we were looking for localized patterns in images with a lot of background whitespace. Accordingly, the technique/approach we adopted was to slice the image into tiles, choose the tiles with most tissue, and reassemble them to create a square image that has a large tissue region.

In many other common problems, such as object detection that we saw in Chapter 10, it would be inappropriate to transform the image by slicing it in any way. However, there might be other requirements in such cases that demand transforming images. One such requirement is that the model should be resilient to variations in orientation of the image (e.g., rotation), the size of the object being identified (zoom factor), and so forth. For example, if the model needs to detect a particular type of object in an image, it should be able to do so irrespective of the orientation of the object in the image, etc. This resilience can be achieved by transforming each original image in multiple ways (e.g., by rotating, etc.) and providing the transformed images along with the original images to the model for learning. This technique thus expands the size of our data and is referred to as *image augmentation*. It helps the model learn to detect patterns in images with arbitrary orientations, zoom factors, etc.

Since such augmentation helps create a much larger corpus of data from your images, it is particularly useful for training deep learning models such as CNNs (see Chapter 16) which require a lot of data.

The specifics of your problem would usually dictate which transformations are suitable; the following are some of the more common augmentations/transformations:

- Rotation by various angles

- Flipping horizontally/vertically

- Zooming in/out

- Shifting horizontally/vertically

- Adding some noise

Libraries and Tools

In this section, we look at various libraries and tools that can be used for data preparation.

Libraries

Data manipulation and analysis libraries usually include functions for aggregation and transformation of data. *Pandas*, for example, is a popular library for processing data in Python – it has functions to aggregate and transform data, including date/time transformations.

If you are working with big data, for example, on Spark clusters, you might use *Spark* library functions for data preparation. Also, the relatively recent *Koalas* library provides a pandas-compatible API to perform Spark operations – this enables data scientists familiar with pandas to work with Spark without a learning curve.

ML libraries usually incorporate functions for common data preparation techniques as well. *Scikit-learn*, for example, provides functions for filling missing values, standardization, one-hot encoding, etc.

There also exist libraries oriented toward a specific class of problem, for example, *natural language toolkit (NLTK)* is a popular library for NLP, which also includes functions for stemming, lemmatization, etc. Similarly, for computer vision, libraries like *scikit-image* and *Keras* provide APIs to ease the task of transforming images.

Tools

In the past few years, tools like Paxata, Trifacta, etc., have gained popularity as they enable data preparation using an intuitive and friendly user interface. This ease of use allows not only data scientists but also analysts and business stakeholders to work on these tools, thus enabling effective collaboration between them in the data preparation step. These tools can also track lineage, that is, all the transformations performed in the data preparation step. This eases reproducibility and auditing.

Data Engineering

There are two broad areas of data engineering activities to support data preparation:

1. Infrastructure and data sources: If the team is working with big data on Spark clusters, etc., and/ or using any tools, then setting up and maintaining the necessary infrastructure falls under data engineering. Also, some tools may need data sources to be configured – these initialization activities also fall under data engineering.

2. Automating data preparation: If/when certain data preparation activities are standardized by the data scientists for some datasets, data engineering can automate and maintain these steps for new data corresponding to those datasets. This helps boost the productivity of data scientists by allowing them to focus on the other steps of the data science process.

Conclusion

In this chapter, we revisited a few data preparation tasks and saw that multiple techniques are available for each task. We also saw that a deep understanding of these techniques is important for deciding which technique is most suited for our problem.

CHAPTER 15

Data Visualization

We looked at data preparation in the previous chapter; let's now delve deeper into the techniques and technologies for *data visualization* which is the next step in our data science process.

We emphasized the importance and benefits of designing effective visualizations with concrete examples while discussing the different classes of problems. We also mentioned how data visualization is a vast subject in itself that covers many different types of charts, legends, layouts, etc. Each of these provides a variety of simple and advanced options to the users for greater control. Also, there are mechanisms to add interactive features to your visualizations or combine existing visualizations to create your own custom visualizations. We will look at some of these general aspects and then delve deeper into a few visualizations and how they could provide insights needed for building effective models in data science. We will conclude the chapter by discussing a few popular libraries and tools in the data visualization category.

© Vineet Raina and Srinath Krishnamurthy 2022
V. Raina and S. Krishnamurthy, *Building an Effective Data Science Practice*,
https://doi.org/10.1007/978-1-4842-7419-4_15

Graphs/Charts/Plots

While some people will use these terms loosely and interchangeably, a few others could give enlightening discourses on how they all mean different things. Without going deeper into that discussion, what we would like to highlight is that these are the basic building blocks using which you can design your visualizations. You might already have used or come across some of these like bar chart, scatter plot, pie chart, etc., but we consider it a useful investment to go beyond these and broaden your awareness of other highly effective ones.

Many of these like bar chart, scatter plot, etc. use a horizontal and vertical axis and display visual elements representing the data. The position or size of each visual element along each axis is derived using the values in the data. Suppose you have data related to demographics of students living in a region. A scatter plot could show each student in this dataset as a circular marker whose position along the horizontal axis is based on the height of the student and position on the vertical axis is based on the weight of the student.

There are other charts that do not use axes like pie chart, treemap, etc. A treemap shows categories in a hierarchy as nested rectangular tiles whose area represents some property of the categories. For example, Figure 15-1 shows the cellular phone sales at a store for different models from different manufacturers.[1] You can see that there is a tile for every manufacturer whose area represents the total sale for that manufacturer. And the tiles for the different models from that manufacturer are nested within the tile of the manufacturer such that the area of each nested tile represents the sale for its corresponding model. For example, there is a large red tile whose area represents the total sale for manufacturer Xiaomi,

---

[1] This is purely *synthetic* data to illustrate a treemap; the data is not intended to represent actual sales of any of the manufacturers mentioned.

and it contains three nested red tiles for the three models of Xiaomi. The area of each nested red tile represents the sale for the corresponding model of Xiaomi.

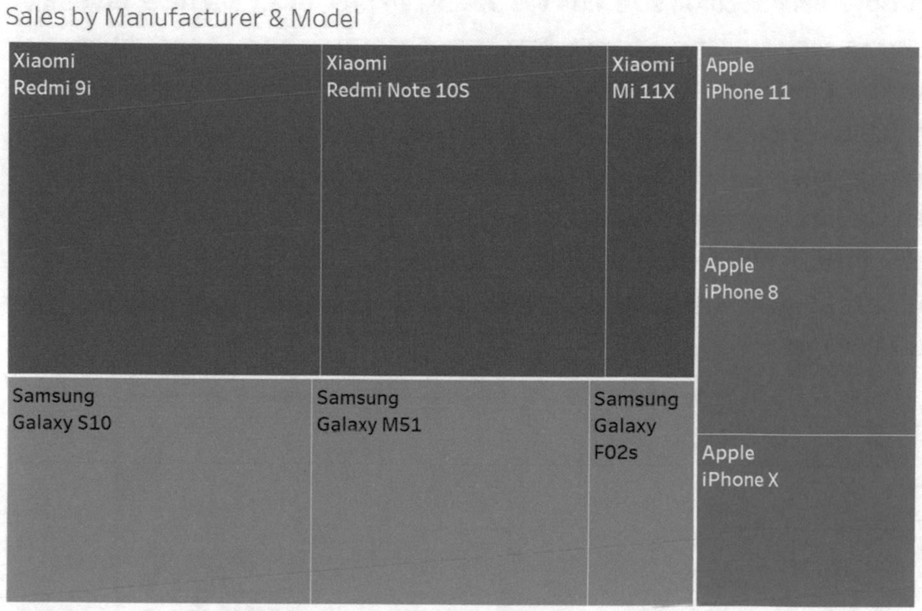

Sales by Manufacturer & Model

Figure 15-1. *Treemap of cellular phone sales*

Another category among the basic building blocks is the node link diagrams. These make use of nodes and links for showing entities and their connections and are useful for visualizing network data.

Legends

You can visualize more variables in existing charts by making use of visual properties like color, size, etc. We discussed previously a scatter plot that shows each student as a marker whose x coordinate and y coordinate are based on height and weight, respectively. You could also add *Gender* (which contains discrete categories *Male* and *Female)* to this visualization by showing markers for male students in blue and markers for female students in green. A discrete legend will be added to the plot that shows what each color represents. Figure 15-2 shows the scatter plot and the discrete legend enabling visualization of Gender along with height and weight.

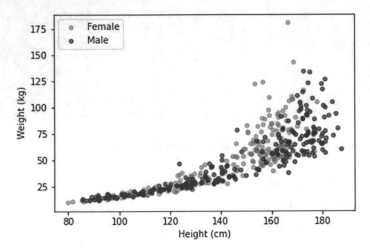

Figure 15-2.   *Scatter plot of Weight vs. Height. Gender is depicted by the color of the marker[2]*

---

[2] The dataset used for all the height/weight plots in this chapter is derived from the NHANES data at https://pypi.org/project/nhanes/

You could also use color to visualize a variable that contains continuous values. The scatter plot example showing height and weight could color the marker for each student by mapping their *Age* to a color from a range of colors. A continuous legend will be added that shows what values of *Age* the colors in the plot represent. Figure 15-3 shows the scatter plot and the continuous legend enabling visualization of an additional variable *Age* that contains continuous values. For example, notice the color of the highlighted marker; you can see in the continuous legend that this color represents an age of around 30.

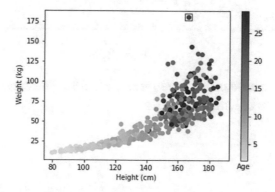

Figure 15-3. *Scatter plot of Weight vs. Height where Age is depicted by colors*

You could also use size property to visualize a variable with continuous values. For example, a bubble plot that shows a bubble for each student (whose x coordinate and y coordinate are based on height and weight) could additionally show *Age* by varying the bubble size. A *Size* legend is added that shows what Age values the different bubble sizes represent. Figure 15-4 shows the bubble plot and the *Size* legend allowing visualization of Age in addition to height and weight. Note that, compared to the earlier scatter plots, we have reduced the number of markers in this plot for visual clarity.

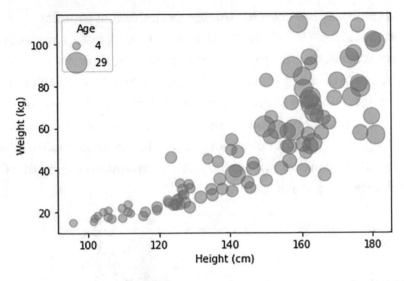

Figure 15-4. *Bubble plot of Weight vs. Height. The size of a bubble indicates the Age of that student*

Layouts

Often you will need to add multiple related charts to your visualization so that you can compare the data across charts. *Layouts* allow you to add multiple charts to your visualization and organize them in different ways. Depending on your need, you can pick the appropriate layout that makes your visualization more effective and conveys more insight into trends. One of the simplest layout is the *overlay* layout that just overlays one axes-based chart on another. Let's say you have a stacked bar chart that stacks the revenue from electronics goods on top of revenue from software for every year. The overall height of each bar thus indicates the total revenue for the corresponding year. On this bar chart, you could overlay a scatter plot that shows the revenue target for each year. Figure 15-5 shows the scatter plot overlaid on the bar chart. Notice that the bar is lower than the scatter marker for year 1990 which means that the revenue target was not met that year as the total revenue was below the revenue target. On the other hand, in year 1995, the total revenue exceeded the revenue target as the bar is higher than the scatter marker for that year.

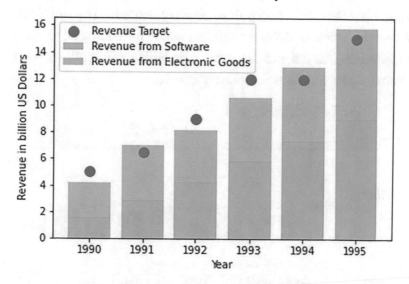

Figure 15-5. *Scatter plot showing revenue target overlaid on stacked bar chart showing actual revenue from electronics goods and software*

Some layouts allow you to organize multiple charts in grids of rows and columns. Some of the layouts in this category require you to manually specify which chart goes into which cell of the grid, while a few others automatically fill the grid with charts based on some rules. Let's say you want to visualize the sales for different car models manufactured by an automobile company, you could use a simple bar chart for this. However, you might want to compare the sales of different models across countries and years. So, instead of using a simple bar chart, you could use the *data lattice*[3] layout and configure it to automatically create a row for every country and a column for every year, thus showing a cell

---

[3] Note that different libraries might use different names for this layout.

for every pair of country and year. And you could specify that each cell should automatically display a bar chart (showing sales of models) for the corresponding country and year. Figure 15-6 shows the data lattice layout showing a bar chart for every pair of country and year. The simple bar chart showing sales for different models would have allowed visualization of two variables (Model and Sale); the data lattice layout allows you to visualize two more variables: Country and Year.

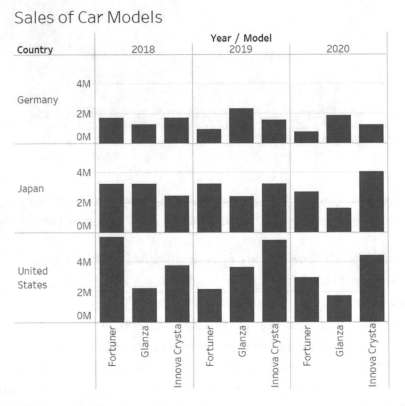

Figure 15-6. *Data lattice of sales for every <country, year> pair. Each cell in the lattice shows the sale per model[4]*

---

[4] This is purely *synthetic* data to illustrate a data lattice; the data is not intended to represent actual sales of any of the car models mentioned.

These layouts often perform many computations behind the scenes for achieving desired functionality like achieving consistency of vertical axis ranges across cells in a row or achieving consistency of horizontal axis ranges across cells in a column.

Options

All charts, legends, and layouts expose options to the users in the form of properties which can be set to different values to avail more features or control the output better. For example, you could use the appropriate option in scatter plot to change the symbol to square shape instead of circular, or you could use the appropriate option to change an axis of an axes-based chart to use logarithmic scale. The spectrum of options varies from the basic ones that result in just cosmetic changes to advanced ones that involve complex calculations and have a significant impact on the visualization. We won't go into further details but encourage you to increase your awareness of different options available as the insight gained from a visualization can be greatly enhanced by using the right options.

Interactive Visualizations

Some tools let you design interactive visualizations which enable a deeper exploration of data or provide dynamic views which are not possible with simple visualizations. Let's again consider the simple bar chart we discussed earlier that shows the sales for car models – each car model is represented as a bar whose height represents the sale for that model. You could add an animation to this visualization that shows how the sales for models changed on a monthly basis. Under the hood, the visualization creates a bar chart (showing sales for models) for every month and displays them in quick succession in chronological order. By observing how the bars increase or decrease with time, you can figure out clearly how the sale for each model changed with time.

Another important interactive feature is the *drill down* feature. When you look at a visualization, you might want to drill deeper into details. Let's say you are looking at a bar chart showing the regional sales of a retail chain in the United States.[5] You might want to analyze further the trends in a particular region and look at the sales in different states of that region. You might decide to go even deeper into a state and look at the sales for different cities in that state. You can achieve this by adding a *drill down* feature to your visualization. When the visualization is rendered, it starts with a bar chart showing sales for regions. Figure 15-7 (A) shows this bar chart. You can then select the bar for a region and choose to drill down into it; this causes the visualization to go to the next level in the hierarchy which is *State* and display the sales for the states in that region. So, if you chose to drill down on the bar corresponding to the *East* region as highlighted in Figure 15-7 (A), you would see the bar chart in Figure 15-7 (B). You can further select the bar for a state and drill down to see the next level which shows the sales for different cities in that state. Figure 15-7 (C) shows the bar chart that would be displayed if you chose to drill down on state *New York*.

---

[5] The sample dataset used in this example is sourced from www.kaggle.com/
rohitsahoo/sales-forecasting

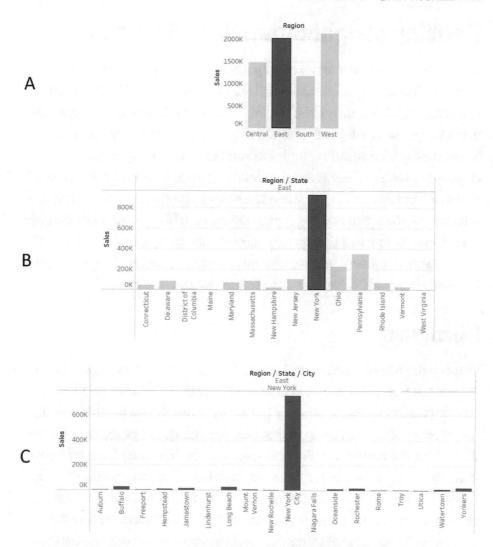

Figure 15-7. *Interactive drill down analysis of sales at a retail chain. (A) Regionwise sales, choosing to drill down into East region. (B) Statewise sales, choosing to drill down into the state of New York. (C) Citywise sales for the state of New York*

Deriving Insights from Visualizations

The sections so far discussed a few general aspects related to data visualization. In this section, we will take a more detailed look at a few visualizations frequently used in data science and how you can leverage them for gaining insights that could help you build effective models. We have already seen some examples of such insights when we discussed classes of problems. For example, while discussing the *regression* class of problems in Chapter 5, we looked at a scatter plot that revealed a linear relationship between the target and feature variable. Based on this insight, we decided to create a linear regression model to capture that linear relationship. Similarly, we had also looked at box plots in Chapter 8 in the context of anomaly detection. Let's look at some more examples.

Histogram

You can use a histogram to look at the distribution of values of a numeric variable. A histogram divides the entire range of values into smaller intervals called bins and shows a bar for each bin whose height indicates the number of values falling in that bin. You can draw several conclusions by looking at a histogram. For example, if all the bars are of similar height, it means that the number of values in each bin is similar. In other words, the values are more or less uniformly distributed across the intervals or bins. On the other hand, if you look at Figure 15-8 which shows the histogram for weights of students in a class, you can see that the bars for intervals 30–35, 35–40, and 40–45 are high and the bars for intervals below 30 or above 45 are very small. This means that there are many students whose weights fall in the intervals 30–35, 35–40, and 40–45 and there are very few students whose weights fall in the intervals below 30 or intervals above 45. In other words, a vast majority of students have weights between 30 and 45.

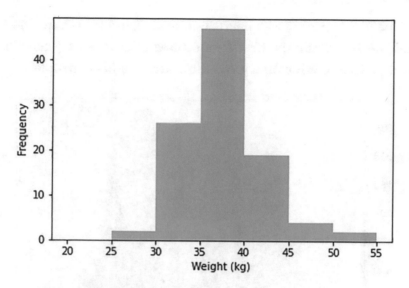

Figure 15-8. *Histogram for weight of students in a class. Majority of students have weights between 30 and 45*

Let's now see how you could use histograms to derive useful insights for building ML models. Let's say you are working toward creating a model that will bc deployed on a wearable device and will predict whether a person has heart condition based on some health parameters like temperature, blood pressure, etc., that it measures. For building this model, let's say you have captured the health parameter values for approximately a thousand normal people and a thousand people with heart condition. You could prepare your data in the data preparation step in such a way that you have a row for each person that contains their parameter values and a label whose value is *Diseased* if the person has a heart condition or *Healthy* if the person is healthy. The variables corresponding to the parameters are your features, and the variable containing the labels *Healthy/Diseased* is your target. Now you want to evaluate whether the feature corresponding to a particular parameter is useful for predicting heart condition. For this, you could plot the histogram of this feature for healthy people and overlay it on top of the histogram of this feature for people with heart condition. Figure 15-9 shows these overlaid histograms for the *Healthy* and *Diseased* class. X axis shows the intervals of feature values and y axis shows the number of people.

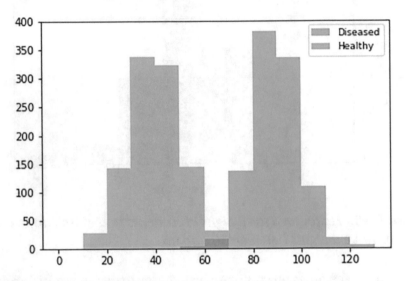

Figure 15-9. *Overlaid histograms for the "Healthy" class and "Diseased" class*

You can see that the histogram for Healthy class has bars from feature value 10 to 70 and the histogram for Diseased class has bars from value 50 to 130. So there is a good separation between the histograms of the two classes – the histogram for Healthy class is shifted left compared to that of Diseased class. Note that there are high bars of Healthy class for feature value less than 50 but no bars of Diseased class for feature value less than 50. So our data is indicating that healthy people often have feature value below 50, but people with heart condition never seem to have a value below 50. Hence, if you come across a case whose feature value is below 50, you could infer that the person might likely be healthy. Similarly, our data indicates that people with heart condition often have a value above 70, but healthy people never seem to have a value above 70. So if you come across a case whose feature value is above 70, you could infer that the person might likely have a heart condition. So we can see that the value of this feature could give some indication about the presence of heart condition in a person. Hence, an ML model could learn to use the value of this feature to try to predict if a person has heart condition. So it will be a good idea to use this feature while building a model that predicts the presence of heart condition. You can thus see how looking at histograms gives you hints about what features could be effective in building your predictive models.

Kernel Density Estimate Plot

Another plot that is commonly used in classification problems is the Kernel Density Estimate plot or KDE plot. The KDE plot estimates and plots the probability density curve for a variable. The x axis in a KDE plot represents the value of the variable, and the y axis represents the probability density. Without going into the mathematical details, let's focus on how to interpret the KDE plot. Figure 15-10 shows the KDE plot for the variable we saw earlier which contains the weights of students in a class – x axis represents weight, and y axis represents the probability density. The area under the KDE curve between two weight values represents the probability of a student's weight falling between those two values.

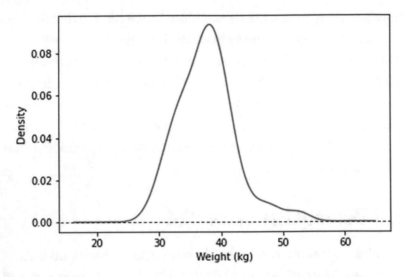

Figure 15-10. *Kernel Density Estimate (KDE) plot for weights of students in a class*

You can see in the figure that the area under the curve between weight 30 and 45 is much more than area under the curve below weight 30. This means that the probability of a student's weight falling between 30 and 45 is much more than the probability of the weight falling below 30. This is because we saw in the histogram in Figure 15-8 that a vast majority of students have weights between 30 and 45. You can thus see that a KDE plot is like a smoother version of a histogram.

The benefit of using a KDE plot instead of histogram becomes evident when you plot multiple distributions. Let's revisit the feature whose distributions for healthy people and people with heart condition were plotted using histograms in Figure 15-9. Let's now overlay the KDE plot for these thousand healthy people on the KDE plot for the thousand people with heart condition instead of histograms as shown in Figure 15-11. The x axis in this figure represents the feature value, and the y axis represents the probability density. You can see that the overlaid KDE plots in this figure look like smooth versions of the overlaid histograms in Figure 15-9, but the benefit you get with KDE plots is that the KDE plots look less cluttered and are more readable than the histograms. The reduction in clutter would be more evident if you were comparing, say, four overlaid histograms with the corresponding four overlaid KDE plots.

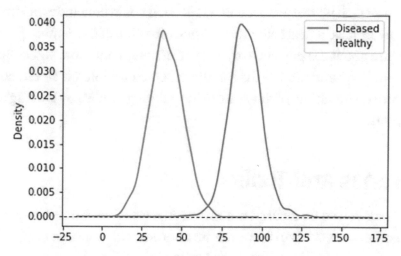

Figure 15-11. *Overlaid Kernel Density Estimate (KDE) plots for the "Healthy" class and "Diseased" class*

Let's now see how you can get insights from KDE plots for building models. We can see in the figure that there is good separation between the KDE plots of the two classes – KDE plot of Healthy class is shifted left compared to KDE plot of Diseased class. Note that the area under the Healthy curve below feature value 50 is large, whereas the area under the Diseased curve below feature value 50 is close to 0. This means that the probability of a healthy person's feature value being less than 50 is high, whereas the probability of the value being below 50 for a person with heart condition is almost nil. So our plots are indicating that the value of the feature for a healthy person will often be below 50 and the value for a person with heart condition will rarely be below 50. Hence, if you come across a person whose feature value is 40, you could infer that the person might likely be healthy. Similarly, the area under the Diseased curve above feature value 75 is large, whereas the area under the Healthy curve above feature value 75 is close to 0. So our plots are indicating that the feature value for a person with heart condition will often be above 75 and the value for a healthy person will rarely be above 75. Hence, if you come across a person whose feature value is 90, you could conclude that they might likely have a heart condition. Since the value of this feature gives you some hint about the presence or absence of heart condition, you could use this feature to build models that predict heart condition. Thus, you could evaluate the suitability of this feature for building models by looking at the KDE plots.

Libraries and Tools

Our discussion so far focused mainly on data visualization techniques. In this section, we will now discuss some libraries and tools that implement a rich variety of such visualization techniques.

Libraries

There are several visualization libraries geared toward data science. For example, in the Python ecosystem, Matplotlib is one of the oldest, and still very popular, libraries. Seaborn[6] is another popular library in Python used by data scientists. We have used these two libraries for creating the scatter plots, histograms, and KDE plots in this chapter.

---

[6] Also based on Matplotlib.

Tools

The space of data visualization tools, also comprising of business intelligence or visual analytics tools, is one of the oldest in the analytics arena. Tools like Tableau have a rich history dating back to the turn of the century. The expansion of data science in the past few years has seen several BI tools expand their capabilities to add support for data preparation and data visualization as needed by data scientists, including integration with Python, etc.

In our experience, Tableau and SAS Visual Analytics are two tools that represent the wide gamut of capabilities offered for data visualization and are popular among data scientists in academia and industry alike. Other popular tools include PowerBI, Looker, etc. – this is a very crowded space with numerous popular tools.[7]

Being aware of this category of tools will enable you to identify if your organization already has a tool (such as a BI tool) which can be leveraged by data scientists as well. This can significantly improve collaboration between the data scientists and other stakeholders. These tools also allow embedding the views and dashboards into existing web applications very easily – it can be very useful to incorporate the visualizations created by data scientists into any existing internal operations portals.[8]

Data Engineering

If the data science team is working with data sizes that can fit on a single machine and using visualization libraries such as Matplotlib, Seaborn, etc., then there aren't many data engineering activities required for the data visualization step.

---

[7] Recent acquisitions of Tableau by Salesforce and Looker by Google continue to rapidly evolve this space.

[8] This especially applies to DSI-Proc projects; see Chapter 23.

But when the data size is large and clusters such as Spark are used, data engineering would ensure that efficient ad hoc queries are supported for data visualization.

In addition to ensuring efficient queries, when BI or visual analytics tools are used for data visualization, the following data engineering activities are typically required:

- Setting up the necessary server infrastructure for these tools

- Configuring the appropriate data sources within those tools

- Any customizations required, for example, any user-defined functions, custom SQLs, etc.

Finally, if dashboards or applications are to be implemented based on the visualizations created by the data science team, data engineering can help spin up prototype applications quickly that reuse the visualizations created by data scientists as part of an interactive dashboard. This can be done using frameworks like Plotly Dash or Bokeh as well – see Chapter 18 for some more details.

Conclusion

In this chapter, we tried to emphasize that data visualization is much more than just bar charts and scatter plots. We discussed some general aspects related to the field of data visualization and also discussed how we can derive insights from visualizations. These insights can help us build effective ML models which is the focus of our next chapter.

CHAPTER 16

Machine Learning

Machine learning, as we have seen, is at the heart of the data science process as it is in this step that the actual models are built. This chapter is dedicated to the ML algorithms/techniques you can use to build models and libraries that implement these algorithms. Awareness of different ML algorithms and an intuitive understanding of the underlying concepts is crucial for the success of the entire data science process. We will start with a general categorization of ML algorithms and then look at a few popular algorithms. We will then discuss model performance evaluation that can help you evaluate the effectiveness of your models. This evaluation helps you choose the best model from multiple candidate models you might have built and also gives you an idea of how well the chosen model is likely to perform when deployed in production.

Categories of Machine Learning Algorithms

ML algorithms can broadly be categorized into three types: supervised learning, unsupervised learning, and reinforcement learning. Let's try to understand what each type means and also look at common examples in each type.

© Vineet Raina and Srinath Krishnamurthy 2022
V. Raina and S. Krishnamurthy, *Building an Effective Data Science Practice*,
https://doi.org/10.1007/978-1-4842-7419-4_16

Supervised Learning

A supervised learning algorithm, as you might have guessed from the name, requires human supervision. As part of this supervision, you need to tell the algorithm what the correct *labels* are for existing observations. The algorithm learns the relationships between these observations and their labels and is then able to predict the label for a new observation. For example, if you are using a supervised algorithm to build a model that can predict whether a new digital payment transaction is fraudulent, you will not only provide the details of the existing transactions (like location of transaction, amount and mode of payment, etc.) but will also need to provide labels *Fraud/Non-Fraud* for these transactions to the algorithm. The model built by the algorithm will then be able to predict which new transaction is fraudulent based on the details of the transaction. We have seen earlier that the variables corresponding to such details (like amount of payment, etc.) based on which prediction is done are called *features* and the variable corresponding to the *labels* is called *target*. Let's again look at the example from Chapter 4 where we were trying to predict whether an interested customer is likely to eventually buy the car or not based on their gender, age, occupation, and annual income. Figure 16-1 shows the data that we passed to the machine learning algorithm. Note that we not only passed the details of past customers (like gender, age, etc.) to the algorithm, but we also passed the labels (Purchased/Not Purchased) for those customers. Hence, the algorithm we used in that example (decision tree algorithm) is a supervised learning algorithm. The figure also points out the features, target variable, and labels for this case.

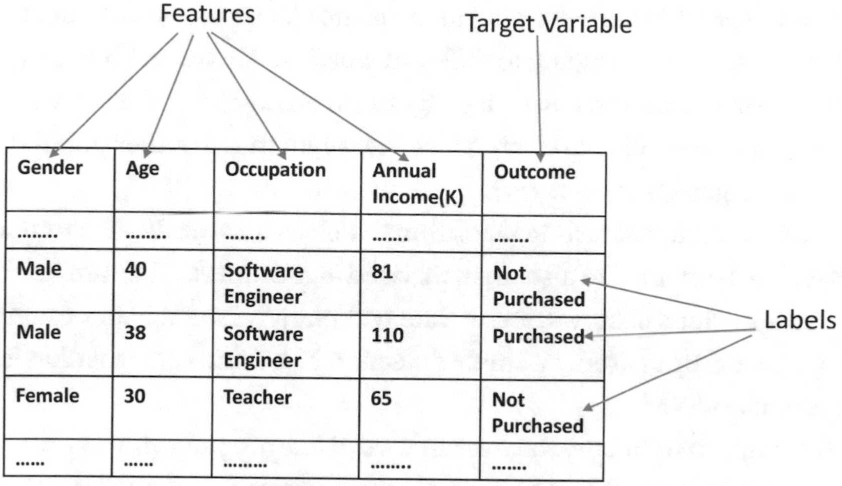

Figure 16-1. Features, target, and labels

Linear regression, logistic regression, decision tree, k-nearest neighbors, naïve Bayes, support vector machine, and neural network are some examples of supervised learning algorithms. Supervised learning algorithms can be further categorized into *classification* algorithms and *regression* algorithms. Classification algorithms predict labels which are classes (e.g., Fraud/Non-Fraud), and regression algorithms predict labels which are continuous values (e.g., salary). *Naïve Bayes* is a popular classification algorithm, and *linear regression* is a popular regression algorithm.

Unsupervised Learning

An unsupervised learning algorithm works without human supervision, that is, you do not provide any labels for the observations. The algorithm tries to learn patterns on its own from the unlabeled data. Clustering algorithms, like agglomerative clustering that we saw in Chapter 7, are examples of unsupervised learning algorithms. A clustering algorithm tries to divide the set of unlabeled observations into groups or clusters such that observations belonging to the same cluster are more similar than observations belonging to different clusters. We saw in Chapter 7, for example, that running a clustering algorithm on customer data can group customers with similar characteristics into segments. Another popular clustering algorithm is *k-means*.

Some anomaly detection algorithms, such as local outlier factor that we saw in Chapter 8, are also unsupervised algorithms as they aim to detect anomalous observations in data without any labels. Other examples of popular unsupervised, anomaly detection algorithms are isolation forest and one-class SVM.

It is important to note that unsupervised learning algorithms are particularly important for KDD/data mining projects – we shall revisit this in Chapter 23.

Reinforcement Learning

We had looked at reinforcement learning in Chapter 11. These algorithms that aim to take decisions to optimize long-term results are rather different in nature from the supervised and unsupervised algorithms, as they interact with their environment and learn based on rewards given for their decisions.

Popular Machine Learning Algorithms

Instead of looking at all ML algorithms available out there, let's focus on only a few popular ones and try to understand how they learn, how they predict, and what kind of insights they give. Knowing these details of the ML algorithms will also be important in Chapter 20 for understanding why data scientists prefer certain algorithms based on the culture (monastic vs. wild west) to which they belong. If you don't wish to go through such details of all these ML algorithms at this point, you could come back to them here when these algorithms are referred to in later chapters.

Linear Regression

The *linear regression* algorithm is one of the most popular *regression* machine learning algorithms. As mentioned earlier, this algorithm builds a *linear regression* model based on the prepared data which is a linear equation that explains how the target variable value can be calculated from the values of features. It is a favorite with many data scientists who often start their initial experimentation on regression problems with linear regression models. The equation created by the linear regression algorithm is used to calculate the target value for a new observation. The equation also provides insight into how the target variable is related to the features.

Let's try and understand how the linear regression algorithm works by revisiting the example from *regression* class of problems[1] where the goal was to predict target *Claim Amount* based on the values of features *Gender, Age, and Smoking Status*. Figure 16-2 shows the prepared data from that example. Recall that *Male* was represented as *1* and *Female* as *0* in Gender feature and *Smoker* was represented as *1* and *Non Smoker* as *0* in Smoking Status feature.

Gender	Age	Smoking Status	Claim Amount(K)
....	....	....	....
0	40	0	9.2
1	50	0	14.9
1	35	1	12.2
....	....	....	....

Figure 16-2. *Prepared data passed to linear regression algorithm*

---

[1] Chapter 5.

Also recall that when we visualized this data, we noticed linear relationships and consequently decided to use the linear regression algorithm. When linear regression algorithm receives this prepared data,[2] it tries to build a linear equation that expresses the target variable value as a weighted sum of the feature values plus a constant term. That is:

$$\text{Claim Amount} = b_0 + b_1 \times \text{Gender} + b_2 \times \text{Age} + b_3 \times \text{Smoking Status}$$

where b_1, b_2, and b_3 are weights for features Gender, Age, and Smoking Status, respectively, and b_0 is the constant term (also called intercept term). As per this equation, the algorithm would predict the Claim Amount for the customer whose Gender = 0, Age = 40, and Smoking Status = 0 to be

$$b_0 + b_1 \times 0 + b_2 \times 40 + b_3 \times 0$$

The column *Predicted Claim Amount* in Figure 16-3 shows the claim amounts that the algorithm would predict for the existing customers using this equation. The error in prediction for an existing customer is the difference between the predicted claim amount and the actual amount claimed by that customer. The column *Prediction Error* in this figure shows the prediction errors for the existing customers. Note that the value in this column is simply the value in the column *Predicted Claim Amount* minus the value in the column *Claim Amount*.

---

[2] We have skipped discussion of feature scaling to focus on the main concepts of linear regression.

Gender	Age	Smoking Status	Claim Amount(K)	Predicted Claim Amount	Prediction Error
....	....	....	....	.....	.....
0	40	0	9.2	$b_0 + b_1 \times 0 + b_2 \times 40 + b_3 \times 0$	$b_0 + b_1 \times 0 + b_2 \times 40 + b_3 \times 0 - 9.2$
1	50	0	14.9	$b_0 + b_1 \times 1 + b_2 \times 50 + b_3 \times 0$	$b_0 + b_1 \times 1 + b_2 \times 50 + b_3 \times 0 - 14.9$
1	35	1	12.2	$b_0 + b_1 \times 1 + b_2 \times 35 + b_3 \times 1$	$b_0 + b_1 \times 1 + b_2 \times 35 + b_3 \times 1 - 12.2$
....	....	....	....	.....	....

Figure 16-3. *Predicted claim amounts and prediction errors for the existing customers*

Squaring the prediction errors for individual customers and adding them gives the overall prediction error across customers. Hence, the overall prediction error is represented by the following expression which is the sum of the squares of expressions in the column *Prediction Error*:

$$... + (b_0 + b_1 \times 0 + b_2 \times 40 + b_3 \times 0 - 9.2)^2 + (b_0 + b_1 \times 1 + b_2 \times 50 + b_3 \times 0 - 14.9)^2 + (b_0 + b_1 \times 1 + b_2 \times 35 + b_3 \times 1 - 12.2)^2 + ...$$

The algorithm tries to estimate b_0, b_1, b_2, and b_3 for which the overall prediction error will be minimum. In other words, it tries to calculate the values of b_0, b_1, b_2, and b_3 for which the earlier expression has minimum value by making use of techniques like gradient descent. In this case, it finds that when $b_0 = -6.9$, $b_1 = 2.1$, $b_2 = 0.4$, and $b_3 = 2.9$, the expression will have minimum value. Once the algorithm has thus zeroed in on the right values for the weights and intercept term, it uses these values to concretize the original equation

Claim Amount = $b_0 + b_1 \times$ Gender + $b_2 \times$ Age + $b_3 \times$ Smoking Status

into

Claim Amount = $-6.9 + 2.1 \times$ Gender + $0.4 \times$ Age + $2.9 \times$ Smoking Status

After rearranging a few terms, the equation is

Claim Amount = 0.4 × Age + 2.1 × Gender + 2.9 × Smoking Status - 6.9

This is the same equation we saw in Chapter 5 (Figure 5-4) which we had mentioned was produced by the linear regression algorithm. We just saw what the algorithm was doing under the hood to come up with this equation. This equation will be used to predict the claim amount for a new customer based on his age, gender, and smoking status. And as we have also discussed earlier, such a linear equation produced by the linear regression algorithm also gives us insights into the relationships between the target variable and features. We saw earlier that, based on this equation, we can tell that Claim Amount increases by 0.4K with every year of age. We can also tell that for males (Gender = 1), Claim Amount is higher by 2.1K as compared to females. And smokers (Smoking Status =1) tend to claim 2.9K more than nonsmokers.

Logistic Regression

Just like many data scientists begin experimentation for regression problems with linear regression, logistic regression[3] is a favorite for initial experimentation for classification problems. Let's try and understand logistic regression using an example similar to the insurance example in the previous section. However, this time, our goal is to predict only whether a new customer will make a claim or not instead of predicting the claim amount. Let's assume we have data from a different insurance company which contains Gender, Age, and Smoking Status for each existing customer like the data in the previous section. But, instead of *Claim Amount,* this data contains a variable called *Claim Status* whose value for a customer is either

---

[3] Lot of interesting content is available online that explains why this algorithm is called "regression" even though it is used so commonly for classification problems.

Claimed or *Not Claimed* based on whether that customer made a claim or not. Now we will try to use logistic regression algorithm to build a model that learns to predict the value of the target variable *Claim Status* based on the values of the features *Gender, Age, and Smoking Status.*[4] Figure 16-4 shows the data from this new insurance company.

Gender	Age	Smoking Status	Claim Status
....	....	....	....
0	30	0	Not Claimed
1	50	0	Claimed
1	40	1	Claimed
......	......	....	....

Figure 16-4. *Features and target variable for logistic regression*

Instead of directly predicting whether a customer will make a claim or not, the logistic regression algorithm learns to predict the probability indicating how likely the customer is to make a claim based on the values of gender, age, etc. For this, the algorithm creates a linear equation (just like the linear regression algorithm) that explains how the probability of a customer making a claim can be calculated based on the weighted sum of their gender, age, etc. However, a simple weighted sum could be greater than 1 or less than 0. The algorithm uses a function called *logistic function* to convert the weighted sum into a value between 0 and 1 for it to be a valid probability.

Figure 16-5 shows how the logistic function is defined and the blue curve in the figure plots the values of this function for different values of input x. As you can see in the plot, the value of the function is 0.5 for x = 0.

---

[4] We have skipped discussion of feature scaling to focus on the main concepts of logistic regression.

This is because the e^{-x} term in the function definition becomes 1 for $x = 0$ causing the overall value of the function to be $1/(1+1)$ or 0.5. As x increases toward large positive values, the e^{-x} term starts becoming close to 0 causing the overall function value to become close to 1. And as x decreases toward large negative values, the e^{-x} term starts becoming very large causing the overall function value to become close to 0. So the value of the function is guaranteed to be between 0 and 1.

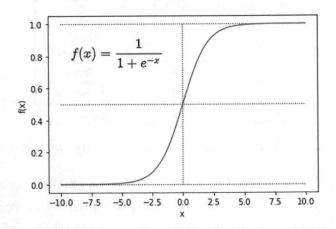

Figure 16-5. *Logistic function*

As mentioned earlier, the logistic regression algorithm uses this logistic function to convert the weighted sum of feature values into a value between 0 and 1 which represents the probability that the customer will make a claim. This can be represented as an equation:

$$p_{claim} = f(b_0 + b_1 \times \text{Gender} + b_2 \times \text{Age} + b_3 \times \text{Smoking Status})$$

where p_{claim} is the probability that the customer will make a claim,
f is the logistic function,
b_0 is the intercept term,
b_1, b_2, b_3 are weights for the features.

Using this equation, the algorithm would predict the probability of making a claim for a customer whose Gender = 1, Age = 50, and Smoking Status = 0 to be

$$f(b_0 + b_1 \times 1 + b_2 \times 50 + b_3 \times 0)$$

The algorithm could also predict the probability of not making a claim by subtracting the probability of making a claim from 1. This could be represented as

$$p_{no\_claim} = 1 - p_{claim} = 1 - f(b_0 + b_1 \times Gender + b_2 \times Age + b_3 \times Smoking\ Status)$$

where **pno_claim** is the probability that the customer will not make a claim.

Using this equation, the algorithm would predict the probability of not making a claim for a customer whose Gender = 0, Age = 30, and Smoking Status = 0 to be

$$1 - f(b_0 + b_1 \times 0 + b_2 \times 30 + b_3 \times 0)$$

The algorithm must predict a high probability of making a claim (p_{claim}) for existing customers who actually made a claim and predict a high probability of not making a claim (p_{no_claim}) for existing customers who didn't make a claim. The column P in Figure 16-6 shows the predicted probability of making a claim (p_{claim}) for existing customers who *made* a claim and predicted probability of not making a claim (p_{no_claim}) for existing customers who *didn't make* a claim. And as we just mentioned, all these values (listed in column P) must be high. So the algorithm will try to find the values for b_0, b_1, b_2, and b_3 for which the values in column P are high.[5] The algorithm will use techniques mentioned earlier for achieving this.

---

[5] This is an extremely simplified explanation that skips a discussion of the actual function which the algorithm tries to minimize.

Gender	Age	Smoking Status	Claim Status	P
....	....	....	....	....
0	30	0	Not Claimed	$1 - f(b_0 + b_1 \times 0 + b_2 \times 30 + b_3 \times 0)$
1	50	0	Claimed	$f(b_0 + b_1 \times 1 + b_2 \times 50 + b_3 \times 0)$
1	40	1	Claimed	$f(b_0 + b_1 \times 1 + b_2 \times 40 + b_3 \times 1)$
......	......	....	....	....

Figure 16-6. *Column P containing either p_{claim} or p_{no_claim} for existing customers*

Let's say the algorithm finds that $b_0 = -80$, $b_1 = 10$, $b_2 = 2$, $b_3 = 10$ are the optimum values for weights and intercept term. It will use these values to concretize the equation

$$p_{claim} = f(b_0 + b_1 \times \text{Gender} + b_2 \times \text{Age} + b_3 \times \text{Smoking Status})$$

into

$$p_{claim} = f(-80 + 10 \times \text{Gender} + 2 \times \text{Age} + 10 \times \text{Smoking Status})$$

Now this equation represents the logistic regression model and can be used to predict the probability of making a claim for a new customer. For example, the probability that a 37-year-old male smoker (Gender = 1, Age = 37, Smoking Status = 1) will make a claim is given by

$$p_{claim} = f(-80 + 10 \times \text{Gender} + 2 \times \text{Age} + 10 \times \text{Smoking Status})$$

$$= f(-80 + 10 \times 1 + 2 \times 37 + 10 \times 1)$$

$$= f(14)$$

So the probability that this customer will make a claim is equal to $f(14)$. We can see in the preceding plot of logistic function $f(x)$ that the value of logistic function for input value of 14 (i.e., *f(14)*) is close to 1. So the probability that this customer will make a claim is close to 1.

Once we have the probability of making a claim for a new customer, we can predict whether he will make a claim or not by comparing this probability with a cutoff. If the probability of making a claim is above the cutoff, we predict that the customer will make a claim. And if the probability is below the cutoff, we predict that the customer won't make a claim. For example, if we chose a cutoff of 0.5 for our logistic regression model, we would predict that the 37-year-old male smoker discussed earlier will make a claim because his probability of making a claim was predicted to be close to 1 which is above the cutoff 0.5. On the other hand, if we had a customer with a predicted probability of 0.3 from the model, we would predict that this customer won't make a claim since his predicted probability is below the chosen cutoff 0.5.

Just like linear regression, logistic regression models are very useful if you want to go beyond just predicting the value of the target variable and want insights into the data and the underlying processes that generate this data. Let's see what insights the logistic regression model we discussed previously gives us. Let's look at the equation for this model again:

$$p_{claim} = f(-80 + 10 \times \text{Gender} + 2 \times \text{Age} + 10 \times \text{Smoking Status})$$

We can see that for larger values of age, the value of the inner expression (which is input for the logistic function in this equation) will also be larger. And the plot of logistic function discussed earlier tells us that as input value becomes larger, the logistic function value becomes larger too. So the probability of making a claim will be larger for larger values of age. This means that older people are more likely to make a claim. Similarly for smokers (Smoking Status = 1), the inner expression increases by 10. With this increase in the value of inner expression, logistic function value also increases. So the probability of making a claim is higher for smokers. In other words, smokers are more likely to make a claim. You could similarly analyze the effect of gender on the likelihood of making a claim.

Let's analyze the equation of the model further to find more insights. We will assume a model probability cutoff of 0.5 for this discussion. Now, let's say we were interested in analyzing the female nonsmokers (Gender = 0, Smoking Status = 0) group. Substituting the values of Gender and Smoking Status for this group in the equation of the model gives us

$$p_{claim} = f(-80 + 10 \times 0 + 2 \times Age + 10 \times 0)$$

which is equivalent to

$$p_{claim} = f(2 \times Age - 80)$$

This reduced equation gives us the probability of making a claim for female nonsmokers group. For any customer in this group, we will predict she is likely to make a claim only when her probability of making a claim p_{claim} is greater than the cutoff 0.5. This will be true when the logistic function value on the right side of this reduced equation is greater than 0.5. From the logistic function plot, we can tell that logistic value is greater than 0.5 when input value ("$2 \times Age - 80$" in this case) is greater than 0. This happens in our case when age is greater than 40. In short, for any female nonsmoker (i.e., any customer in this group), we end up predicting she is likely to make a claim if her age is above 40. So what this effectively conveys is that female nonsmokers are likely to claim if they are above 40 years of age. We can get similar insights for other groups like male smokers, female smokers, etc.

Support Vector Machine

Support vector machine (or SVM) is another machine learning algorithm that data scientists very often use for classification problems though it can also be used for regression problems. We will try and understand this algorithm using a very simple classification example.

Let's say our data contains two features *f1* and *f2* and a target variable *t* whose value is either *N* (representing *Negative* class) or *P* (representing *Positive* class). This data is shown in Figure 16-7.

f1	f2	t
......	....	....
1	4	P
4	2	N
......	......	....

Figure 16-7. *Simple data with two features and target*

Let's plot the positive observations (whose target value is P) as red square markers and negative observations (whose target value is N) as green circular markers on a scatter plot as shown in Figure 16-8. The x coordinate of each marker is based on f1 value of corresponding observation, and y coordinate is based on the f2 value. You could visually imagine a line that seems to separate the positive and negative observations. This imaginary line is shown as a dotted line on the plot. Now you can yourself classify a new observation easily using this imaginary line. You will first plot the new observation on the scatter plot based on the values of f1 and f2. You will then check which side of the dotted line the new observations falls in. If it falls in the side that contains the red markers, you will predict that the new observation must be positive (i.e., you will predict the target value to be P). And if it falls in the side of green markers, you will predict that the new observation must be negative (i.e., you will predict the target value to be N). This is the general idea on which the SVM algorithm is based.

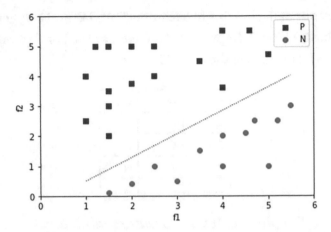

Figure 16-8. *Scatter plot for our simple data and the imaginary separating line*

SVM algorithm in general tries to find a hyperplane in the n-dimensional space (corresponding to n features) that separates the existing observations of one class from the observations of the other class. Let's call one class *positive* and the other class *negative*. So SVM tries to find a hyperplane that will separate the positive observations from negative observations. If a new observation falls on that side of the hyperplane which contains the positive observations, the new observation will be predicted to be *positive*. And if the new observation falls on the other side, SVM will predict that it belongs to *negative* class. When the data has just two features, the hyperplane is simply a straight line just like the imaginary separating line in the previous figure. If the data has three features (i.e., data is three dimensional), the hyperplane is simply a plane and so on.

Data shown in the previous figure (which had two features) is linearly separable which means that it is possible to find a straight line that separates the two classes. In general, when you are dealing with data that has *n* features, you will say the data is linearly separable if it is possible to find a hyperplane in the n-dimensional feature space that separates the two classes. And you could use a *linear SVM* to find this hyperplane for linearly separable data which can then be used to predict the class for a new observation.

However, data is not always linearly separable. Let's look at a popular toy example to understand this. Figure 16-9 shows this toy data with just one feature *f1* and target *t* whose value could be *P* (positive) or *N* (negative). Figure 16-10 shows the plot for this data in which you can see that the data is not linearly separable because you cannot find a hyperplane that separates the positive and negative observations. For such cases where the data is not linearly separable, you could use a *nonlinear SVM* to separate the classes.

f1	t
......	....
-5	P
1	N
3	P
......	....

Figure 16-9. *Toy example data*

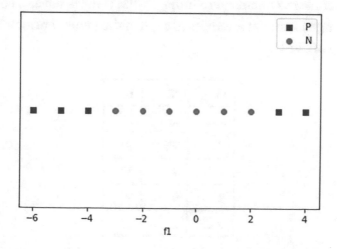

Figure 16-10. *Plot for toy example data*

We would naturally want to understand how a nonlinear SVM can manage to separate the classes even when data is not linearly separable. Let's take the case of the single feature data discussed earlier which is not linearly separable. Let's say you add a derived feature *f2* to this dataset whose value is simply square of f1 value (i.e., f2 = f1^2). Figure 16-11 shows the toy data with the derived feature added, and Figure 16-12 shows its scatter plot. You can see that now it is possible to find a hyperplane (shown as dotted line on the scatter plot) in the two-dimensional space which separates the classes. To predict the class for a new observation, you can derive its f2 value using the f1 value and use both these values for plotting the new observation in the two-dimensional space in order to check which side of the hyperplane it is falling in. So we can see how adding features (like the derived feature we just saw) to data that is not linearly separable could make it possible to find a separating hyperplane. A nonlinear SVM can achieve the effect of adding such features (without really having to add them) by using a technique called *kernel trick*. Since this technique gives the effect of adding those features, a nonlinear SVM can separate the classes in data that is otherwise not linearly separable and hence can accordingly classify new observations. Needless to say, there are many other variations and details pertaining to SVM that we haven't covered. But the preceding discussion attempts to explain the general principles behind the working of SVMs.

f1	f2	t
......	...	....
-5	25	P
1	1	N
3	9	P
......	...	....

Figure 16-11. *Toy data with derived feature f2 = f1^2*

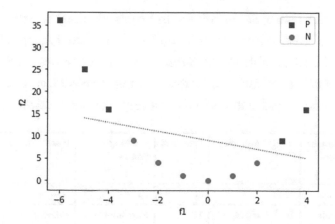

Figure 16-12. *Scatter plot for toy data with derived feature*

Decision Tree

Decision tree algorithm is another popular supervised machine learning algorithm that is used for both classification and regression problems. We already saw an example of decision tree when we discussed classification problems. Let's try and understand decision tree algorithm in more detail with another example. Let's say you are building an app for the employees of your organization which can monitor their health and give timely warning about onset of various illnesses. One of the features of this app indicates whether the user is at risk of heart disease. Behind the scenes, the app will use a machine learning model to predict whether the user is likely to have heart disease. Your job is to build this model using the available data that has roughly an equal number of healthy people and people with heart disease. Figure 16-13 shows a snapshot of the data for adults that we will use for building this predictive model. *Gender* and *Smoking Status* in the table are straightforward. *Weight Category* column can have one of the three values: *Normal* (indicating that the person is in the normal weight range for their height and gender), *Underweight* (indicating that person is below the normal weight range), and *Overweight* (indicating that person is above the normal weight range). *Exercises* column indicates whether the person exercises

225

regularly or not. *Health Status* column indicates whether the person is healthy or has heart disease. We will try and build a simple model that predicts the value of target variable *Health Status* based on the values of other four columns which are our features for this example. In reality, you would want to use more sophisticated features to build a very accurate model.

Gender	Weight Category	Exercises	Smoking Status	Health Status
....	....	....	....	....
Male	Underweight	Yes	Non Smoker	Healthy
Female	Overweight	Yes	Non Smoker	Healthy
Male	Normal	No	Smoker	Heart Disease
....	....	....	....	....

Figure 16-13. *Snapshot of data for predicting heart disease*

If we give these features and target variable to the decision tree algorithm, it will build a decision tree model. A decision tree model is simply a tree[6] in which non-leaf nodes inspect values of features and leaf nodes predict the target value. Figure 16-14 shows a partial view of the decision tree model built by the decision tree algorithm for the previous data. You can see that the model inspects the value of *Exercises* feature in the first non-leaf node and goes right[7] if the value is *Yes* and goes left if the value is *No*. If the value is *Yes*, it then checks the value of the feature *Smoking Status* in another non-leaf node. If the value of *Smoking Status* is *Smoker,* it goes right, and if the value is *Non Smoker,* it goes left to a leaf node. This leaf node predicts the target value as *Healthy*. Other non-leaf and leaf nodes could be similarly explained.

---

[6] A tree is a representation that looks like an inverted real-life tree: with a root node at the top and leaf nodes at the bottom.

[7] Reader's right.

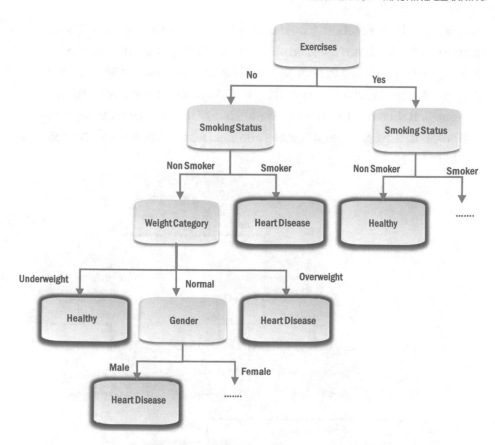

Figure 16-14. *Partial view of the decision tree model for predicting heart disease*

To make a prediction for a new observation, the model will simply start at the root node and traverse down the tree. At each non-leaf node, it will inspect the value of a feature of the new observation and take the corresponding branch. It will keep doing this till it has reached a leaf node and will finally predict the value corresponding to the leaf node. Let's say we want to make prediction for an overweight male employee who does not exercise and does not smoke (Gender = Male, Weight Category = Overweight, Exercises = No, Smoking Status = Non Smoker). Red arrows in Figure 16-15 show how the tree is traversed for this employee for making the prediction. The model will start at the root node *Exercises* and take the left[8] branch corresponding to *No*. It will again take the left branch corresponding to *Non Smoker* from node *Smoking Status* and take the rightmost branch corresponding to *Overweight* from node *Weight Category*. It thus reaches the leaf node *Heart Disease* (surrounded by red rectangle in the figure) and hence predicts *Heart Disease* for the employee.

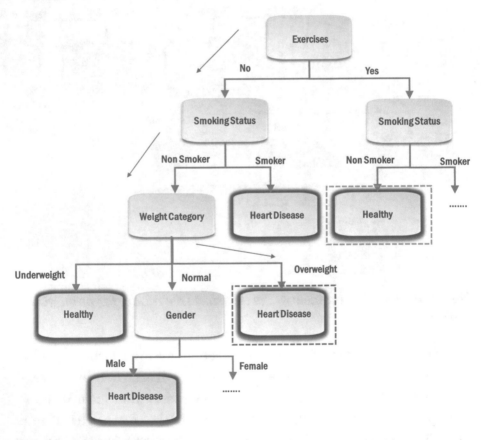

Figure 16-15. *Traversing the decision tree for predicting heart disease for the employee*

---

[8] Reader's left.

Let's take a step back and understand why the model predicts *Heart Disease* when a person reaches this leaf node inside the red rectangle. The model knows from the tree structure that if a person reaches this leaf node, they must belong to the group of non-exercising nonsmoking overweight people. And the model observed that all people in this group in the data it was provided had heart disease.[9] So the model confidently predicts *Heart Disease* for this person. Similarly if a person reaches the leaf node inside the green rectangle, the model knows that they must belong to the group of exercising nonsmoking people and all people in this group in the data were healthy. So the model confidently predicts this person as *Healthy*. The important point to note here is that the model confidently predicted the target value as *Heart Disease* in the first case because the leaf node he reached corresponds to a group (non-exercising nonsmoking overweight people) which has a very high predominance of people with heart disease in the data provided. And the model confidently predicted the target value as *Healthy* in the second case because the leaf node he reached corresponds to a group (exercising nonsmoking people) which has a very high predominance of heathy people in the data provided. So we can see that, to be able to confidently predict the target value, it is important that the leaf nodes should correspond to groups that have a very high predominance of one class (Healthy or Heart Disease). Or we could say in short that the leaf nodes need to have a very high predominance of one class.

The algorithm uses measures like entropy to evaluate whether a node has a very high predominance of one class. Just like the leaf nodes inside the red and green rectangles correspond to certain groups as mentioned previously, every node in the tree corresponds to a certain group. For example, the node to the right of the root node corresponds

---

[9] This is true for our data even though it is not visible in the partial view we have shown in Figure 16-13.

to the group of exercisers. If a node corresponds to a group in which P_H fraction of people are healthy and P_{HD} fraction of people have heart disease in the data, the entropy of the node is defined as

$$\text{Entropy} = - P_H \times \log_2 P_H - P_{HD} \times \log_2 P_{HD}$$

If a node has a very high predominance of healthy people, P_H will be close to 1 and P_{HD} will be close to 0. Since P_H is close to 1, $\log_2 P_H$ is close to 0 and hence "- $P_H \times \log_2 P_H$" is close to 0. Also since P_{HD} is close to 0, "- $P_{HD} \times \log_2 P_{HD}$" is also close to 0. Hence, entropy is close to 0. If a node has a very high predominance of people with heart disease, P_{HD} will be close to 1, and P_H will be close to 0. It is easy to see using the entropy equation that for this case too, entropy will be close to 0. So this means that entropy is close to 0 whenever there is a very high predominance of one class. Let's see what the entropy value is when no class is predominant, that is, the number of healthy people is roughly equal to the number of people with heart disease in the data for the group corresponding to the node. So for this case, both P_H and P_{HD} are close to 0.5, and hence, we can calculate the entropy using the entropy equation:

$$\text{Entropy} = - 0.5 \times \log_2 0.5 - 0.5 \times \log_2 0.5$$

$$= - 0.5 \times -1 - 0.5 \times -1$$

$$= 1$$

So entropy is close to 1 when no class is predominant. So we can conclude that entropy is very low (close to 0) when there is a very high predominance of one class and very high (close to 1) when no class is predominant. Since we want the leaf nodes to have a very high predominance of one class, we will want the entropy for leaf nodes to be very low.

Now we can finally look at how the algorithm creates the tree. The algorithm starts with the root node which corresponds to the group of "all" people which has roughly equal number of healthy people and people with heart disease in our data. So no class is predominant in the root node. It then splits the root node on that feature from the feature set for which the child nodes have a high predominance of one class. So it will pick the feature for which the child nodes have the lowest entropy. It then repeats this for each child node, that is, it splits each child node further using the feature that results in children with high predominance of one class (or lowest entropy). And it keeps doing this to build the tree. Thus, the algorithm keeps splitting to create nodes with high predominance of one class. Hence, by the time it has reached the leaf nodes, there will be a very high predominance of one class. This is the reason that the leaf node in the red rectangle earlier had a very high predominance of class *Heart Disease* (the group of people corresponding to this leaf node had people with heart disease only and no healthy people as we saw earlier) and the leaf node in the green rectangle earlier had a very high predominance of class *Healthy* (the group of people corresponding to this leaf node had only healthy people and no people with heart disease as we saw earlier). And as we saw earlier, a very high predominance of one class in a leaf node gives the model the confidence to predict that class as the target value for the person who has reached that leaf node during prediction.

Decision tree models also provide insights into the trends within data and the underlying processes. For example, you can tell looking at the tree that if a person exercises and does not smoke, the decision tree will predict that person to be healthy irrespective of that person's gender and weight category. More specifically, the important insight we gain is that *even an overweight person is likely to be healthy* if that person exercises and does not smoke.

Decision tree algorithm is also popular because it is applicable in many different scenarios that one is likely to encounter. The example we saw earlier did not have any numeric feature, but the decision tree algorithm can work with numeric features as well for making predictions. We saw an example of this in Chapter 4, where the algorithm created a tree that used the numeric feature *Age* for predicting which interested customers are likely to buy the car. Also, the example we just saw in this section is a classification problem, but the decision tree algorithm can also be used for regression problems.

Random Forest

A close relative of the decision tree algorithm is the random forest algorithm. Random forest algorithm can also be used for classification as well as regression problems. We saw that the model created by the decision tree algorithm is simply a decision tree. The model created by the random forest algorithm, on the other hand, is a forest of decision trees. So the random forest algorithm, instead of trusting the prediction from a single decision tree, forms a team of multiple decision trees each of which gives its prediction for a new observation. The predictions from all the trees are considered to arrive at the final prediction for the new observation.

For classification problems, each decision tree in the forest predicts the class which it thinks the new observation might belong to. In other words, each tree recommends a class for the new observation. The class that is recommended by the largest number of trees is chosen as the final predicted class. Let's assume we gave the data of healthy people and people with heart disease from previous section to the random forest algorithm which builds a forest of trees. Figure 16-16 shows how the trees collaborate to predict whether a new employee has heart disease. You can see that 80 trees think this new employee is healthy and 20 feel the employee has heart disease. Since a larger number of trees think the employee is healthy, the model predicts that the employee is healthy.

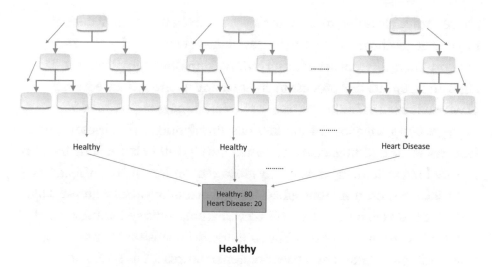

Figure 16-16. *Prediction with random forest for a new employee*

For regression problems, each individual tree in the forest predicts a numeric value for the new observation. The model averages the predicted values from all trees and returns the average value as the final target value for the new observation.

If you look deeply at the way the decision tree algorithm learns from the data and builds the tree, you can understand why a decision tree often overfits the data using which it learned. This means that a decision tree is often able to predict very well the target values for those observations which it used for learning but might not perform very well for new unseen observations. The random forest algorithm solves this problem and improves the performance on new data by consulting multiple decision trees.

To consult multiple decision trees, the random forest algorithm needs to first create those multiple decision trees from the single dataset of observations and features that it was provided. The algorithm manages to do this by varying the observations and features while building each tree. For each tree, the algorithm randomly chooses observations with replacement from the original dataset till a new dataset with same number of observations as the original dataset gets created. Since the algorithm is *replacing*, some of the observations in the original dataset might get chosen multiple times, and some observations in the original dataset might not get chosen at all. So the new dataset will have the same size but contain a different set of observations from the original dataset. The algorithm repeats this process to create many different datasets each of which is used to build one tree – this technique is called *bootstrap aggregating* or *bagging*. On similar lines, the algorithm also tries to vary the features while building each tree. When the algorithm is deciding the best feature for a split in any tree, it only looks at a random subset of features and picks the best from that subset instead of looking at all features. This further causes each tree to use different features in its splits. The crux of the story is that each tree gets built differently because each tree learns from a different dataset and uses different features for its splits. And multiple such different trees collaborate to improve performance.

Gradient Boosted Trees

Gradient boosted trees is another popular algorithm that makes use of multiple decision trees. Let's focus only on regression problems in this discussion to understand how this algorithm works and how it is different from random forest algorithm. Random forest algorithm builds multiple trees independently of one another where each tree learns to predict the numeric target value itself. For a new observation, each tree tries to predict the target value, and predictions from all trees are averaged to arrive at the final target value that should be predicted for this observation. *Gradient boosted trees* algorithm on the other hand creates trees sequentially where the first tree learns to predict the numeric target value and each subsequent tree learns to predict the error made by the previous tree. While predicting for a new observation, the first tree predicts a numeric target value, and each subsequent tree predicts the error made by the previous tree. The idea is that if you can predict the numeric target value and if you know beforehand the errors in your prediction, you can adjust for those errors to improve your prediction.

Let's look at a concrete regression example to understand this in more detail. Let's assume the data for our example contains three features *f1, f2, and f3* and a continuous-valued target variable *t* as shown in the top-left table in Figure 16-17. Note that there is an observation where f1 is 5, f2 is 7, and f3 is 2 and the corresponding target value *t* is 10. Our goal of course is to build a model that closely predicts the value of target *t* using the values of the three features. If we pass this data to the gradient boosted trees algorithm, it will build trees sequentially as mentioned earlier. Figure 16-17 shows a simple scenario where the gradient boosted trees algorithm builds two trees using this data. The algorithm takes the prepared data with the features and target (top-left table in the figure) and builds the first tree on the left which learns to predict the value of target using the feature values. The algorithm now uses the first tree to predict the target values for existing observations which are shown in column *predicted_t* of bottom-left table. You can see in this table that the first tree predicts a target value of 8 for the existing observation whose f1 is 5, f2 is 7, and f3 is 2, whereas the actual target value was 10. So the first tree makes an error of 2 (= 10 minus 8) for this observation.

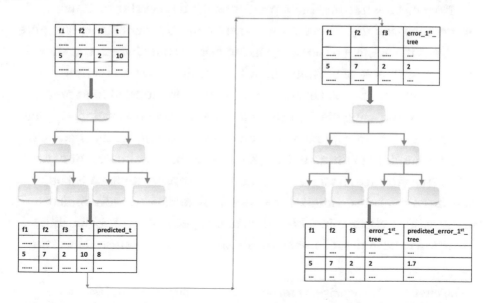

Figure 16-17. *Gradient boosted trees with two trees*

The algorithm now builds a second decision tree that can predict the errors that the first tree will make in predicting target values. For this, the algorithm calculates the error made by the first tree for each existing observation which is the difference between the actual target value and target value predicted by the first tree (i.e., *t* minus *predicted_t* in bottom-left table). The top-right table shows the errors made by the first tree (in column *error_1ˢᵗ_tree*[10]) along with the feature values for existing observations that are passed to the second tree. One of the rows in this data tells the second tree that the error made by the first tree is 2 when f1 is 5, f2 is 7, and f3 is 2. The second tree uses this data to learn to predict the errors that the first tree will make. Once the second tree has learned, it can be used to predict the errors that the first tree makes. The additional column *predicted_error_1ˢᵗ_tree* in the bottom-right table shows the errors that the second tree predicts will be made by the first tree for the existing observations. For example, for the observation whose f1 is 5, f2 is 7, and f3 is 2, the second tree predicts that the first tree will make an error of 1.7, whereas the actual error made by the first tree was 2.

Now that the trees are built, predicting the target value for new observations is simple. Let's say we have a new observation which is quite similar to the existing observation in our original data (which was shown in the top-left table of previous figure). So for this new observation too, f1 is 5, f2 is 7, and f3 is 2. Let's see how the gradient boosted trees predict the target value using the feature values for this new observation – notice how this prediction approach explained next tries to make the predicted target value close to the actual target value for this new observation (we will assume the actual target value for the new observation to also be 10 like the existing observation since the new observation is very similar to the existing observation, but this actual target value will obviously be unknown to us in practical scenarios). Now, for these feature values, the

---

[10] The errors will be negative for rows where actual target value is less than predicted target value.

first tree will predict a target value of 8 (we can tell this from the bottom-left table of previous figure). Now the second tree is used to improve this prediction and make it closer to actual target value. For these feature values, the second tree will predict an error of 1.7 by first tree (we can tell this from the bottom-right table in previous figure). The predicted target value from the first tree will now be corrected using the error of the first tree as predicted by the second tree to get the final target value that will be predicted for this observation. So the predicted error given by the second tree (1.7) is added to the predicted target value from the first tree (8) to get the corrected target value (9.7) that gets finally predicted for this observation. Thus, the final predicted target value is close to the actual target value (which we assumed to be 10 as mentioned earlier).

Let's see how we can improve the predictions further. We saw in the bottom-right table previously that the actual error made by the first tree is 2 when f1 is 5, f2 is 7, and f3 is 2, but the second tree predicts the error to be 1.7. This means that the second tree itself has an error of 0.3 for these feature values. So you could configure the algorithm to build a third tree that can predict the errors of the second tree. This is shown in Figure 16-18. You can see in the figure that the third tree learns from the data passed to it that the error made by the second tree is 0.3 when f1 is 5, f2 is 7, and f3 is 2. And when the third tree is in turn asked to predict the error made by the second tree for these feature values, it predicts 0.25 as you can see in the figure. Once the three trees are built, when we make a prediction for the new observation (whose f1 is 5, f2 is 7, f3 is 2), the first tree will predict that the target value is 8, the second tree will predict that the first tree will make an error of 1.7, and the third tree will predict that the second tree will make an error of 0.25. So the final predicted target value will be equal to the predicted target value from the first tree (8) plus error of the first tree as predicted by the second tree (1.7) plus error of the second tree as predicted by the third tree (0.25) which is equal to 9.95. Hence, the third tree further helps us make the final predicted target value closer to actual target value (which we assumed to be 10).

You can configure the algorithm to use more and more trees sequentially in a similar fashion. And even when you have many trees, while predicting for a new observation, the predictions by all trees are added, and the resulting sum is predicted as the final target value. This can be represented as a simple equation:

Final Predicted Target Value = Prediction by 1st tree + Prediction by 2nd tree + Prediction by 3rd tree + Prediction by 4th tree + Prediction by 5th tree + ...

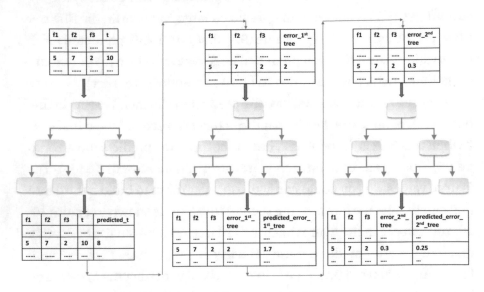

Figure 16-18. *Gradient boosted trees with three trees*

Artificial Neural Network

Artificial neural networks (ANNs), or simply neural networks, are among the most talked about and glorified machine learning algorithms that are based on the way the biological neurons function in the brain. They are being used to solve the most complex problems and are the target of extensive research across the globe. Deep learning, as we saw in Chapter 1, is based on neural networks. The journey of setting up an effective data science practice is likely to go through a phase of evaluating the need for and building expertise in ANNs. There also exist special kinds of ANNs like convolutional neural network (CNN), recurrent neural network (RNN), etc., each of which has some unique characteristics that make it especially suited for specific types of problems. Instead of discussing all kinds of ANNs, we will focus in this section on understanding the general principles behind ANNs which will help us understand their strengths as well as limitations compared to other ML algorithms.

Our brain consists of billions of interconnected nerve cells called neurons. Each neuron receives signals from other neurons, processes them, and produces its own signal which is further passed on to other neurons. In a similar way, artificial neural networks consist of several interconnected artificial neurons. Each such artificial neuron receives inputs from other neurons and does some calculations to produce an output which is passed on to other artificial neurons. Let's revisit the problem we discussed in Chapter 6 where our goal was to infer/predict the category of an email based on the text in the email body. Figure 16-19 shows a partial view of the data we prepared in that chapter which contains a row for each email. You might remember that this prepared data contains a feature for every base word in the vocabulary and also contains the target variable *Category*. The value of a feature for an email is equal to the number of times the corresponding base word occurred in that email. And the value of the target variable for an email obviously indicates the category of that email.

context	...	security	fix	release	...	...	design	...	...	Category
1	...	1	1	0	...	...	0	...	...	Product Development
0	...	0	0	1	...	...	0	...	...	Product Development
0	...	0	0	0	...	...	1	...	...	Research Work
0	...	0	0	0	...	...	0	...	...	Research Work
0	...	0	0	0	...	...	0	...	...	Trainings
0	...	0	0	0	...	...	0	...	...	Trainings
...	...	...	...	...	...	...	...	...	...	....
...	...	...	...	...	...	...	...	...	...	....

Figure 16-19. *Features and target for email data*

We will convert the single target variable *Category* into three target variables corresponding to the three possible categories: Product Development, Research Work, and Trainings. Figure 16-20 shows the prepared data[11] that has been transformed[12] to have three target variables which can be seen in the last three columns. If an email belongs to a certain category, the value of the corresponding target variable for that email is 1 and the other two target variables have a value of 0. For example, the first email in the figure belongs to category *Product Development,* so the value of target variable *Product Development* is 1, the value of target variable *Research Work* is 0, and the value of target variable *Trainings* is also 0. Let's now build an artificial neural network that can predict the values of the three target variables using the values of the features.

---

[11] We have skipped discussion of feature scaling to focus on the main concepts of artificial neural networks.

[12] We saw similar transformations when we converted categorical variables into numeric variables in Chapter 14.

context	...	security	fix	release	...	...	design	...	...	Product Development	Research Work	Trainings
1	...	1	1	0	...	...	0	...	...	1	0	0
0	...	0	0	1	...	...	0	...	...	1	0	0
0	...	0	0	0	...	...	1	...	...	0	1	0
0	...	0	0	0	...	...	0	...	...	0	1	0
0	...	0	0	0	...	...	0	...	...	0	0	1
0	...	0	0	0	...	...	0	...	...	0	0	1
...	...	...	...	...	...	...	...	...	...	...	...	...
...	...	...	...	...	...	...	...	...	...	...	...	...

Figure 16-20. *Features and new target variables*

We will build a neural network with a simple and common architecture that consists of layers where each layer contains some artificial neurons. And neurons within a layer generally receive inputs from neurons in the previous layer, do some computations on them, and pass on the results to neurons in the next layer. Figure 16-21 shows the neural network we have designed for predicting the three target variables from the values of the features. You can see in the figure that our neural network has four layers. The neurons in the input layer will take the values of the features for an email, and the neurons in the output layer will predict the values of the three target variables for that email. This neural network could be improved in many ways by using more advanced functions/techniques, but as mentioned earlier, we will focus mainly on the basic principles and leave out such details. Let's walk through this neural network to understand it in more depth.

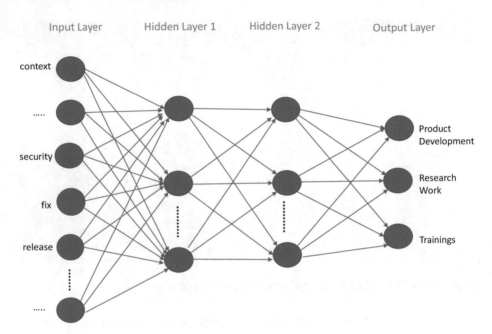

Figure 16-21. *Our neural network for predicting the category of an email*

The first column in this figure is the *input layer* and contains a neuron for each feature. Note there is a neuron for feature *context*, a neuron for feature *security*, and so on. Each neuron in this layer simply receives the value of the corresponding feature for an email and outputs the same value without changing it. The output of each neuron in the input layer (which is simply a feature value as we just saw) is fed to all neurons in *hidden layer 1*. Thus, each neuron in the first hidden layer receives all feature values as input.

The neurons in *hidden layer 1, hidden layer 2,* and *output layer* are different from neurons in the *input layer*. What each neuron in these three layers does is similar to what we saw in logistic regression. It calculates the weighted sum of its inputs, adds a bias, and uses the sigmoid function to convert the resulting value into a value between 0 and 1. This can be represented as an equation:

$$\text{output} = f(b_0 + b_1 \times ip_1 + b_2 \times ip_2 + b_3 \times ip_3 + \ldots)$$

where **output** is the output of the neuron,

f is the sigmoid function whose definition is the same as the logistic function,

b_0 is the bias,

ip_1, ip_2, ip_3... are inputs to the neuron,

b_1, b_2, b_3... are weights for the inputs.

So we can say that each neuron in these three layers performs some computations on its inputs using its list of weights (including the bias) to produce the output. And the output of each neuron in first hidden layer is passed to all neurons in *hidden layer 2*. And output of each neuron in the second hidden layer is passed to all neurons in *output layer*. Note that the output layer has three neurons corresponding to the three target variables. So each neuron in the output layer outputs the predicted value of the corresponding target variable for the email.

In a nutshell, we could say that the neural network takes feature values of an email in the input layer and performs multiple computations on these feature values using the weights of the neurons in order to predict the values of the three target variables in the output layer. But how does the neural network know what values of weights in the neurons will produce the correct target values from the feature values? The neural network learns this from the data we provided to it which contains features and the three target variables for existing emails.

Let's understand this in more detail. The neural network begins by initializing the weights of all neurons to some values.[13] It will then look at the first email in the provided data and pass its feature values to the input layer. Computations will be performed on these feature values in different layers using the weights of neurons to produce three predicted target values. Figure 16-22 shows the feature values for the first email on the left and the predicted target values on the right of the network. The neural network then measures the error in prediction for this email by comparing these

---

[13] For example, random values.

predicted target values with the actual target values for this email which are known from the data provided. It then adjusts the weights of the neurons in the network in such a way that the error for this email decreases. The figure also depicts these steps of measuring the error and adjusting the weights. Let's take a closer look at the process of adjusting the weights. The error in prediction for this email depends on the actual target values and predicted target values. The predicted target values themselves depend on the feature values for this email and weights of neurons. So we could say that the error depends on the feature values, weights of neurons, and actual target values for the email. Since the feature values and actual target values for this email are fixed as present in the data, the error for this email ends up being a function of the weights of neurons.[14] So the neural network could use techniques similar to gradient descent to change the weights from their current values to new values in a way that the error decreases.

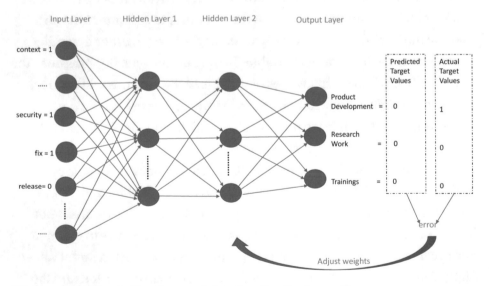

Figure 16-22. *Adjusting weights for the first email*

---

[14] Similar to how the overall prediction error in linear regression was a function of the weights b_0, b_1, b_2, and b_3.

The neural network then performs these steps of adjusting the weights to reduce the error (which it performed for the first email) for all other emails as well. With the new weights, the neural network should make less errors in predicting the target values for existing emails. And then the neural network repeats this entire process of adjusting the weights for all emails one more time to reduce the errors further. It continues to repeat this entire process many times till the errors for existing emails have minimized. At this stage, for the existing emails, the neural network is able to predict target values that are close to the actual target values. Figure 16-23 shows that the neural network now predicts target values that are close to the actual target values if you feed it the feature values of the first email. So the network predicts a value close[15] to 1 for the target variable *Product Development*, value close to 0 for *Research Work,* and value close to 0 for *Trainings* for the first existing email. However, the real benefit comes from the fact that the neural network is now able to predict reasonably well the category for even new incoming emails that it hasn't seen earlier.[16] For example, if a new incoming email has similar text as the first existing email (and hence similar feature values), the neural network will still predict a value close to 1 for target variable *Product Development*, value close to 0 for *Research Work,* and value close to 0 for *Trainings.* In other words, the neural network will be able to correctly predict that the new incoming email belongs to the category *Product Development.*

---

[15] Figure 16-23 shows the predicted target value for product development to be *exactly* 1 for simplicity. The predicted target values for other two target variables are shown to be *exactly* 0 in the figure for the same reason.

[16] Assuming that the neural network after learning from a large set of existing emails will generalize well for new emails.

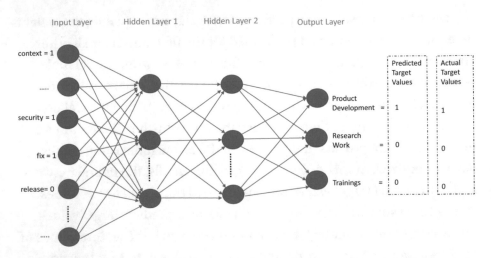

Figure 16-23. *Predictions for the first email after the neural network has learned*

Like we just saw, the neural network might do a great job of correctly predicting the category for new incoming emails. However, the network doesn't give us a simple picture of how it is doing the predictions unlike some other models we discussed earlier. If you recall our discussion on linear regression, you might remember that a linear regression model gives you a simple equation that explains how the value of target variable is calculated using the feature values. And that equation gives many insights about the underlying processes. However, with neural networks, all we know is that many neurons are doing lots of computations to arrive at the predicted target values. We don't have a simple picture that explains how the target values are related to feature values.

Finally, let's talk a bit about designing neural networks. For this problem, we chose to have two hidden layers in our network. If you decide to use neural networks for your problem, you will need to decide how many hidden layers your network should have and how many neurons each hidden layer should have. We won't dwell further on this aspect but recommend a study of the approaches used to decide the appropriate number of hidden layers and neurons.

Convolutional Neural Network

We discussed ANNs and also mentioned a few special kinds of ANNs in the previous section. In this section, we will talk a bit about one such special kind which is known as *convolutional neural network (CNN)*. Because of the way CNNs are designed, they are highly effective for problems related to images (like *image classification)*, but they have also been found to be useful for problems beyond images in recent times. What mainly makes a CNN different from a regular neural network we saw earlier is the additional layers it places before the usual layers of a regular neural network.

Let's say your company manufactures a surveillance camera and now you want to build a model that can tell whether a picture taken at close range by the camera belongs to a person, an animal, or a vehicle. This is an *image classification* problem because the goal here is to predict which class out of the three classes (Person, Animal, Vehicle) the image taken by the camera belongs to. This problem is similar to the one in previous section where we wanted to predict which category out of the three categories (Product Development, Research Work, Trainings) the email belongs to. So you can build a regular neural network (similar to the one we saw in the previous section) to predict the class for the image. This neural network too will output the predictions in the output layer when you pass it the feature values of an image in the input layer. But how do you get the feature values for an image? You will obviously need to have some mechanism in place to extract feature values from an image so that you can pass them to your regular neural network for it to make predictions.

Or you could instead use a *convolutional neural network (CNN)* that does not require you to explicitly extract feature values from the image. A CNN itself has additional layers that extract feature values from an image which are then passed on to a regular neural network for making predictions. Figure 16-24 shows a high-level view of the CNN we have designed for predicting the class of an image taken by the surveillance camera. The CNN takes the image as input and passes it through the convolutional and pooling layers as you can see in the figure. Convolutional layers apply filters containing weights to the image – each filter uses its weights to calculate the weighted sum of pixel values from a portion of the image, thus producing a calculated value for that portion; the filter does this for all portions of the image resulting in a matrix of calculated values (containing a calculated value for each portion of the image as explained) which is known as a feature map. Pooling layers reduce the size of the feature maps – this is often done by retaining only the largest value or the average value from each small chunk of a feature map. The next step seen in the figure is *flattening* which flattens/converts the generated feature maps into a plain one-dimensional vector of feature values. As you can see in the figure, this feature value vector is passed on to the regular neural network which outputs the predictions in its final (rightmost) layer.

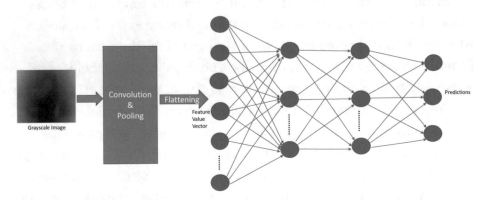

Figure 16-24. *CNN for predicting the class of an image taken by surveillance camera*

This CNN learns to correctly predict the class for an image using a process that is similar to the learning process we discussed earlier for the regular neural network. The CNN will require a set of existing images and a label for each image indicating the class to which the image belongs. It will then calculate and assign such values to filter weights and neuron weights that will produce the correct predictions for existing images. And with these appropriate values of filter weights and neuron weights, the CNN could correctly predict the class for a new unseen image as well. This is the 10000-foot view of the learning process that skips many details.

Since a CNN has a few layers in addition to the usual layers of a regular neural network, there are some additional design aspects you need to consider while designing a CNN. Refer to Chollet (2018) for a coverage of some of these aspects. You could also explore standard architectures available out there[17] and see if any of those work well for your problem.

Evaluating and Tuning Models

ML algorithms that we discussed earlier learn from the data to build models. Let us now turn our attention to one of the key steps in the scientific method: evaluating the performance of a model. This is also referred to as model testing.

In practice, model evaluation and tuning often go hand in hand. In this section, we look at how models are evaluated and tuned.

Evaluating Models

To objectively determine whether a model is performing well, we need to check how it performs on *unseen* data, that is, data that is not used for creating the model. In order to achieve this, we set aside some of the data from the original dataset for testing; this data set aside is called the *test data* and is usually represented as a percentage of the total dataset. All data except the test data is used by the ML algorithm to *train* the model and is referred to as the *training data*. Thus, if you hear something like a "70-30 split," or "we set aside 30% for testing," it means

---

[17] Such as EfficientNet that we saw in Chapter 10.

Dataset => Train data (70%) + Test data (30%)

The model thus trained on the training data is used to predict the target values for the observations in the test data. The performance of the model on the test set is evaluated by checking how close these predicted target values are to the actual target values. For example, for classification problems, we could check what fraction of the observations in the test set have a predicted target value which is the same as the actual target value. This is known as *accuracy* of the model. There are numerous other metrics for evaluating the performance of models for classification problems like *precision, recall, F1 score, AUC,* etc. Similarly there are metrics for regression problems like *mean squared error, mean absolute error, R squared,* etc.

How this *train-test* split happens is one of the most important factors to ensure that the data science process, that is, the scientific method, is applied correctly and successfully. We have seen several cases where a claim is made to having created a good model, but the model does not perform well in production – one of the primary reasons is that something was overlooked in the train-test split.

There can be several aspects to carefully consider in how the train-test split is done, depending on the specifics of the data and the problem being solved. The following are a few common considerations and nuances:

- Distribution of data: When a train-test split is done, it could be important to ensure that the distribution of the data in the test set is similar to the original dataset. For example, consider the example of predicting health status based on gender, smoking status, etc., that we saw earlier in this chapter. Now suppose the percentage of healthy people in this dataset was 80%, then it could be important that the test set also has 80% healthy people. You could then rely on the test set as a representative of the real world in terms of the distribution of data.

- Grouping of data: Suppose you interacted with various people as part of a survey in which you have done a one-to-one clinical session with each person. In each session, you have captured multiple voice recordings of that person along with a label indicating the overall emotion of the person (positive vs. negative). The label for a session applies to all recordings of that person in that session, so your data effectively has recordings and their labels. Your goal is now to predict the emotion based on a voice recording, that is, its tonality. Now, if you simply do a train-test split, it is possible that given one person, some recordings of that person will go into the train set and others into the test set. When a model is trained with this train set and evaluated on this test set, you are effectively testing on same persons who were used for training. A high performance on this test set does not guarantee a high performance in production where it will encounter new persons that were not in our dataset. In such cases, it is important that all the recordings of one person are entirely in the train set or entirely in the test set, that is, the recordings are *grouped* based on the individual and the *groups* are assigned to train and test sets.

In today's age of advanced high-level ML libraries, it can be rather quick and easy to build initial models. But deep understanding of the data, how it is collected, etc., are required to ensure that model performance testing – the cornerstone of the scientific method – is done correctly. We would like to reiterate that these are not points relevant only to amateur data scientists; in a business setting with business outcomes to be achieved, some of these can get overlooked even by seasoned data scientists in large teams.

Tuning models

ML algorithms typically provide various "knobs" to tune how they build the model. For example, the random forest algorithm allows you to specify the number of trees, maximum depth of the tree, etc.

The "knobs," or parameters to the algorithm that are used to specify how training should happen, are referred to as *hyperparameters*. And determining the right combination of values for the hyperparameters that results in the best model performance is referred to as *hyperparameter tuning*. For example, you might find out in your scenario that you have the best performance with random forest for the combination of hyperparameter values in which the number of trees is 30, maximum depth of tree is 8, etc.

The simplest way to perform hyperparameter tuning is to train models with various combinations of hyperparameter values using the train set and determine the combination whose model performs the best on the test set. And the model corresponding to the best combination is chosen as the final model. However, with this approach, we end up choosing the final model by *seeing* the test set – a gross violation of the scientific method which demands that the test set be "*unseen*".

To address this issue, the train set is typically split further to create a "validation set" as shown in Figure 16-25.

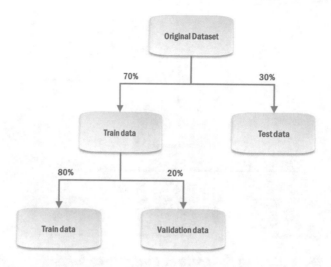

Figure 16-25. *Train-validation-test split*

With this train-validation-test split, we would determine the best combination of hyperparameter values as described earlier, using the train set and the validation set (instead of the test set). And the model trained using the best combination thus determined is finally evaluated for performance on the test set. This ensures that the final model performance on the test set is in fact on unseen data.

Note that many of the aspects to be taken care of during the train-test split would also apply to the train-validation split: for example, the distribution of data in the validation set being appropriate, etc.

Cross-Validation

The notion of creating a train-validation split can be generalized further. For example, after creating the train-test split, let us split the train data into multiple parts called "folds." Figure 16-26 shows such a split that creates three folds.

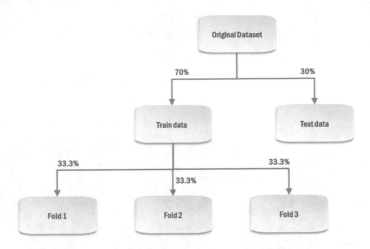

Figure 16-26. *Splitting the train set into three folds*

We then train models treating each fold as the validation set in turn. That is, we first train models using data from folds 1 and 2 with various combinations of hyperparameter values and determine how the combinations perform against fold 3 as the validation set. We repeat this step two more times for the second and first folds, each time using the selected fold for validation and the remaining two folds for training.

We would then know which combination of hyperparameter values is performing consistently well in all the three cases and can choose this combination of hyperparameter values as the most optimal. This technique is referred to as cross-validation and ensures to a greater degree that the choice of optimal hyperparameter values is generic (i.e., not restricted to a single validation set).

In case of cross-validation also, it is important to ensure that the folds are created appropriately, since each fold will be used for validation (i.e., evaluation) as well, for example, the distribution of data in all the folds being appropriate, all observations of a group being part of a single fold, etc.

In practice, there are several variations on this theme of cross-validation. The simplest variation occurs if only one combination of hyperparameter values is used in the previous process – in this case, cross-validation is used only for model testing. The more complex *nested* cross-validation strategies use multiple folds for both validation and test data.

Libraries and Tools

There are numerous ML libraries; we shall only name a few popular ones in the Python community. Note that the R community too has similar support for various ML algorithms.

ML libraries in Python:

- Scikit-learn is one of the most widely adopted ML libraries in Python – it is commonly used for all ML algorithms except deep learning.

- XGBoost is one of the most popular libraries for gradient boosted trees.

- Keras (with TensorFlow 2.0) and PyTorch are a couple of widely used deep learning libraries.

Deep learning libraries often require GPUs or clusters of GPUs for model training. Cloud services like Amazon, Azure, and Google can be used to spin up GPUs as needed. Frameworks like Horovod are useful to simplify distributed deep learning.

Libraries like Hyperopt and Ray Tune are popular for efficient hyperparameter tuning.

In Chapter 18, we shall look at some other advanced visual tools – multimodal PAML tools – that can be used for ML.

Data Engineering

Data engineering is primarily required when dealing with a large amount of data for training models.

Certain ML algorithms can run on a cluster of machines for faster training; in this case sizing and maintaining these clusters, with efficient access to the data, falls under data engineering.

In case of deep learning, clusters of GPUs are often used. In this case, the infrastructure needs to be set up to ensure that latency of data access does not become the bottleneck to training models. This activity also falls under data engineering.

Conclusion

We discussed categories of ML algorithms in this chapter and looked at a few ML algorithms in detail. We discussed how these algorithms work, how they make predictions, and what kind of insights they provide. We also talked about model evaluation and tuning and mentioned a few popular ML technologies. The next chapter focuses on deploying and using the ML models in production systems for inference.

Further Reading

For a coverage of ML techniques, refer to James et al. (2013). For hands-on examples of ML in Python, refer to Géron (2019). Specifically for deep learning, we recommend Chollet (2018).

References

Chollet, Francois. *Deep Learning with Python*. NY, USA: Manning, 2018.

Géron, Aurélien. *Hands-on Machine Learning with Scikit-Learn, Keras & Tensorflow, 2nd ed.* Sebastopol, CA: O'Reilly, 2019.

James, Gareth, et al. *An Introduction to Statistical Learning*. New York: Springer, 2013.

CHAPTER 17

Inference

Once models are created in the machine learning step, they need to be deployed as part of real-world processes and production systems. This is done in the *inference* step of the data science process.

In the inference step, we perform the tasks required to push the models to the production systems so that they can be used by other applications and to monitor the performance of these models.

Figure 17-1 shows the various activities, techniques, and technologies that go into this last mile of data science. In this chapter, we shall cover Figure 17-1 in detail. We first cover the model release process, wherein the models created during internal experimentation are prepared to be pushed to the production systems. Then, we cover the production system itself, including how the models are deployed, used for predictions/inferences by applications, and monitored. We shall cover the diagram starting from the bottom and moving upward in the numeric sequence indicated in the boxes/arrows. While doing so, we shall discuss the various components, techniques, and technologies used in each activity. We shall then touch upon a few factors to consider while choosing between open source and paid tools for inference. Finally, we shall mention the data engineering aspects involved in inference.

© Vineet Raina and Srinath Krishnamurthy 2022
V. Raina and S. Krishnamurthy, *Building an Effective Data Science Practice*,
https://doi.org/10.1007/978-1-4842-7419-4_17

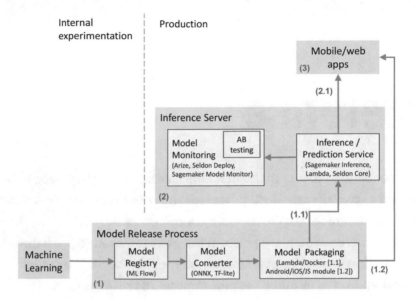

Figure 17-1. *Inference: steps and components; technology examples are mentioned in parentheses within the boxes*

Model Release Process (1)

When the data science team has created a model and is ready to deploy it to production, the model release process is triggered. This is the starting point of the inference step.

The model release process packages the model so that it is ready to be deployed to the production systems. Let us take a look at each component and activity in the model release process.

Model Registry

The models created by the data science team in the machine learning step are stored in a **model registry**. Models in the model registry are typically versioned. Models would also have a life cycle, for example, *under testing,* *in production,* etc.

MLFlow is a popular open source choice for implementing a model registry. It also allows linking models back to the original experiments that created the models[1] – this enables traceability and reproducibility of experiments.

Some dev environments (see Chapter 18) provide an in-built model registry as well. Databricks, for example, integrates MLFlow into its dev environment.

Model Converter

A model created by the data science team is typically represented initially in the technology stack that they use, for example, if the data science team uses Python and ML libraries such as *scikit-learn*, then a Python *pickle* file would represent an ML model. The pickle file would capture, say, the structure of a decision tree or the equation of a linear regression model. This ML model typically needs to be *converted* to a form suitable for deploying to the targeted production systems.

Model converter involves converting ML models either to an interexchange format or for a target system such as mobile/web apps. Let us briefly look at both these options and when they are used.

Interexchange Format

Several ML libraries and platforms exist in various programming languages – we saw some of these in Chapter 16. To enable interoperability among these, interexchange formats are developed in the machine learning community. An interexchange format

- Specifies a representation of ML models that is agnostic to programming languages and ML libraries

---

[1] The MLFlow API, invoked as part of the experimentation code in the machine learning step, enables this.

- Provides *inference runtime libraries* in various popular production system languages such as Java, Python, etc., to invoke the models

- Motivates ML library developers to provide APIs that can save the models in the interexchange format

The advantage of using an interexchange format is that though the data scientist may build a model in one language (say Python or R) using any ML library, the converted models can easily be invoked in various production technology stacks (such as Java, Python, JavaScript, or Swift) using appropriate inference runtime libraries.

The classical PMML[2] and the recent ONNX[3] are a couple of examples of popular interexchange formats. In our experience, ONNX is currently the preferred choice as it supports a wide range of ML models and has integrations with a large number of popular ML libraries[4] in multiple languages (Python, R, etc.).

Target System

In some cases, a model can be converted directly to target a specific production system,[5] without using an interexchange format. This is possible if the ML library tech stack is standardized across the data science and software engineering teams. For example, if *TensorFlow* is agreed as a standard across the teams, then the TensorFlow models can be converted using *TensorFlow Lite, Tensorflow.js,* etc., to target systems such as mobile/web apps, where the model must execute directly on the user's device/browser.[6]

---

[2] https://wikipedia.org/wiki/Predictive_Model_Markup_Language
[3] https://onnx.ai/
[4] Such as the ones we saw in Chapter 16.
[5] Refer to the "Mobile and Web Applications" section for examples of when this may be appropriate.
[6] Or on IoT devices as well.

Model Packaging

Model packaging involves creating a deployable artifact from the converted model. The type of artifact depends on whether the model is to be deployed to a server or an end user's system (e.g., mobile app/web browser).

- When a model is to be deployed to an inference server (1.1), then the type of artifact could be an AWS Lambda function, a Docker container, etc.

- When a model is to be deployed to a mobile or web application (1.2) so that it runs on the user's mobile device or browser, then the artifact would be an Android/iOS/JavaScript module or library that can be used within the mobile or web application.

In both cases, the converted model (e.g., ONNX model) is included as part of the artifact.[7] This artifact is then deployed to production systems (1.1, 1.2) – the models can then be invoked by the applications, which we shall look at next.

Production

The models created by the data science team are used by applications in production systems. We shall now look at how these applications typically *invoke* the models that have been deployed.

---

[7] In case of (1.2), occasionally the converted model is directly integrated without packaging into a module. This depends on the low-level design of the app.

Inference Server (2)

The most common scenario is to expose the models as REST APIs, so that they can be invoked by any applications (2.1). You would also need to monitor how the models are performing in production to determine whether the performance of the models is acceptable or deteriorating over time. We are referring to the component that encapsulates these responsibilities as the *inference server*.

Let us briefly cover these two responsibilities of the inference server.

Inference/Prediction Service

This refers to the services (most commonly REST APIs) that expose the models. Typically, data engineers or software engineers can easily implement a REST API layer on top of the packaged models.

But if there are a large number of models, or if you need the ability to scale rapidly to several thousands of concurrent requests, etc., you may instead want to consider using services such as Amazon Sagemaker Inference, Seldon, Algorithmia, etc. In our experience, we have also found *serverless* techniques rather appropriate. For example, Amazon API Gateway coupled with AWS Lambda is a cost-effective way to deploy models that can scale easily.

Model Monitoring

To know how effective the models are, you need to know when the predictions given by a model turned out to be correct or incorrect. Let's refer to the example in Chapter 4 on classification – depending on whether a prospective sale materialized or not, we can determine whether the prediction given by the model was correct or not. Often a model in production tends to start *drifting* over time, that is, increasingly starts giving incorrect predictions. Detecting this early and fixing/upgrading the model is essential.

To enable this, all the predictions generated by a model would need to be stored for future analysis by the data science team. Also, whenever we know the true outcome, we should store that too, so that *model drift* can be detected. This data will also be useful to determine how a new candidate model compares with older models.

Model monitoring is often coupled with some form of AB testing, that is, two or more model variants are deployed at the same time, and some percentages of the inference requests are routed to each variant. By analyzing how each variant performs in production, we can determine which variant is the best and use it as the primary model, that is, route most of the inference requests to it.

A few cloud services that focus on monitoring models are mentioned in Figure 17-1.

Data obtained from model monitoring is also used in further iterations of the data science process – we shall revisit this point in the "Data Engineering" section.

Mobile and Web Applications (3)

This broadly refers to applications built by your company as well as third-party applications that wish to use your models. There are two typical ways in which an application can invoke a model:

1. The applications will invoke the APIs exposed by the inference server to get predictions using the models (2.1).

2. The models are integrated into your mobile or web app (1.2) such that the models run directly on the user's mobile device/web browser. These are typically cases where low latency is required and/or when a mobile app needs to be able to function

offline without Internet connectivity. Examples
include suppressing audio noise in real time during
an online conference[8] or detecting health condition
of a user from their voice captured on their mobile
device.

ML Ops

The discipline of releasing and maintaining models in production is
referred to as ML Ops. This has evolved as a discipline in the past couple of
years and broadly covers both the blocks of *model release process* and the
inference server.

Correspondingly, a dedicated ML Ops *role* is also increasingly seen in
data science teams – we shall look at this role in more detail in Chapter 21.

Open Source vs. Paid

Several organizations are beginning to adopt data science and are facing
difficulties in deploying the models to production systems. As a result,
there are numerous tools and cloud services in this rapidly expanding
space.

For the *inference* step, we would recommend using open source
frameworks to the extent possible or use tools that have an open source
strategy.

For example, you could begin by using MLFlow for model registry,
ONNX for model conversion, Docker for model packaging, and simple
custom deployments for the inference service.

---

[8] Typically done using a deep learning model that is trained to produce clean
audio from noisy audio.

In the early stages, you can simply store model predictions directly to your data lake or data warehouse.[9] At some point, you would begin to have several models in production, and deploying and monitoring the models at scale would start gaining importance.

Once you reach a stage where a more advanced tool may seem more effective for all these activities, you can then consider using a paid tool, possibly with an open source strategy. You may want to begin by adopting the new tool for some of the components in an incremental fashion. For example, you could begin by using open source Seldon[10] for the *model release process* and the *inference/prediction service* and later at an appropriate juncture adopt their enterprise solution[11] that covers the entire *inference server* as well.

Data Engineering

All the activities in the inference step can be considered as a part of data engineering. When the number of models in production increase and the team grows, a small, specialized MLOps group can be segregated if needed. Refer to Chapters 21 and 22 for more details.

Also, from the data engineering perspective, the data captured from model monitoring is on par with the rest of the data, that is, the model monitoring system is yet another data source. Here, we circle back to the data capture step of the data science process – the data about the predictions given by a model and its performance (evaluated against the true outcomes) is used in the further iterations of the data science process to tune and upgrade the models.

---

[9] See Chapter 13.

[10] That is, Seldon Core.

[11] That is, Seldon Deploy.

Conclusion

In this chapter, we covered the various activities involved in the inference step of the data science process. We also touched upon a few tools and libraries typically used in the various activities for specific purposes and covered a few pointers related to choosing between open source and paid tools.

The predictions and performance of a model in production are effectively a new data source for the data capture step of the data science process. This loop forms the maximal iteration – from data capture to inference, back to data capture – of the data science process that we first saw in Chapter 1.

CHAPTER 18

Other Tools and Services

In this chapter, we shall look at an assortment of tools, libraries, and services. These are typically cutting across all the layers that we have seen in the earlier chapters, so we are covering them separately in this chapter.

Not all the tools are essential always; we have included both essential and good-to-have tools in the following list. It is important to start small and incrementally evolve by adding more complex, advanced tools to boost productivity – being aware of the various categories of tools, libraries, and services in this chapter would be helpful during this evolution.

Development Environment

The dev environment is used by data scientists and data engineers to write the code for all the steps in the data science process from data capture to machine learning. If you are just starting out with one or two data scientists, and you are able to make the data available to them in CSV files, they can simply do the analysis on their respective machines using an IDE[1] of their choice, such as Spyder or RStudio. But often a data science team works in a highly collaborative environment, coding in environments such

---

[1] Integrated development environment.

© Vineet Raina and Srinath Krishnamurthy 2022
V. Raina and S. Krishnamurthy, *Building an Effective Data Science Practice*,
https://doi.org/10.1007/978-1-4842-7419-4_18

as *notebooks* that are in a shared location for discussion with the rest of the team. Ideally, the notebooks should also support collaborative editing by multiple data scientists simultaneously.

Jupyter notebooks are the most common environment for data scientists. Other popular environments are Databricks, Sagemaker Studio, JupyterHub, and Zeppelin. Some of these allow a mix of R/Python/SQL in a single notebook, which can be useful if your data science team has a mix of these skills.

The dev environment should also allow the data science team to register common, standard libraries to ensure the entire team is working with the same versions of the various libraries.

We shall look at how a dev environment is used in conjunction with all the other components in Chapter 19.

Experiment Registry

An experiment registry is where all the experiments executed by the data science team would be stored. An experiment registry needs to support the following:

- Store parameters, plots, metrics, etc., that contain details of an experiment.

- Search for experiments using tags/keywords, etc.

- Compare multiple experiments based on parameters and results.

- Maintain a link to the notebook/source code version used to execute the experiment. This is crucial to track lineage and be able to reproduce experiments.

- Store models in a model registry[2]; each entry in the model registry would be linked to the original experiment to allow traceability of models back to experiments and corresponding source code and data.

MLFlow is a popular open source experiment registry that offers the aforementioned capabilities. Some dev environments bundle an experiment registry as part of their offering.[3]

The experiment registry acts as a central, long-lived repository of all the activities of the data science team in your organization. It is thus essential to maintaining business continuity of the data science team. By storing the history of all experiments and lineage, it also helps ensure the necessary scientific rigor by enabling reviews and reproducibility of the experiments.

Compute Infrastructure

Compute resources serve three broad purposes in the operations of a data science team:

- Providing servers to host the dev environment. This includes, for example, a JupyterHub server that is scalable according to the needs and the size of the team. In cloud-hosted environments such as Databricks, this may be taken care of by the service provider.

- Providing the compute resources for executing the notebooks/scripts written by the data science team. This includes any scalable clusters (such as Spark clusters), GPU machines, etc., for the data preparation and machine learning steps in the data science process.

---

[2] We covered model registry in Chapter 17.
[3] Databricks, for example, integrates MLFlow into its environment.

- Providing servers for hosting visualization tools[4] (e.g., Tableau) and SQL query engines[5] (e.g., Presto) when applicable.

Compute resources can belong to any of the following categories:

- Individual machines (physical machines on-prem, or cloud services like AWS Ec2). Typically used for

  - Data science when the data can fit on a single machine

  - Hosting a server or a third-party tool

- Compute clusters such as Spark (on-prem, or a service like Databricks or Amazon EMR)

- GPU machines (single or multi-GPU)

- Cluster of GPUs using a framework like Horovod

- Container hosting services such as Amazon ECS.[6] Typically used for complex ML jobs packaged as Docker containers or tools/libraries that can be deployed using Docker

AutoML

One of the motivations of AI is to automate a lot of the repetitive work done by humans. What if we aim to automate the work done by data scientists? This is the vision of AutoML.

---

[4] Covered in Chapter 15.
[5] Covered in Chapter 13.
[6] Elastic Container Service.

In a primitive sense, what does a data scientist do? They merely attempt various data preparation operations and try various kinds of models with different parameter settings to arrive at the best model. What if an algorithm were to simply brute-force and try all the popular models such as XGBoost, LinearRegression, NeuralNetworks,[7] and so forth? We already begin to see the underpinnings of AutoML here.

To run through various models, and neural network architectures, is not an easy task, of course. AutoML solutions employ several advanced techniques and heuristics to optimize the search to arrive at a good model.

Purpose of AutoML

AutoML serves two primary purposes:

- Democratizing data science: AutoML services allow, say, software engineers to use the power of data science without knowing data science. In a way, AutoML is to data science now, what SQL was to data processing since the 1980s. Just like SQL allowed folks with less programming skills to declaratively query for data, AutoML is beginning to allow engineers to apply the scientific method to data by automating many of the challenging steps in the data science process.

- Automating the repetitive tasks of data scientists: Data scientists need to do a lot of manual tuning and repeated experimentation with minor variations. They also often perform a *model sweep*, which is to run experiments using various candidate modeling

---

[7] Searching through the various architectures of a neural network to determine the best architecture is referred to as Neural Architecture Search or NAS. The EfficientNet family of models we saw in Chapter 10 was a result of NAS.

approaches to narrow down a promising avenue of
continued research. In all these areas, AutoML can help
the data scientist by automating these repetitive tasks.
In this sense, AutoML is to data scientists what SQL is
to software engineers – software engineers don't need
a declarative language; they can write the complex
programs required to query data. But nevertheless,
SQL makes their job easier by automating the repetitive
programming task of efficiently querying data from
multiple tables, etc.

AutoML Cautions

It is important to be cautious in the use of AutoML. If someone in the team
is using AutoML, it is important that they know how to evaluate model
performance, so that they can determine if the resulting models are good
enough. They also need to have a complete understanding of the data
being fed to the AutoML and the formulation of the problem itself (which
is the target variable, which are the features, etc.). A person with these
skills is referred to as an ML engineer these days – refer to Chapter 21 for
more details.

AutoML does not reduce the need for domain understanding –
particularly when it comes to identifying the right features and some
domain-specific data preparation steps. For example, your goal may be to
predict when the fuel stock at various gas stations in a region would need
replenishment, so that you can then optimize the dispatch of fuel to the
gas stations from the main terminal. In this case, it may seem at first sight
that we need to predict the inventory of a gas station. But inventory will
typically not have a clear pattern – what is more likely to have a pattern
is the sales at a gas station. The sales may depend on day of the week,
whether a day was a holiday, the weather, and so forth. Once we have a
model that can predict sales, we can deduce the future inventory based

on current inventory and future sales. From the future inventory, we can determine when the inventory will be low and need replenishment. Even if one is using AutoML, this kind of problem formulation still needs to be done by the data scientist or ML engineer.

While some data preparation aspects such as normalization or missing value handling can be done by AutoML, the primary focus of AutoML is to automate the machine learning step. A human still needs to execute the other steps of the data science process.

Tools and Services

AutoML tools and services come in various flavors. We mention an assortment here:

- Open source libraries such as

  - Auto-sklearn, which builds on top of scikit-learn to provide AutoML functionality

  - AutoGluon which is open sourced by Amazon

- Cloud services such as Amazon Sagemaker Autopilot, Google Cloud AutoML, and Azure Machine Learning support AutoML. In addition to the machine learning step, they may also support data preparation steps to varying extents, for example, featurization for text, images, etc.

Some tools may support hyperparameter tuning in an automated fashion and refer just to this as AutoML. Since the term AutoML is not clearly defined in the market, it is important to check the detailed capabilities of a tool or service that claims to provide AutoML.

Multimodal Predictive Analytics and Machine Learning

Multimodal Predictive Analytics and Machine Learning (PAML)[8] tools offer advanced capabilities to support the end-to-end data science process at big data scale. This includes

- Ability to define data preparation and machine learning workflows in a visual, no-code UI.

- Hooks for data scientists and data engineers to plug in custom code into the visual workflows.

- Integrating with notebooks for data scientists who prefer coding.

- Ability to share experiments and their results with other team members. This may also include various roles such as editor, reviewer, etc.

- Tracking data lineage across experiments to enable auditing, and reproducibility and traceability of experiments.

- Seamlessly deploying the models to production without writing additional code.

- Monitoring the models in production, AB testing, etc.

Multimodal PAML tools differ largely with respect to which of these capabilities are provided out of the box, on the one hand, and to what extent customizations are allowed, on the other.

---

[8] This term is coined by Forrester.

SAS Visual Data Mining and Machine Learning (VDMML) in conjunction with the SAS Viya suite of products is one of the most comprehensive PAML tools in the market currently and supports all the capabilities mentioned earlier.

KNIME Analytics Platform is an open source tool that supports visually defining data science workflows for the entire data science process. KNIME Server is a paid enterprise tool to enable collaboration and interactive execution of workflows.

Multimodal PAML tools are especially useful if you have citizen data scientists[9] and data analysts working with the data science team.

In our experience, while multimodal PAML tools can boost productivity for most common experimentation flows, they can tend to be a hurdle when it comes to highly complex, intricate variations in experiment design. The decision of adopting a multimodal PAML tool is not one to be taken lightly – various factors need to be considered to ensure they boost productivity and collaboration rather than slow down data scientists. This decision is usually highly specific to your team composition and business needs. If your team does feel a need for low-code/no-code tools for data science, then beginning with an open source option like KNIME Analytics Platform is usually a prudent approach – based on its adoption and usefulness, more expensive and advanced options can be considered.

Data Science Apps/Workflows

There is often a perception that a data science team is operating in a silo. This perception is typically caused because the primary outcomes exposed by the data science team are the models which cannot be used easily outside of the data science team, for example, when software engineers are needed even to build a prototype application on top of the model to showcase the model's capability.

---

[9] See Chapter 21 for understanding the role of citizen data scientist.

The primary reason for this has been the mismatch in technology stacks –while data scientists use languages such as R and Python, creating a prototype application to showcase a model requires classical web app skills of JavaScript, web server, REST APIs, etc. To address this problem, there are a couple of approaches that we see in the industry today[10]:

- Enable data scientists or data engineers to quickly create prototype apps that can invoke their models/scripts using a technology they are familiar with. Plotly Dash and Bokeh are examples of this – they allow quickly prototyping web applications using only Python code.[11] So, any models/visualizations created by the data scientists/engineers can directly be plugged in to quickly create an interactive web application.

- For data science teams that use a visual workflow tool, the models can be exposed using guided analytic workflows. These workflows created by a data scientist/engineer can be executed interactively using inputs from a user on a web app. An example of this is KNIME Server.

These approaches enable the data science team to include other stakeholders, data analysts, and citizen data scientists as part of the data science process.

---

[10] If you happen to be using an advanced tool such as SAS VDMML, then this is readily available already. So, you wouldn't need these approaches.

[11] An equivalent in the R ecosystem is Shiny.

Off-the-Shelf AI Services and Libraries

There are several AI services and libraries that are oriented toward specific classes of problems:

- In some cases, such as time series forecasting or recommender systems, the model depends on your specific data – so these services train a model using your data and then provide APIs for inference.

- In other cases, such as problems related to processing images, text, speech, etc., these services provide APIs for inference directly, because they have already trained models using their own data. This is because, for example, the sentiment of a text or the emotion in a human face is universally applicable to any dataset. These libraries/services typically allow customizing the model using your training data as well.

Some of the popular AI services and libraries are mentioned in Table 18-1.

Table 18-1. *Examples of AI services/libraries*

Class of problem	Examples of services/libraries
Time series forecasting	Prophet, Amazon Forecast
Recommender system	Amazon Personalize, Google Recommendations
Natural language processing	Amazon Comprehend, Azure Text Analytics, Google Natural Language
Computer vision	Amazon Rekognition, Azure Computer Vision, Azure Video Analyzer for Media
Speech processing	Amazon Transcribe/Polly, Azure Cognitive Speech Services, Google speech to text

Apart from this, one can find numerous libraries that are specific to a particular domain such as medical imaging, etc. Typically you would want to explore whether any such libraries/services – preferably open source – exist for your domain, which you can leverage.

The skills needed to make effective use of these AI services and libraries are similar to the skills required to use AutoML. Thus, ML engineers – who we encountered in the AutoML section earlier – are often ideally placed to leverage AI services/libraries as well.

When to Use

If you are building an application that involves a class of problem covered in Table 18-1, it may be prudent to begin by using one of the corresponding services. This may require much less investment compared to if you were to build a model from scratch yourself. It can also hasten your time to market and allow you to focus on getting the basic functionality of your application out in the hands of users. The same applies if you would like to automate some processes in your organization using some of the capabilities mentioned earlier.

While we can rely on these services to a great extent as they are used by several organizations, there is no guarantee on how it will perform in your specific business and domain. Thus, it is important to evaluate the performance of the models critically in any case.

If your product or application aims to differentiate itself in the market by leveraging your own domain expertise and data, then it would make sense to create your own models. In this case, it would still be useful to use the previously mentioned services as a baseline benchmark.

One final aspect to consider, as always with cloud services, is security. It is important to read the fine print – some cloud services may use your data to continually improve their services, and you may need to opt out from them explicitly.

Open Source vs. Paid

The field of data science is based largely on open source libraries and frameworks as we have seen in the earlier chapters.

While paid tools can offer various benefits, it is important particularly for data science to not get locked down to a tool or vendor. Doing so will reduce flexibility of operations and might also limit the talent pool for your hiring.

It is often a good compromise to choose a tool that builds on top of open source technologies. This enables you to limit the extent of vendor lockdown while using the capabilities of the paid tool to boost productivity. An example of a tool that does this exceptionally well is the Databricks platform.

- Databricks notebooks can easily be exported to/ imported from open source Jupyter notebooks.

- Databricks compute clusters are based on the open source Spark.

    - Databricks query engine uses the open source SparkSQL.

- Databricks clusters are preloaded with popular open source ML libraries.

- Databricks Delta is based on the open source storage layer, Delta Lake.

- Experiment and model registry in Databricks is based on the open source MLFlow.

Various other tools follow a similar open source strategy to varying extents. If you decide to choose a paid tool that does not have an open source strategy, then it is a significant strategic decision that would need strong arguments in its favor, specific to your business and data science team.

Conclusion

In this chapter, we saw an assortment of various categories of tools that are used across multiple steps of the data science process.

With this chapter, we wrap up our coverage of techniques, tools, and technologies. In the next chapter, we shall look at a reference architecture that illustrates how the various technologies discussed in Part 3, so far, come together in executing the entire data science process.

CHAPTER 19

Reference Architecture

So far, we have covered the various tools and technologies that are used by a data science team to execute the various steps of the data science process. In this chapter, we shall now look at a reference architecture that can be tailored and used for your data science team's operations. The reference architecture brings together the various tools and technologies that we have seen so far, to enable the data science process for rapid experimentation and deployment.

Figure 19-1 shows the reference architecture. We have already looked at the individual components in the earlier chapters of Part 3 – this chapter covers how they all come together.

It is important to note that not all blocks are necessary to begin with – depending on the kinds of data science projects and the data science culture, different blocks would evolve over time. But eventually once your team reaches a level of maturity, nearly all these blocks would be needed.

At a high level, there are two aspects to data science as seen in Figure 19-1: the systems that support the data science experimentation activities and the production systems that consume the models created by the data science team.

In this chapter, we shall walk through Figure 19-1 in detail. We shall first look at the experimentation side, followed by the transition from experimentation to production. Generally, we shall walk through the blocks in the numeric sequence indicated in the boxes/arrows.

© Vineet Raina and Srinath Krishnamurthy 2022
V. Raina and S. Krishnamurthy, *Building an Effective Data Science Practice*,
https://doi.org/10.1007/978-1-4842-7419-4_19

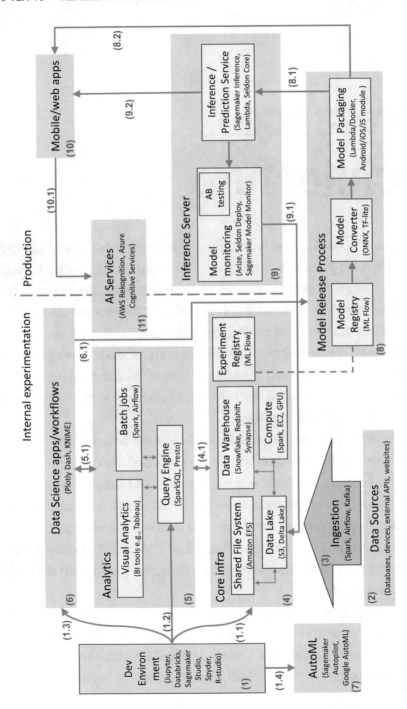

Figure 19-1. *Reference architecture for enabling data science operations*

Experimentation

In this section, we cover the various components pertaining to the experimentation activities of the data science team.

Dev Environment (1)

We had briefly covered development environments in Chapter 18. Here, we look at more details on how a dev environment is used with all the other components in the reference architecture.

(1.1) The dev environment should allow a seamless access to the core infra:

- All the data in the data lake/warehouse should be accessible (with access controls) using common mechanisms such as SQL, pandas, Spark, etc.

- The data scientists should be able to scale the compute capacity as required. This includes scaling up/down a single machine, as well as potentially a cluster of machines, depending on the size of data and the type of analysis.

- The data scientists should be able to easily register their experiments in the experiment registry, along with the candidate models and lineage of the data.

(1.2) If you have a big data setup where a query engine such as SparkSQL or Presto is used, then the data science team should be able to run SQL using this query engine.

(1.3) If the data science team is exposing some of the models to other internal stakeholders using simple applications or workflows, it would be good to enable integration between the dev environment and these applications/workflows. For example, KNIME Server, which can be used for this like we saw in Chapter 18, allows invoking workflows using REST APIs – such APIs can thus be invoked from the dev environment to execute workflows.

(1.4) The data science team may need to access AutoML services on the cloud, such as Amazon Sagemaker Autopilot, Google Cloud AutoML, etc.

Data Sources (2)

There could be several data sources, internal and external, that are relevant. We had covered these in Chapter 13.

Data from these multiple data sources are ingested (3) into the central data lake/warehouse (shown inside 4) for analysis by the data science team.

Ingestion (3)

We had looked at aspects related to ingestion in Chapter 13. The goal of ingestion is to have the data available in reasonably organized form in the data lake or warehouse (in 4).

Core Infra (4)

This is the core of the experimentation sandbox infrastructure, on which all the other systems are based. Broadly, this comprises of data storage, compute, and experiment registry components.

We had covered data storage, that is, data lake, data warehouse, and shared file system in Chapter 13.

We had covered compute infrastructure and the experiment registry in Chapter 18.

Analytics (5)

A lot of the data analysis by the data scientists will likely happen within the dev environment (1) using the core infra (4). But in slightly larger teams working on big data, the following needs begin to be felt:

- If the team has a data analyst or a citizen data scientist[1] who may not have great programming skills, using **visual analytics** tools can boost productivity. Visualizations created using these tools can fetch data using a query engine or directly from the data lake/warehouse (4.1). We covered data visualization and BI tools in Chapter 15.

- Data engineers or data scientists may write **batch jobs** that automate the steps from data preparation to machine learning. These could yield transformed data, or analytics results, which are written back into the data lake/warehouse (4.1). The batch jobs could also be executing ML experiments, in which case the experiment details are written to the experiment registry (also 4.1).

- If your infrastructure does not include a data warehouse and your data scientists/analysts prefer to use SQL, a **query engine** may be necessary to provide SQL support. The query engine is capable of filtering/aggregating data from across multiple datasets in the data lake and warehouse (4.1). We had looked at the query engine in Chapter 13.

---

[1] Data analysts and citizen data scientists are described in Chapter 21.

285

Data Science Apps/Workflows (6)

We covered data science apps/workflows in Chapter 18. Note that

- The models used in these applications/workflows are typically fetched from the model registry (6.1).

- Any data required by the applications/workflows is typically accessed using the analytics query engine (5.1).

- Visual analytics can also be embedded into the data science applications/workflows (5.1).

AutoML (7)

AutoML services were covered in Chapter 18. The AutoML services used would need access to the data for training the AutoML models.

In case you are planning to use *cloud* AutoML services but have an *on-prem* setup of the core infra (4), your IT team may need to facilitate your data science team to use AutoML from their dev environment (1.4).

Having covered the experimentation side, let us now see what steps/components are required to ensure that the models created by data scientists see the light of day as part of a production system.

From Experimentation to Production

When a model created by the data science team is to be deployed to production systems, the model release process (8) is triggered. In Chapter 17, we had covered this model release process as well as the subsequent inference server (9) and the mobile/web applications (10).

The predictions generated by the models would be stored back in our data lake (9.1) for monitoring and future analysis – this too was touched upon in Chapter 17.

AI Services

AI services (11), such as for speech processing, computer vision, time series forecasting, etc., were covered in Chapter 18. These services are typically exposed as APIs and SDKs, and can be invoked directly from mobile or web apps (10.1).

Typically, the data science team[2] would perform some experiments to evaluate the fitment of an AI service for your specific use case before it is used in production – this is why we have depicted the AI services component as cutting across the experimentation and production systems.

Conclusion

In this chapter, we covered a reference architecture that can be tailored to your specific needs. We also covered the usage of various components in this reference architecture to support the data science process.

We shall revisit the reference architecture in Chapter 23 – there we shall look at how the type of data science project influences the need for various blocks of the reference architecture.

---

[2] Possibly an ML engineer, see Chapter 21.

CHAPTER 20

Monks vs. Cowboys: Praxis

In Chapter 3, we had first looked at the two cultures of data science and how to determine which culture is likely more relevant to a problem at hand and to your business in general. Now, having covered the various techniques used in the steps of the data science process, we are ready to understand how the two cultures differ in the way they practice data science. This is the focus of this chapter.

Understanding these cultural differences in praxis is useful in three ways: first, this can enable you to determine which techniques would and should be used by your data science team to align with the desired culture – this is illustrated by Figure 20-1 later in this chapter.

Second, when you are building the team, you can try to onboard data scientists that tend toward the desired culture for your business; the cultural differences summarized in this chapter will help identify the culture to which a candidate data scientist predominantly belongs. We shall be revisiting this aspect in Chapter 22 in the context of forming the data science team.

Third, the deeper understanding of the goals and techniques covered in this chapter can be useful for regulatory compliance as well, in the context of explainability. We shall cover this in Chapter 23.

© Vineet Raina and Srinath Krishnamurthy 2022
V. Raina and S. Krishnamurthy, *Building an Effective Data Science Practice*,
https://doi.org/10.1007/978-1-4842-7419-4_20

So, in this chapter, we shall elaborate on how the two cultures approach modeling in practice – this primarily relates to the machine learning step of the data science process and, to some extent, the data preparation step. It is in these two steps that the chief differences occur in practice.

We shall begin with a brief, slightly more formal, recap of the goals of creating data science models. We shall then summarize how various ML techniques fare in regard to achieving these goals, and the goals that each culture deems relevant. This effectively provides a framework to identify the techniques typically preferred by the two cultures. Finally, we shall expand on Table 3-1 to include the differences seen in practice between the two cultures.

Note that, throughout the rest of this chapter, we refer to various ML techniques that were covered in Chapter 16. You may find it useful to refer back to that chapter as needed to refresh your understanding of a technique or some of its finer details.

Goals of Modeling

Recall from Chapter 3 that the primary purposes of a model are

- Explaining observations by estimating the underlying *truth*: this can be broken down further into two granular goals, *simplicity of representation* and *attribution.*

- Predicting values for future observations: this can be broken down further into two granular goals, *interpretability of prediction* and *accuracy of prediction.*

In this section, we shall describe these four goals with a few examples of how various techniques contribute toward each of them.

Estimating Truth: Simplicity of Representation

Truth is ever to be found in simplicity, and not in the multi-plicity and confusion of things.

—Sir Isaac Newton[1]

We tend to prefer – and believe in – ideas and representations which are simpler, as being closer to the truth. The quest for a "unified field theory" or "grand unified theory" in physics is a flagship example of this timeless human thirst to *simplify* – having separate theories for different kinds of physical forces in nature is indicative of "multiplicity" and "confusion" and begs, demands, simplification.

A single equation, like $E = mc^2$ or $F = ma$, is the simplest representation and strikes us with its elegance. Techniques like linear/logistic regression aim at this level of simplicity – to achieve this simplicity, data scientists are often willing even to sacrifice accuracy of prediction. Similarly, a polynomial equation, and, more generally, any equation that represents a curve (or *surface* in n-dimensions), is an elegant, simple representation.

Let us check out a few other representations:

- A linear SVM, in which the truth is represented by a single line[2] that separates the observations, is also rather simple and very close to linear regression in terms of simplicity. Nonlinear SVM, on the other hand, is a more complex representation.

---

[1] Sourced from The Newton Project "Untitled Treatise on Revelation (section 1.1)." <www.newtonproject.ox.ac.uk/view/texts/normalized/THEM00135>

[2] Or more generally, a hyperplane.

- A decision tree is a simple, but slightly cluttered representation; there is a sense of "multiplicity" when we look at the various nodes that need to be traversed, etc. – we don't get the same impact of elegant simplicity as we get by looking at an equation.

- Random forest, etc., are rather complex – we sense both multiplicity and confusion in the representation, resulting from the randomness and large number of trees.

- Deep neural networks are the most complex representations – hundreds of neurons and thousands of weights convey an overpowering sense of multiplicity and confusion to the human mind trying to make sense of it all. While it can be argued that mathematically a neural network is just a collection of equations,[3] the more layers it has, the more complex it seems. This complexity is increased further when we add layers with more complex representations as in CNN, RNN, etc.

Estimating Truth: Attribution

When the observations are composed of values of several attributes/ features, one of the fundamental aspects of "truth" is understanding which of those attributes are most important, that is, which of the attributes are most significant in determining the value of the target variable. We refer to this goal as *attribution*.[4] Recall that we had looked at etiology in Table 3-2; attribution is the technical basis to determine etiology.

---

[3] That is, the equations that map inputs to an output at each neuron.

[4] This does not seem to be a standard term in the industry yet, but we find it rather apt.

Let us revisit a few examples we saw in Chapter 16 in the context of attribution:

- Linear regression: If the coefficient/weight of a feature is zero in the linear equation, it would obviously mean that target value is unaffected by the value of this feature. In other words, the value of this feature is not useful for determining the value of the target variable. We can also see from the equation that if all the features have the same range of values (e.g., using min-max scaling[5]), a feature with a higher weight[6] can be regarded as having a greater effect on the value of the target variable – and thus, more important.

- Decision tree: Recall that each node is split using that feature from the set of available features for which the child nodes have a high predominance of one class, that is, that feature is picked from the set for which the child nodes have the lowest entropy. This means that a decision tree is capable of comparing features and determining which feature is better or more important. This capability can provide a mechanism to rank the features by their importance.

- Random forest: We just discussed a mechanism that can help us determine the importance of features in a decision tree. We can consider the importance of each feature in all the decision trees of a random forest to arrive at the overall importance of the features in the random forest.

---

[5] See Chapter 14.

[6] Absolute value of the weight to be more precise.

- Deep learning: There is no intuitive notion of how the relative importance of features can be gauged. Recent developments, particularly in the field called "explainable AI," can help determine important features – but these approaches can be rather complex in themselves and less intuitive. And if it becomes extremely complex and unintuitive, then it usually doesn't feel like "truth."

Note that in all these cases, based on the ML algorithm used to create the model, a data scientist adopts some notion of determining the importance of features. They then draw conclusions about attribution, that is, announce some features as "important." As we can see, this is only a relative notion of importance – it may thus feel like a somewhat arbitrary foundation for attribution, unless the attribution mechanism is both intuitive and rigorous. Achieving this intuition and rigor can be a tall order, but fortunately as we saw in Chapter 3, many real-world business problems do not demand etiology and attribution.

Prediction: Interpretability

This goal refers to the need for us, humans, to be able to understand and interpret how the model is generating a specific prediction for a new observation. In other words, we as humans need to be able to *interpret* each step that a model took to reach the target prediction from the input observation. Let us look at a few examples:

- The interpretation of an equation, such as that of linear regression model, is extremely straightforward.

- In case of a decision tree, we can look at the tree and understand which branch the new observation will follow at each node based on the value of a feature in order to arrive at the prediction. Predictions given by such a model are thus highly interpretable.

- In case of a random forest, it can be extremely difficult to have a detailed look at the numerous trees to understand how they made their predictions and accordingly interpret the final prediction. Thus, even though random forests can give some notion of which features are important (i.e., support attribution), they are not as interpretable.

- We saw in Chapter 16 that a neural network doesn't give us a simple picture of how it is doing the predictions – such a model is thus one of the least interpretable.

Prediction: Accuracy

This simply refers to the notion that we want our model to accurately predict values of the target variable for future, unseen observations. Note that this goal does not include any notions of whether we as humans are able to understand (interpret) why the model predicts something – it only talks about the goal of getting the prediction right. At the time of writing, in terms of power of accurate predictions

- Deep learning techniques seem to outperform the rest, especially for perception-related problems such as NLP, computer vision, etc.

- Random forest and gradient boosted trees[7] generally seem to be the favored techniques for all other kinds of problems. We saw in Chapter 16 how these algorithms improve their predictions.

---

[7] Particularly XGBoost.

Having looked at the four goals and some examples of how a few techniques fare toward achieving these goals, we can look at a more formal "grading" matrix to capture these notions for all techniques – this matrix also helps identify which techniques are typically preferred by each culture.

Grading ML Techniques

In the previous section, we discussed how each purpose of modeling can be broken into two goals each, resulting in the four goals of modeling. We also discussed a few examples of how various techniques fare against these goals. This is summarized by the grades[8] we've given in Figure 20-1 – the figure also shows how the two cultures differ in the way they approach these goals and how this determines the techniques that they usually prefer. We had seen in Chapter 3 that the monastic culture focuses on both purposes, so all four goals are equally relevant to monks as shown in the table. The wild-west culture focuses only on the purpose of predicting values, so the goals toward the bottom of the table are more relevant to cowboys. Consequently, since the ML techniques toward the left have generally high grades in all four goals, these techniques are preferred in monastic culture. Similarly, techniques toward the right have very high grades for the bottom goals and hence are preferred in wild-west culture.

---

[8] Various data scientists might give slightly different grades.

ML technique Goal	Linear, logistic regression	SVM (linear)	Decision Tree	SVM (non-linear kernel)	Gradient Boosting, Random Forest	Deep learning
Simplicity of representation	A+	A+	A	A	B	C
Attribution	A+	A+	A+	B	A	C
Interpretability of prediction	A+	A+	A+	A	B	B/C
Accuracy of prediction	B	A	B	A	A+	A+

All goals equally relevant to monks

Goals increasingly relevant to cowboys

Increasingly monastic techniques

Increasingly wild-west techniques

Figure 20-1. *Some ML techniques graded for each goal of modeling, and how these grades influence the preferred techniques of the two cultures*

The following are examples of the (somewhat subjective) reasoning behind a couple of cases:

- Random forest gets a high grade (A+) for accuracy of prediction, but a slightly lower grade (A) for attribution. This is because while the algorithm does identify important features, there can be cases where these are not as reliable – see Efron (2020) for one such example.

- Deep learning gets a high grade (A+) for accuracy of prediction and poor grade (C) for attribution. It gets a somewhat ambiguous grade of B/C for interpretability of prediction, because

  - The interpretability varies depending on the complexity of the neural network.

  - There is ongoing advancement in this field of interpreting/explaining deep learning predictions, for example, class activation maps for CNN, etc. These interpretations would likely not be clear/crisp enough to merit an A, but they can be useful enough to occasionally warrant a B.

While we have only mentioned a few techniques covered in this book, the structure and framework of Figure 20-1 can be used to grade any ML technique and determine how well it is suited to particular goals, hence to a particular culture (and thereby to the business problem at hand).

ADVANCED NOTE: OTHER TECHNIQUES

The following are a few classical monastic techniques that we haven't covered elsewhere in the book:

- *Statistical tests*: Statistical tests such as t-test, chi-square test, etc., are frequently used by monks in their journey of finding the underlying truth. For example, statistical tests could be used to determine which features are significant.

- *Akaike information criterion and Bayesian information criterion*: Commonly referred to as AIC and BIC, these are used to choose the best model among a set of candidate models. To do this, they take into account both performance of the models on train data and complexity of the models. Complex models with more parameters are penalized.

We refer to these techniques in the next section.

Cultural Differences

Table 20-1 summarizes all the differences between the two cultures – it elaborates on a few points in Table 3-1 and also adds a few new points based on our coverage earlier in this chapter.

Table 20-1. *Monastic vs. wild west: final edition*

Factor	Monastic culture	Wild-west culture
Mindset	Find the underlying, eternal truth (nature) which led to (caused) the observations	Find what works *now.* Can update frequently. Empiricism is the only eternal truth
Purposes	Estimation of *truth* behind the observations, which enables prediction and deeper, accurate causative insights	Predictive accuracy is the primary goal Causation is often a casualty. Causative insights are either irrelevant, less accurate, or just good to have
Evaluation	How close to the truth is my estimation?	Am I getting the predictions as accurately as I wanted to?
Evaluation – what is evaluated	The estimated "truth" includes attribution as well as interpretable and accurate predictions by a model. Also, models with simpler representations are preferred	Primary focus is on accuracy of predictions by a model. Interpretability of predictions and attribution are occasionally good to have
Domain expertise	Domain understanding significantly leveraged to craft features; this is because attribution is a primary goal, so features that are well understood are preferred	Lesser domain expertise often suffices when the techniques used automate feature extraction; for example, using CNN, relevant features are automatically extracted from an image

(continued)

Table 20-1. (*continued*)

Factor	Monastic culture	Wild-west culture
How many features used for modeling	Try to avoid "the curse of dimensionality." Find a few features that contain most information – this reduces model complexity and facilitates attribution	Any additional information can help improve predictive accuracy and is useful. Techniques like deep learning, gradient boosted trees, etc., can be used even with hundreds of features
ML techniques	Prefer the ones with a high grade for all the goals in Figure 20-1	Prefer the ones with grade A+ for "accuracy of prediction" in Figure 20-1
Attribution	Statistical tests, important features as identified by the ML model	Important features as identified by the ML model
Model performance evaluation	Statistical tests, AIC/BIC, cross-validation[9]	Cross-validation
Model upgrade frequency	Can take longer to create a model. But once created, since it represents a long-term truth, upgrades are less frequent	Models are typically created quickly and upgraded often through rapid iterations as new data is obtained

---

[9] Covered in Chapter 16.

> ### UNSUPERVISED LEARNING AND THE TWO CULTURES
>
> Our coverage has primarily focused on supervised learning techniques where the cultural differences are rather striking. But such differences can occasionally be seen in the context of some unsupervised techniques such as anomaly detection techniques as well.

Conclusion

In this chapter, we elaborated on the differences between the two data science cultures that were first introduced in Chapter 3.

It was Leo Breiman who first highlighted the existence of two such cultures when it comes to creating models from data. His original paper, the comments by D.R. Cox and Brad Efron, and Breiman's responses are in Breiman (2001). Using our terminology, we would say that Breiman was apparently the first monk to leave the monastery and venture into the wild west. After years of doing data science there, including contributions to techniques like random forest, he returned to the monastery with not only a new set of techniques but also a new perspective – the aforementioned article details Breiman's journey and the welcome he got from a few monks when he returned to the monastery.

Our description of the two cultures is largely based on our personal experience. These two cultures have been given various names in the past – for the record, our "monastic" culture is somewhat akin to Breiman's "data modeling" culture, and our "wild-west" culture is somewhat akin to Breiman's "algorithmic modeling" culture. It is important to note though that the implications and details of how the two cultures practice data science have evolved since Breiman's original paper – particularly during the Big Data era (starting around 2006–2010) and then the deep learning revolution (since around 2013).

A more recent survey of the two cultures is Efron (2020). This paper, along with the Breiman discussions mentioned earlier, helped us put some structure around our observations of the two cultures. Efron (2020) also provided the very useful term "attribution" that we have adopted.

We shall see how the various factors covered in this chapter are useful while building the data science team in Chapter 22.

In Chapter 23, we shall see how the choice of culture is influenced by the type of data science projects. We shall also revisit the goals of modeling and Figure 20-1 in the context of explainability.

Summary of Part 3

In Chapters 12 to 18, we covered the various techniques and technologies used in the data science process. In Chapter 19, we saw how they all come together in a reference architecture to support the operations of a data science team. Finally, in this chapter, we covered more details of how the two data science cultures differ in the way they practice data science, particularly in regard to their choice of ML techniques.

Thus far in the book, we have covered the business and technological aspects that need to be factored into building a data science practice. In the next, final part, we shall look at the practical aspects of building a data science team and executing data science projects.

References

Breiman, Leo. "Statistical Modeling: The Two Cultures." *Statistical Science* 2001: 199–231.

Efron, Bradley. "Prediction, Estimation, and Attribution." *Journal of the American Statistical Association* 2020: 636–655.

PART IV

Building Teams and Executing Projects

In the previous parts, we covered the business and technical aspects around data science. In this final part, we shall focus on some important (but often neglected) practical aspects which are crucial for doing data science *effectively*. We will cover the practical aspects around building and structuring data science teams and managing data science projects.

We first cover a skills framework in Chapter 21 – this elaborates the various skills that are needed for roles that are typically seen in a data science team. In Chapter 22, we look at typical team structures that are built around this skills framework for effective execution. Finally in Chapter 23, we cover a few important aspects around managing data science projects such as the types of data science projects, ensuring data quality in these projects, regulatory aspects that must be kept in mind when working on these projects, etc.

CHAPTER 21

The Skills Framework

Recall the notion from Chapter 1 that *the application of the scientific method to data using software is referred to as data science.* Data science is thus fundamentally an interdisciplinary activity at the cusp of data analysis and software engineering. As a team leader, you would periodically need to determine the roles necessary to your team and ensure that the appropriate team members with the right mix of data analysis and software engineering skills are available for that role.

The various roles typically seen in a data science team, and the degree of each type of skill required for the roles, are shown in Figure 21-1.

© Vineet Raina and Srinath Krishnamurthy 2022
V. Raina and S. Krishnamurthy, *Building an Effective Data Science Practice*,
https://doi.org/10.1007/978-1-4842-7419-4_21

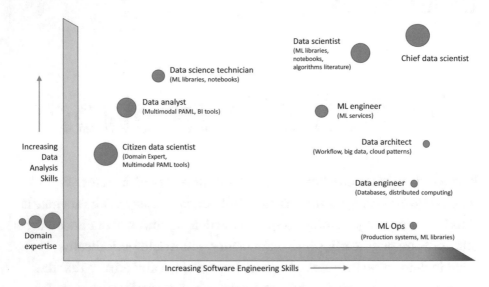

Figure 21-1. *The skills framework. Roles are depicted as a combination of skills required along three dimensions: data analysis, software engineering, and domain expertise*

As seen in the figure, in addition to the two dimensions of data analysis and software engineering, there is a third dimension – *domain expertise*, represented by the size of the bubbles. The different roles require a combination of these skills to varying extents. In the rest of this chapter, we shall cover the three dimensions of skills, followed by the various roles and their responsibilities.

The Three Dimensions of Skills

The three types of skills that are necessary for a data science project are *data analysis, software engineering,* and *domain expertise*. Let us look at each of them to understand what they entail.

Data Analysis Skills

Data analysis simply refers to the ability to gain insights from data. This can vary from simple reports (e.g., sales trends) to statistical techniques (e.g., correlation analysis to find which products typically sell together) and machine learning algorithms.

Conceptually, the thought process that goes into data analysis does not necessarily require software skills – indeed, many of the techniques used by data scientists today were well established by the first half of the 20th-century and predated computers. While software tools help make data analysis faster and more accurate, *using* these tools does not necessarily require software engineering skills – for example, tools such as Microsoft Excel have been the default choice for data analysis for decades, even for advanced analysis as done by quants in finance.

Software Engineering Skills

Software engineering is of course a vast discipline in itself. Within the specific context of data science, software engineering skills are needed for coding the various steps of the data science process. Some relevant aspects include

- Design and efficient implementation of analytic algorithms: There are several open source libraries for data science. But occasionally a need arises to implement an algorithm tailored to your needs or modify an open source algorithm.

- Data preparation: Collating, cleansing, and preparing datasets at scale, including data pipelines.

- GPUs and deep learning: State-of-the-art deep learning algorithms and neural networks require clusters of GPUs and finely tuned data flow paradigms for efficient model training. Several performance tuning aspects in such setups require software engineering skills.

- Productionizing ML models: Deploying models to production requires software engineering skills to integrate the model into the production technology stack at scale.

For effective, end-to-end data science solutions, these software engineering skills are indispensable.

Domain Expertise

Deep understanding of the domain, and how the data relates to the domain, is essential to formulate the right problem statement, determine the data science approach to solving the problem, and, finally, to evaluate the correctness of the solution. Several data science problems are oriented toward automating the routine work conducted by experts in domains such as finance, retail, healthcare, etc. – in these cases, the domain expertise of these folks is critical to the success of the data science team.

Refer to Chapter 20 for a discussion around how the domain expertise requirements depend on the data science culture.

An effective data science team thus requires these three kinds of skills: data analysis, software engineering, and domain expertise. We shall now look at the typical roles in a data science team and how these roles require a combination of skills along these three dimensions.

The Roles in a Data Science Team

Refer to Figure 21-1 where the various roles are shown along with the level of skill in each of three dimensions that each role typically requires. We shall now cover each of the roles, along with their responsibilities in a data science team.

It is important to note that these are "roles" rather than individuals – a single individual may perform several of these roles, especially during the incubation phase of the team. We shall cover these aspects around building and structuring teams in the next chapter.

Citizen Data Scientist

A citizen data scientist is the foremost domain expert in the company. They know the business processes and how the data maps to the real world.

Given their domain knowledge, a citizen data scientist typically determines the scope of a data science project and also influences the data strategy[1] of the company. They also enable the chief data scientist and others to understand the domain in increasing depth.

They work closely with the chief data scientist in formulating the problem statement and participate actively in the data science process iterations – especially the design of experiments and evaluation of model performance from the domain perspective.

Having expertise in the domain, often they do not have a high degree of data analysis or software engineering skills. Thus, they rely on advanced tools[2] which make it easier for people like them to create initial baseline models using their domain knowledge. Data scientists then build upon this baseline during further iterations of the data science process.

---

[1] *Data strategy* refers to the overarching vision around the capture and utilization of data oriented toward achieving business goals.

[2] For example, multimodal PAML tools such as SAS VDMML – refer to Chapter 18.

Data Analyst

This is a traditional role in most organizations and something you might be familiar with. Data analysts are experts in the domain. They typically use BI tools along with query languages such as SQL, but their programming expertise may be limited. They can extract insights from data using various visualization and statistical techniques.

If your company already has a data analyst, it would be great to involve them in a consulting fashion. Given their domain expertise of the products and business processes, they are often ideally positioned to evaluate model performance in production systems and the business impact of incorporating data science models in the operations of your organization.

Data Science Technician

This is a term we have coined for folks who are moderately skilled in programming and have knowledge of libraries such as scikit-learn, Keras, Matplotlib, etc., that are used in the data science process. They can thus rapidly execute experiments and evaluate model performance. On the other hand, they are yet to gain the scientific expertise to *design* new experiments independently – in this sense, they can be regarded as apprentice data scientists.

In large data science teams, data science technicians are crucial to execute experiments rapidly and precisely; this enables the data scientists to focus on experiment design and innovating novel techniques.

ML Ops

ML Ops requires understanding of both, the models that the data science team creates, and the production systems that the engineering/IT team creates and maintains. This is a niche role that is oriented primarily toward the *inference* step of the data science process.

ML Ops is responsible for the deployment, maintenance, and monitoring of models in the production systems.

Typically, ML Ops members would need to be familiar with the techniques and tools mentioned in Chapter 17.

Data Engineer

A data engineer performs the data engineering step of the data science process. They are thereby responsible for storing, tracking, transforming, evaluating, and maintaining the data assets for use by the entire data science team. Data engineers typically fulfil the following responsibilities:

- Perform most of the activities in the data capture step of the data science process. This includes ingesting data from the data sources identified by the domain experts and data scientists and facilitating easy access to the data.

- Automate repeatable data preparation and data visualization steps that crystallize through multiple iterations of the data science process.

- Ensure seamless availability of the data for the machine learning step, including possibly for distributed learning with big data.

- Perform the ML Ops role in small teams.

- Maintain any BI or PAML[3] tools along with the rest of the data infrastructure.

---

[3] Refer to Chapter 18.

Data Architect

The data architect is responsible for deciding the entire data and compute infrastructure aligned with budgetary constraints. This includes the choice of tools that are best suited for the data science team. Given the interdisciplinary team, the data architect needs to ensure that the architecture enables smooth collaboration among all the roles across the various steps in the data science process.

We had looked at a reference architecture for data science teams in Chapter 19. The data architect is responsible for tailoring this reference architecture to the specific needs and constraints of your organization.

ML Engineer

The last few years have seen a tremendous rise in AI services on the cloud and AutoML. We covered these in Chapter 18. As we saw in that chapter, an engineer could use such a service or library to create a model, for example, to predict the inventory requirements at a store. For this, they would need to understand the domain and the data, but does not have to know the details of the data science process, ML techniques, etc., that go into the creation of the model.

This has led to the relatively new *ML engineer* role – an engineer with a good understanding of the domain who can use these services and libraries and evaluate the resulting models to ensure they meet the desired goals.

Compared to the data science technician role, ML engineers require less data analysis skills since they do not need to know the data science process fully. But ML engineers would need to have stronger engineering skills in order to use the AutoML libraries and cloud services effectively.

Software engineers can easily be upskilled to ML engineers with minimal training of ML basics such as model performance evaluation, combined with a knowledge of the AI/AutoML services and libraries.

If you are following a wild-west approach, or need to do quick PoCs with existing cloud services before investing significantly into hiring data scientists, it may be a good idea to bootstrap the team with an ML engineer.

Data Scientist

As we see from Figure 21-1, a data scientist has a good mix of skills across all three dimensions. Typically, a data scientist is skilled at applying the scientific method tailored to the domain they are working in. Correspondingly, they work closely with the domain experts to gain deep understanding of the business and the domain.

In a small team, they may work with the chief data scientist to help design the experiments and also execute them. In large teams, the data scientist may focus on designing experiments with the chief data scientist and delegate the execution to data science technicians and ML engineers. They also work with data engineers, defining requirements for the data pipeline. As the data preparation and data visualization steps become more repeatable, the data scientist works with the data engineers to automate these steps for rapid iterations.

A data scientist usually has a deep understanding of the algorithms – they can thus modify existing open source implementations when necessary. Some data scientists can also create new algorithms and techniques as required.

Chief Data Scientist

The chief data scientist is ultimately responsible for the overall data science team. They have a mix of skills in all the three dimensions that enable them to move smoothly across data analysis, software engineering, and domain/business aspects.

They are the primary owner for formulating the problem to be solved, setting the data and experimentation strategy required, defining a roadmap, and getting it executed with the support of the other roles. We shall discuss the chief data scientist role in more detail in the next chapter.

Deviations in Skills

The depiction of some of the roles in Figure 21-1 represents our idealistic view, and deviations from these are not uncommon in practical scenarios; particularly, the ideal data scientist and chief data scientist depicted here are generally regarded as unicorns. In many teams, the other roles usually augment and fill in for any shortcomings in the skills of these primary roles, for example, if a (chief) data scientist has less software engineering skills, then other engineers such as the data architect, data engineer, or ML engineer fill in to compensate for this.

The choice of culture (monastic or wild west) can also tend to influence which skill (data analysis or software engineering) is predominant in a data scientist. For example, the software engineering skills of a monk may possibly be lesser than the ideal depicted here.

Conclusion

In this chapter, we covered a skills framework to explain the various roles that go into forming an interdisciplinary data science team. Which of these roles are required in a team depends on the specifics of the data science culture and the business – we covered some of the aspects in the descriptions of each of the roles.

In the next chapter, we shall look at aspects around building and structuring a data science team composed of these roles.

CHAPTER 22

Building and Structuring the Team

In the previous chapter, we saw the various roles and skills that go into forming an interdisciplinary data science team. In this chapter, we shall look at a few typical team structures that are seen in practice and then cover some pointers around hiring data scientists, with a particular focus on the chief data scientist.

Typical Team Structures

In this section, we shall first look at the minimal team composition required to begin data science activities. Then we shall look at a typical composition of a large team that is mature and operational, that is, a team that creates several models that are deployed to production systems and are generating value for the business. After covering these two extreme points in the data science journey, we shall look at a few factors regarding how teams evolve and grow from the incubation structure toward the mature, operational structure.

Small Incubation Team

Once you have ascertained that you are ready to embark on the data science journey, you would typically begin by onboarding a chief data scientist. Depending on the complexity of the problem, you may hire an additional data scientist. Or if you are planning to rely on AutoML and AI services,[1] you can hire an ML engineer instead.

As discussed in Chapter 2, it is crucial to make the data available to data scientists. As data scientists continue to analyze the data, they may request for additional data or highlight issues in the data. To service these requests from the data scientists, you may need a data engineer as well.

With such a team composition, the data engineer would own the data capture step of the data science process. As data scientists progress through iterations of the data science process, the data engineer can also automate some parts of the data preparation and data visualization steps. This will allow the data scientists to increasingly focus on the machine learning step of the data science process.

The data scientist or data engineer would perform the inference step as well; typically, the initial models will be packaged into a simple script that can be invoked by the IT/engineering team. In this early stage, it may not make sense to invest in advanced ML Ops processes.[2]

Mature Operational team

Figure 22-1 shows a typical structure of a team that has grown to become mature and fully operational.

---

[1] Covered in Chapter 18.

[2] ML Ops was covered in Chapter 17.

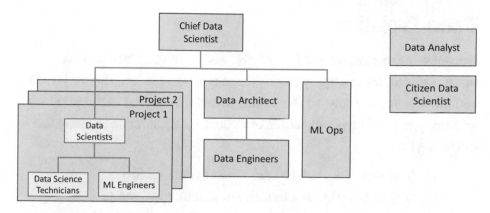

Figure 22-1. *Typical structure of a mature, operational data science team*

Such a team typically has multiple projects being executed simultaneously. Several of the current and past projects would already have resulted in models deployed into production systems.

In this case, each project typically has a group of data scientists, data science technicians, and ML engineers working on it. The data scientist(s) typically define an experimentation strategy and specify the experiments to be executed. Data science technicians and ML engineers execute the experiments. The composition of the team within each project depends on the type of project – this is covered in more detail in the next chapter.

The data engineering activity is performed by a team of data engineers, often led by a data architect. This team supports all the data science projects.

A dedicated ML Ops team ensures that models are deployed, upgraded, and monitored in an automated fashion. If advanced ML Ops tools are used, then typically this team can be rather small, consisting of just one or two members.

All these roles effectively report to the chief data scientist, who is responsible for coordinating the overall execution. The chief data scientist also draws insights and distils common techniques across the multiple projects.

The data analyst and citizen data scientist roles, if present, collaborate with the rest of the team on various projects as needed.

Team Evolution

Once the incubation team successfully executes a couple of projects, more opportunities to apply data science typically present themselves. As you grow your team toward the mature structure covered in the previous section, you would typically strive to maintain a right balance along the following lines:

- The proportion of data scientists to data science technicians/ML engineers: For scaling the team in a cost-effective manner, it can be useful to allow the data scientists to increasingly focus on experiment design rather than coding and execution.

- Offloading data preparation to data engineers: Once the data scientists have identified the typical data preparation activities such as data cleansing and data transformations, you can enable the data scientists to offload these steps to the data engineers. Ideally, a data scientist should spend minimal amount of time in preparing data.

- Offloading inference activities: While the data scientists need to be aware of the production requirements (e.g., acceptable latency during inference), it is not very productive to make them package the models for production deployments. It would be good to offload the inference step to a data engineer or ML Ops at the earliest.

- Adopting advanced tools vs. hiring: Encouraging the data science team members to adopt tools can reduce the need for data engineers and ML Ops. Examples of such tools include advanced IDEs that increase collaboration and ease of provisioning compute clusters, experiment and model registry, ML Ops tools, etc.[3]

- Rapid execution vs. best practices: To ensure business continuity and reproducibility of all the experiments, it is crucial to inculcate best practices such as the use of an experiment registry, tracking lineage of datasets, and so forth. When these are introduced, the team may feel it is an overhead – but once inculcated, the day-to-day operational overhead tends to be insignificant, especially if the right tools[4] are used.

The Key Hire: Chief Data Scientist

For the role of the chief data scientist, one of the most important factors to evaluate is: how many of the models that they created have been deployed to production systems or used in strategic decisions. A solid track record of production experience with models is crucial to ensure that the chief data scientist has an outcome-based mindset and has collaborated with other teams – such as engineering teams and management stakeholders – in the past to create end-to-end solutions.

Next, in addition to the usual technical credentials, there are two main aspects to consider when you are trying to find a chief data scientist suited to your business: first, which culture you feel is suitable to your business – monastic or wild west – and, second, whether you want to hire a chief data scientist full time or get a consultant. We shall cover each of these briefly.

---

[3] Refer to Chapter 19 to recall how these various tools are used together.
[4] Such as ML Flow for experiment registry, etc.

Evaluating the Culture

Recall from Chapter 3 that typically, based on your business needs, you can identify which of the two data science cultures is more suited. If you have thus identified which culture is more suited to your business, then you would want to evaluate the chief data scientist to determine the culture they might predominantly belong to.

If the chief data scientist is of the "right" culture, then the rest of the team typically inculcates the same culture from the chief data scientist – they would instill the requisite culture in their team members and also hire new data scientists that belong to a similar culture.

We have seen some of the differentiating factors between the two cultures in Chapters 3 and 20. Accordingly, the following are a few pointers for identifying which culture a candidate data scientist might predominantly belong to:

1. Look at the problems that they have worked on in the past. Did those problems require a monastic or wild-west approach? Refer to Chapter 3 for pointers in understanding this.

2. Look at the techniques they have used to solve these problems, and map them to Chapter 20. Do they seem to have a background indicative of an inclination toward monastic or wild-west techniques?

3. What is the academic background of the candidate? In our experience, if the candidate has

    •   A masters or doctorate in statistics, they are likely to be closer to the monk end of the culture spectrum. (Refer to Chapter 3 for the data science culture spectrum.)

- A computer science background, they are likely to be closer to the cowboy end of the culture spectrum.

- Some other scientific background, for example, natural sciences, then they are likely to be in the middle of the culture spectrum.

Note that these pointers would apply to hiring any data scientist. Specifically in regard to the chief data scientist role, the body of work (points 1 and 2) would be the primary indicator of culture. The factors based on academic background (point 3) are observations based on our experience working with data scientists across the cultural spectrum.

Hiring vs. Getting a Consultant

In the very initial stage when you are considering bootstrapping the data science team, it may be prudent to get a consulting chief data scientist who can help

- Formulate the problem

- Ensure that the necessary data is available

- Ensure that data science is, in fact, the right approach to solve the problem[5]

- Define the data and experimentation strategy

The consultant can also advise whether using AI services or AutoML might fulfil your needs. If initial experiments can be done using AI services or AutoML, you can then assign an ML engineer to work under the guidance of the consultant. If you do not have an ML engineer

---

[5] See Chapter 2.

available, you can likely upskill a smart software engineer in your existing IT/software development team to become an ML engineer quickly.[6]

If the consultant suggests that existing AI services or AutoML may not be a good fit, then you can consider hiring a senior or chief data scientist, depending on complexity of the problem and the potential RoI you see from the pilot data science project.

Data Engineering: Requirements and Staffing

Let us look at a few factors that determine the data engineering requirements of your team and how to fulfil them.

If you are incubating a monastic culture, there is less likelihood of requiring heavy infrastructure such as clusters of GPUs, etc. Typically, in these cases, the data scientist would prefer to work on a single, dedicated machine where the data is available. In this case, the data engineering activities might be intermittent rather than ongoing.

If you are incubating a wild-west culture, then your data scientists will likely be working with big data and also require clusters of machines, including possibly GPUs. There are typically much more data engineering activities to be performed in this case.

In any case, it is possible that you wouldn't need a full-time data engineer at the early incubation stage; if so, there are a couple of options:

- A data scientist could perform the data engineering activities if they are conversant with the data sources in your organization.

---

[6] Recall from the previous chapter that software engineers can easily be upskilled to ML engineers with minimal training of ML basics such as model performance evaluation, combined with a knowledge of the AI/AutoML services and libraries.

- Carve out some time from a software engineer in your IT/engineering team who works on the database side. If this is done, then the productivity of your data scientists would be optimal.

Notes on Upskilling

You may have heard that data engineers can be upskilled to data scientists. While this may be true in some cases, we often find data engineers lacking the requisite background in data analysis and the thought process required to apply the scientific method effectively.

If upskilling is your primary staffing strategy, then data engineers, just like software engineers, can often be upskilled to ML engineers to begin with. Once they show promise as ML engineers, you can then consider upskilling them to data scientists.

Conclusion

We covered the typical team structures and evolution and some pointers regarding hiring data scientists, particularly the chief data scientist.

In the next chapter, we shall revisit the team structures in the context of various types of data science projects.

CHAPTER 23

Data Science Projects

We began this book with an introduction to the data science process in Part 1. Then in Part 2, we saw the various classes of problems that could be relevant to your business and how the data science process is applied in each of those cases. In Part 3, we looked at the various techniques and technologies that go into executing each step of the data science process, culminating in a reference architecture that can be tailored to your specific team. And in the last couple of chapters, we have seen the various roles that go into forming an interdisciplinary team that executes the data science process end-to-end.

The data science team (previous two chapters) applies the techniques and technologies (Part 3) to various classes of problems (Part 2) using the data science process to realize a business outcome (Part 1). A data science *project* is the overarching activity that encompasses all these aspects that go into yielding a desired business outcome. In this final chapter, we shall look at various practical facets of data science projects.

We first cover the four common types of data science projects and the typical business outcomes they yield; we also cover how the project type influences the data science process, reference architecture, data science culture, etc.

In the following sections, we cover various aspects related to managing data science projects and teams. We first cover a critical aspect often considered too late in the data science journey – evaluating the performance of a team using KPIs. Then we cover aspects of data quality and data protection/privacy – these are usually the skeletons in the closet

© Vineet Raina and Srinath Krishnamurthy 2022
V. Raina and S. Krishnamurthy, *Building an Effective Data Science Practice*,
https://doi.org/10.1007/978-1-4842-7419-4_23

that folks often tend to shy away from during regular operations. We then look at the legal and regulatory considerations unique to data science projects. We finally wrap up by looking at cognitive bias and how/when to guard against it in data science projects.

Types of Data Science Projects

Four common types of data science projects and the typical business outcomes expected from each type of project are shown in Table 23-1.

Table 23-1. *Types of data science projects and typical business outcomes*

Project type	Typical business outcomes
Knowledge discovery from data (KDD)	Novel, actionable insights derived from existing data
Data science infusion in processes (DSI-Proc)	Improvements in existing business processes. Can also lead to new business models
Data science infusion in products (DSI-Prod)	Increase in customer engagement with an existing product, increased adoption of the product
Data science-based product (DSBP)	New "intelligent" product built upon data science models

Using Table 23-1, you can identify which type of project best suits your business needs. This also helps set expectations about the outcomes accordingly with the team as well as other stakeholders.

In the following subsections, we cover some examples of each type of data science project and summarize some typical traits of each type of data science project.

Knowledge Discovery from Data/Data Mining

Extracting novel, actionable insights from existing data is referred to as *knowledge discovery from data (KDD)* or *data mining*. The following are some examples:

- The classical example is identifying patterns in user transactions to enable effective sales and marketing strategies. For example, suppose your organization operates a retail store/chain and has captured data of several users and transactions. Using this data, you want to cluster users with similar purchase patterns or identify products that often sell together.[1] These kinds of insights can then enable cross-selling campaigns.

- Suppose your organization manufactures some heavy equipment such as earth-moving machines. You have already created an industrial IoT solution that is gathering various data about the operations of the machines such as telemetry data. Other in-house or dealer applications in your organization capture data such as the sales or rentals of your equipment, its operating conditions such as the type of soil, etc. Given all this data that has been captured over a few years, you are eager to extract further insights from this. At this stage, you are not sure what kinds of insights to expect, but anything useful along the lines of how the operating conditions or users of the equipment affect the performance of the equipment could be useful. A KDD project can explore the data to extract such insights. A concrete outcome could be insights into, for

---

[1] We saw a similar example in Chapter 7.

example, how the soil conditions, operating hours, and
the equipment handlers impact the fuel consumption
or the maintenance needs of the equipment.

TERMINOLOGY CHAOS: DATA MINING AND KDD

The terms *data mining* and *KDD* are used in a few different flavors. Some, for
example, regard data mining as one of the steps in KDD. In this book, however,
we are using the terms data mining and KDD interchangeably.

Also, a common expansion of KDD is Knowledge Discovery *in Databases*. We
prefer the more generic term Knowledge Discovery *from Data*, since the data
can be sourced from websites, APIs, streams, etc., in addition to databases.

Finally, as elaborated in this section, we regard KDD/data mining to now be
subsumed under data science as *one* type of data science project.

Data Science Infusion in Processes

Data science can play a key role in improving existing processes within an
organization[2] or processes in which an organization participates.

The following are a few examples of such projects:

- In a company that stores liquids in large tanks, the
  operations at a terminal typically involve activities
  such as monitoring the tanks, maintaining the liquids
  in a certain temperature range, and pumping liquids
  into/out of the tanks from/into trucks or railcars for
  transport. The various activities involve electrical
  machinery such as pumps, heaters, etc., and result

---

[2] When used to optimize the internal operations of an organization, then the
project also has some elements of the classical notion of operations research
(OR). This can be felt in the first example that follows in the main text.

in utility costs. Given data of past operations, current liquid volumes in tanks, and estimated arrival of trucks/railcars, data science models can be used to predict the latest time by when certain activities (e.g., heating) would need to happen at various tanks. These predictions can be fed into a scheduling algorithm that schedules the activities – adhering to predicted time constraints – in such a way that the peak electricity usage at the terminal is minimized. This would result in cost savings.

- Consider a company that manufactures a product for home medical use, for example, a urine strip for monitoring of cancer patients. In this case, the process would typically involve the strip being dispatched to a clinician/doctor who decodes the color readings to arrive at pathology metrics. With modern computer vision techniques, this can be digitalized such that a photo of the strip (taken by the patient using their mobile device) can be analyzed to extract the color readings, converted to pathology metrics, and shared with the clinician/doctor in an automated fashion. This improves the overall process and the experience of the patient.

- In some cases, automating some internal processes using data science models can lead to new business models as well. For example, suppose a company manufactures chemical enhancers to improve the yield of certain chemical processes at, say, a refinery. To recommend the right mix of enhancers for a particular refinery, the company would have experts analyze the input raw materials and other environmental factors at the refinery. If you have collected data from several such past analyses, it may be possible to now automate it using data science models. The models would learn from the past decisions of experts that led to improved yield and accordingly provide recommendations of the enhancer mixture for any new client/chemical process. Once this critical piece of the process is automated, it can open up opportunities to provide self-serve platforms to the clients where they can input all the parameters about raw material, environment, etc., and get recommendations of the enhancer mixture that can improve yield.

Data Science Infusion in Products

Technology products in various domains tend to benefit by adding "intelligence" obtained by infusing data science models. For example:

- Suppose your company creates software products for collaboration and productivity. One such product, a virtual integrated workspace, allows users to use various modes of communication such as chat, audio/video conferencing, emails, and other tools like calendar, notes, etc., from within a single integrated interface. Data science-driven capabilities that can be infused into such a product include

  - Automatically understanding the intent of an email, chat, or audio call and carrying out the action requested. For example, creating calendar events or booking conference rooms as requested in the email, etc.

- Automatically generating transcripts and action-item notes for meetings, including automated actions such as setting up follow-up discussions, etc.

- Suppose your company manufactures IoT devices and provides a software platform for monitoring the devices and their usage and controlling the devices remotely including specification of policies, etc. In this case, data science-based models can be added to the product that help detect any abnormal readings (i.e., anomaly detection) and enable use cases around predictive maintenance.

- Suppose your company sells IT security products that detect abnormal network traffic or resource usage. You may have embedded AI using a rule engine, but customers are now reporting that false alarms are rather high in some cases. Adding data science-based anomaly detection techniques can improve the performance of your product and thereby the customer experience.

- Suppose your company manufactures CT scan machines. While high-radiation doses capture high-quality scans, a high-radiation dose can be less safe for the patients compared to low-radiation doses. But the patient-safe scans obtained using low-radiation doses can have more noise, look blurry, etc., which can make the interpretation/diagnosis unclear. By analyzing past scans obtained from low- and high-radiation doses, deep learning techniques can learn to convert a noisy scan (obtained from reduced radiation dose) to a high-quality scan. Infusing the CT scan machine with such technology can enable high-quality CT scans using low-radiation doses.

- Recommendation systems, voice-augmented interfaces, etc., are other common examples of infusing data science into existing products.

- If your company provides an online video conferencing solution, then denoising the participant audio in real time can be done using data science models. In this case, a model is trained on data of clean audio and noisy audio (e.g., background sound of traffic, dog barking, child crying, etc.) to remove the noise. One of the challenges in such a system is that the audio denoising has to happen in real time so that the participants do not experience lag during the meeting. Offering such a capability can be a differentiator in the market leading to increased customer adoption.

Data Science-Based Product

Due to the rapid increase in various easy-to-use libraries and tools for data science, various companies are now building products that are entirely based on data science models. Note that the main difference between such DSBP projects and the DSI-Prod projects we saw earlier is that in case of DSBP, the product cannot exist without data science models; in case of DSI-Prod, on the other hand, data science adds some useful functionality to an existing, functional product. The following are a few examples of DSBP projects:

- If you are building a mobile app for wellness that can detect health conditions using audio samples of the user, you would be relying entirely on data science models to accomplish this. As part of the business strategy, you may begin with one or two health conditions such as respiratory distress, etc., and, over time, increase the number and variety of health conditions that you are able to detect.

- As part of the business strategy, you may also want to provide APIs that can detect health conditions using audio samples. Such APIs can be used, for example, by external companies that create, for example, telehealth applications, etc.

- These days, it is more common to build an API platform first and build your mobile app on top of this API platform. In this way, you can monetize the mobile app as well as leverage it as a prototype of the capabilities of your API platform.

- If you provide APIs, then from the perspective of the clients of your APIs, you are providing an AI service.

- Several products are built using computer vision technologies in the fields of surveillance, medical imaging, etc.

Typical Traits of Data Science Projects

Table 23-2 captures some typical traits of the various types of data science projects. While these traits are largely based upon our experience, they can also be logically derived from our earlier coverage in the book. This table is intended to be an indicative reference[3] when starting new projects or building a team – it can help determine the direction to take, set expectations of stakeholders and team members, and serve as a starting point to estimate budget and areas of allocation.

---

[3] Deviations specific to the project at hand are not uncommon.

Table 23-2. Traits of data science projects

Type of project	Data Science Process	Data Science Culture	Team Structure	Reference Architecture	Typical Artifacts
KDD	• Data Capture would be completed prior to project kick-off • Inference: Deploying & monitoring models needed less often, and kept simple.	• Monastic, as the goal is to uncover insights	• 1-2 data scientists • Data analyst / citizen data scientist • Part-time data engineer	• Interactive tools for ad-hoc Data Preparation & Data Visualization	• Insights and conclusions documented • ML models • Experiments captured in slide-decks or in experiment registry (e.g. ML Flow)
DSI-Proc	• Data Capture would be typically completed prior • Inference involves integration with existing systems/applications used in the processes.	• Monastic preferred, to enable the analysts to easily understand & validate the models w.r.t. domain • If wild-west adopted, human-in the-loop typically essential	• Similar to KDD. • Would additionally involve engineers for integration and ML Ops activites.	• Data Science applications using tools such as Plotly Dash e.g., to test the models before integrating with the processes • Leverage any existing systems using APIs etc. for Inference • Model monitoring and feedback design needed to gauge improvement in processes	• Data Science application/portal to showcase models to stakeholders before integrating in the process. • Service (e.g. REST API) that is integrated into existing systems used in the process.
DSI-Prod	• Data Capture would be typically completed prior • Machine Learning and Inference: Model-tuning / configuration per customer may be needed for B2B product	• Wild-west, as the goal typically is to add functionality (with accuracy) to existing product rather than uncovering insights	• ML engineers if AI services are used; else data scientists • Data engineers are key to ensure automated data pipelines for continuously arriving data	• Similar to DSI-Proc. (Data Science applications may not be needed, as the product itself can be used to invoke the models.)	• Service or library – encapsulating the model is integrated into product. • REST APIs • Javascript/Java/Swift libraries for browsers and mobile devices.
DSBP	• Data Capture from your product or using services like Amazon Mturk • End-to-end automation, including ML Ops.	Depends on goals • Typically wild-west. • Monastic if research to advance the field is a business strategy.	Grow towards the mature team structure of Figure 22-1.	All components of Figure 19-1 typically needed.	Deployable, functional product (including automation from new data availability to model upgradation as needed).

KPIs

Key performance indicators, or KPIs, are used to quantify the performance of a team and the overall progress toward the goals. In this section, we shall mention a few KPIs and metrics that can be used for data science projects or the overall team. Note that we are not covering business KPIs such as RoI, etc., that determine the contribution of the data science team to the business; rather we are covering operational KPIs that are used to track the performance of the data science team against its own goals. It is assumed that the goals of the data science team have already been mapped to desired business outcomes (see Chapter 2). If you have a mature practice with multiple projects, then you may want to capture the KPIs at a project level and aggregate them for tracking the overall team performance.

Model Performance

This is the KPI that determines how well a given model is performing. Achieving a desired model performance is typically the immediate goal of a data science project.

An appropriate metric of model performance needs to be determined – refer to the coverage of model performance evaluation and metrics in Chapter 16.

Each iteration or sprint of a project should capture the improvement in model performance, which indicates the progress of the core data science.

The model performance KPI ensures the team is progressing in the *right* direction and captures the progress made; the other metrics mentioned in the following only track how *efficiently* the team is working toward that direction.

Experimentation Cycle Time

The *experimentation cycle time* KPI is the aggregate metric that captures the overall time taken to complete an experiment. This captures how quickly the data science team is able to iterate through experiments.

WHAT IS AN EXPERIMENT?

Note that the notion of an "experiment" is rather subjective and specific to the problem at hand and the techniques used. It can also evolve based on which stage the project is in. For example, in the early stages of a project, evaluating each type of ML algorithm or various possible datasets could each be an experiment. Once a certain ML approach and datasets are identified, then one specific iteration of model training and tuning could be regarded an experiment.

Thus, what constitutes an "experiment" is something that the data scientists will identify.

To continually improve the experimentation cycle time, several auxiliary metrics can be useful, some of which are shown in Table 23-3. Addressing the areas of improvement specific to any of the metrics will result in improving the overall experimentation cycle time.

Table 23-3. *Auxiliary metrics related to experimentation cycle time*

Metric	Description	Relevant steps of data science process
Dataset curation effort	Effort involved in curating a dataset of interest. This involves capturing relevant data, exploratory analysis, and preparing data for ML	Data capture, data preparation, data visualization
Model training effort	Efforts taken for training models and analyzing resulting models and their performance. Data size, infrastructure, etc., play a role here. If a model takes too long to train because the infrastructure is suboptimal, data scientists may spend time waiting – this time should also be included here	Machine learning
Model testing effort	Given a model, effort required to "test" the model on a new dataset. This involves any effort required to transform the test dataset to appropriate format, using the model on the test set, and evaluating model performance on the test set The data size, infrastructure, etc., play a role here as well	Machine learning
Model deployment effort	Once a model is approved, how long does it take before it is "live" on the targeted production system(s)? This gauges the effectiveness of the entire ML Ops pipeline	Inference
Model monitoring effort	Effort required for the data science team to analyze production model performance. This includes the ability to get a clear picture of all the relevant data and resulting predictions/ insights given by a model	Inference

Effort-Cost Trade-Offs

Note that in the preceding table, we have typically included *effort* as the metric. One common way to reduce efforts is to procure tools, for example, such as the ones we saw in Part 3 for the various steps of the data science process. Like for any other project, data science projects also involve an appropriate trade-off among the following factors:

- If manual effort is not reduced, what is the opportunity cost?

- How much manual effort of the data science team will be saved by using a tool? What is the cost equivalent of this effort?

- How much would a tool cost?

Data Quality

Data quality is often a polarizing topic of discussion within a company, particularly so within the data science team. When you have data coming in from multiple sources and have set up data pipelines to capture data meant for being used by data scientists in the data science process, the expectation of a data scientist is that the data is of "good quality." But often what a data scientist means by "good quality" turns out to be different from what the software or data engineers interpret as "good quality" – this leads to discovery of issues rather late in the data science process. It is not uncommon to see several man-months of effort wasted due to a data quality issue that was uncovered too late.

In this section, we shall first cover the importance of data quality and how the severity of impact resulting from data quality issues could vary depending on the type of the data science project. Then, we look at a few dimensions of data quality, which will help "define" data quality appropriately for your team. Then, we shall touch upon some aspects around measuring and ensuring data quality. Finally, we shall look at the typical reasons why data quality often takes a backseat and how to address these reasons. Our focus in these sections is on making sure that the data is of expected quality before data scientists begin work on it in the data science process.[4]

Importance of Data Quality

To understand the importance of data quality, let us consider the kinds of issues that can arise when poor-quality data is used for data science and the potential severity of the impact resulting from such issues.

Issues Arising from Poor-Quality Data

One commonly expected type of issue that would arise is that the data scientists are unable to create a model with sufficiently good performance. This is a relatively less serious issue – as soon as this occurs, you could go back and check the data quality more rigorously. The time lost is less and hence might be tolerable in this case.

The more serious issue, and one which is often overlooked, is that a data scientist might actually arrive at a model (using poor-quality data) which seems to perform well – this happens when the underlying test data is also of poor quality and gives a misleading perception of good performance. This can occur surprisingly often especially in the wild-west culture, for example, with deep learning techniques where you look only at predictive accuracy rather than obtaining and validating the insights provided by a model. When such a model – built using data with quality issues – is deployed in production, it will perform poorly or erratically.

---

[4] However, once this expected quality is ensured, data scientists themselves can also play a role in improving the quality further in the data preparation step of the data science process.

Then it is often assumed at first to be an issue with the model, for example, maybe the model wasn't tested on sufficiently large amount of test data, so it is not generalizing well for production scenarios. Only after that, quite late, does the attention shift to validating the data quality. In this way, the underlying data quality issues are uncovered rather late, and significant effort of the data science team could have been wasted by then.

Severity of Impact

The severity and nature of impact of these issues would depend on your business and the problem being solved. Nevertheless, the type of data science project typically can help arrive at some initial approximations of severity/nature of impact. This is shown in Table 23-4.

Table 23-4. *Impact of data quality based on project type to help arrive at some initial approximations of severity/nature*

Type of project	Severity of impact	Nature of impact
KDD	Critical	Results/insights from KDD projects are often used to define novel strategies or initiate new product development. Since these are usually high-cost investments, the impact could be correspondingly higher if the results of KDD projects are found to be incorrect
DSI-Proc	Moderate – high	If the model infused into a process performs poorly in production, the improvements in the process may not occur to the extent envisioned/desired. Thus, the RoI would be lesser than anticipated. The impact could be much higher if reliance on the model with minimal supervision led to worsened process efficiency

(continued)

Table 23-4. (*continued*)

Type of project	Severity of impact	Nature of impact
DSI-Prod	Low – moderate	Since the product was sustaining the business already, if a new functionality introduced does not perform as expected, the impact is relatively low. Moderate impact could be expected if many users engaged with the new functionality, and a poor experience led to customer churn
DSBP	High	Since the entire business relies on the data and resulting models, the impact would be high. But in this case, the issues and impact also tend to get highlighted (and addressed) much sooner as the model is the primary focus of the customer-facing product. Thus, we categorize impact as high rather than as critical

Determining the appropriate trade-off between the severity of impact of poor-quality data against the amount of effort to be expended in mitigating the risk by ensuring data quality – this *risk-effort trade-off* is one of the cornerstones of a data quality program. In the following sections, we shall touch upon various aspects that go into evaluating this trade-off.

Dimensions of Data Quality

The first, big hurdle in ensuring data quality lies in defining it. For a data science practice, the definition is best driven by the chief data scientist in collaboration with the data architect or data engineers.[5]

---

[5] In organizations where data stewardship practices exist, the data stewards would be consulted to understand the existing dimensions and tailor/enhance them as needed.

341

This ensures that everyone is aligned with the definition and the resulting data quality requirements, as well as the state of data quality at any point in time.

The definition of data quality typically takes the form of identifying various dimensions along which quantifiable metrics can be determined. The choice of dimensions may vary from one organization to another. As the data science practice matures, the choice of dimensions often evolve as well – more dimensions may get added, or existing ones refined further. In any case, there are a few typical dimensions that are seen repeatedly – Table 23-5 captures some of them.

Table 23-5. *Dimensions of data quality*

Data quality dimension	Quality question addressed
Consistency	Are there unexpected differences in the data at multiple steps in the data pipeline?
Validity	Is data available with the expected range of values, data type, and format?
Completeness	Are all the attributes of every observation available?
Usability	Are the observations usable by the data science team? This is decided by the data scientist according to the specifics of the data analysis undertaken. For example, in some cases, invalid or incomplete observations might still be usable
Accuracy	To what extent does the data reflect the real world?

For a more general, rigorous, and detailed coverage of the various dimensions of data quality, refer to Chapter 13, "Data Quality," of DAMA (2017).[6]

Once you have identified the relevant dimensions, it is time to consider how the data quality will actually be *measured* along these dimensions.

Measuring Data Quality

When it comes to measuring data quality along the dimensions identified, a couple of initial questions encountered are "which data do we measure?" and "what level of quality is acceptable for the various dimensions?".

A common approach to address these is to "mark" various datasets as bronze, silver, or gold as shown in Table 23-6.

Table 23-6. *Grading datasets based on intended purpose and expected nature of data*

Grade	Purpose	Expected nature of data
Bronze	Early-stage exploration to understand the data that is available; feasibility analysis of a data science project	Raw data that has not been processed in any way
Silver	Early iterations of the data science process, more oriented toward data preparation and data visualization steps	Data that is transformed to standard formats, cleansed, and any basic errors such as invalid values, inconsistency across tables, etc., have been identified and marked
Gold	Creating data science models	Observations of interest, with requisite quality, distilled from multiple silver tables

---

[6] In Table 23-5, we have tailored some of the dimensions in regard to typical data engineering and data science activities.

Accordingly, the goal is that gold data should be of high quality (scoring high in all quality dimensions), silver data can be of somewhat lower quality, and all other data can be regarded as bronze data – bronze data quality may not be measured at all or be of poor quality.

Given this kind of categorization of the data assets, it would now make sense to first put in all the efforts necessary to ensure the quality of gold datasets used in your current, immediate projects. Once the entire pipelines leading up to the gold data for your current projects are ensured to be of acceptable quality, you can invest further effort in measuring the quality of other silver and bronze data depending on your strategic needs and the resources available.

Ensuring Data Quality

Once the dimensions have been identified and the datasets graded, typically scripts are written to automate the following:

- Measuring data quality for the relevant datasets

- Updating data quality metrics as new data arrives

- Triggering alerts (e.g., email notifications) if any severe data quality issues are detected

These scripts are typically written and maintained by the data engineering team.

ML techniques can also be used for assisting in data quality improvements. Refer to Using Machine Learning for Improving Data Quality (2021) for an overview of this area.

Resistance to Data Quality Efforts

When one identifies in hindsight that scientific efforts were wasteful because the data was of poor quality, in addition to the business impact, this also tends to have a significant negative impact on the morale and motivation of the data scientists. Having a *scientist* work with data that is not verified for quality is fundamentally against the spirit of the discipline. In any other scientific field, one does not expect scientists to work with such data, but in case of data science, we have often seen leaders and managers not focusing on data quality sufficiently until it's too late.

An underlying root cause for this is that once a data scientist comes on board, it is deemed more productive (profitable) to try to create models – typical expectations tend to be along the lines of "when will a model be delivered for …?" or even "how many models are planned to be delivered in the first quarter?" – and revisit data quality only if any issues are actually encountered later.

In such a situation, the resulting perception is often that there isn't sufficient time or bandwidth to define "data quality" properly, measure the data quality metrics, and ensure requisite quality of data – this is the main resistance to data quality efforts.

An informed trade-off analysis can usually help evaluate if this resistance is justified. During the trade-off analysis, it is important to fully appreciate the nature and seriousness of the issues that may arise if data quality is not verified. An objective analysis of the trade-offs between severity of the impact of poor data quality (covered earlier in this section) and the available bandwidth/resources will help objectively determine how much effort can be expended toward data quality.

Data Protection and Privacy

Data protection/privacy is a vast topic and affects all aspects around storage and usage of data in an organization. It is so significant that in many companies, a dedicated chief information security officer (CISO) is tasked with ensuring data protection and privacy. Various regulations for data protection are extant, such as

- Generic regulations, for example, GDPR

- Industry-specific regulations such as HIPAA for health information, etc.

The regions/country an organization operates in and the business vertical it belongs to determine the applicable data protection and privacy regulations (such as those mentioned here). An organization accordingly adopts standards and compliance requirements that it needs to adhere to. While several factors need to be considered in complying with these regulations, there are a few common, important aspects in regard to data used for data science. We shall touch upon these in this section.

Encryption

Typically, the data collection, storage, and processing would be encrypted with appropriate mechanisms to comply with the standards set in your organization for security and regulatory compliance.

It is important to ensure that these mechanisms are also followed by the data science team during various steps of the data science process. The following are a few examples of such organizational standards and how they apply to the data science team:

- The data lake or data warehouse that the data science team uses should be encrypted. Similarly, if your processes allow data scientists to download this data to their machines, then their machines also need to be encrypted.

- Any processing of data should be done over secure channels, such as HTTPS/TLS. This may include the ways in which data scientists download data or how the data transfer happens between machines in a cluster, such as a Spark cluster or a cluster of GPU machines.

Access Controls

It is important to ensure that data access is limited to the right team members. For example, if a data scientist is working on a specific project, then they should be given access only to the tables and rows that are needed for their analysis. Various data lakes and warehouses support access control mechanisms for this purpose.

Occasionally, for exploratory purposes, a data scientist may need access to more data, or even the entire data lake – in these cases, expanded access can be given for a limited period of time.

It may also be useful to restrict write access to certain data; for example, you may define a policy to ensure that gold data is written to/ updated by only certain authorized data engineers or data scientists.

Finally, in case some members in the data science team have access to protected or identifiable information, all such access needs to be audited.

Identifiable/Protected/Sensitive Information

Personally identifiable information (PII) refers to attributes such as name, phone number, address, etc., that can be used to identify a specific individual. Even voice recordings are potentially PII since an individual can potentially be identified using their voice.

Protected information expands the scope of PII to include any other information collected about an individual using your services that can be used to identify the individual. For example, as per the US Health Insurance Portability and Accountability Act (HIPAA), Protected Health Information (PHI) includes information such as the medical record number, health insurance details, etc., of an individual in addition to the PII information covered earlier.

Finally, certain regulations may cover aspects related to the processing of "sensitive" data. For example, as per GDPR (Article 9), sensitive data includes

> *personal data revealing racial or ethnic origin, political opinions, religious or philosophical beliefs, or trade-union membership, and the processing of genetic data, biometric data for the purpose of uniquely identifying a natural person, data concerning health or data concerning a natural person's sex life or sexual orientation …*

> —GDPR (Article 9)

It is important the data science team is aware of these concepts as required by the compliance goals of the organization and that they *actively* try to *not* access or use PII, protected, or sensitive information unless it is absolutely necessary. And even when it is necessary, access needs to be given in a controlled manner.

For example, suppose you are building a data science-based product that analyzes voice samples to detect health conditions. Once you have ascertained that data scientists do need access to the audio files containing the voice samples, then the following are a couple of questions you should consider while enabling access:

- Can we restrict access to audio files to only certain data engineers or data scientists who will execute data preparation to extract numeric features from the audio samples? This way, PII access is highly restricted while the rest of the team can use the numeric features (not PII) for modeling, etc.

- Are audio files collected from multiple countries? If so, what are the regulations in each country w.r.t. processing of PII? For example, it is likely that the countries require that PII should not leave the country – any processing of PII needs to happen in that country itself. If so, how can we architect the system and define processes such that data scientists are able to use the audio files for creating models while adhering to these constraints?

These are usually nontrivial challenges; the solutions would depend on the data architecture, infrastructure, and compliance requirements of your organization. This often requires the chief architect, data architect, chief data scientist, and chief information security officer to work together to define a holistic strategy that enables data science in compliance with regulations.

Finally, if you are using (or planning to use) any cloud services, it is important to check that those services comply with the regulatory requirements of your organization. For example, if you are using AWS to store and process healthcare information in the United States, you would need to check that the AWS services you use are HIPAA compliant (they often are).

Federated Learning

Often organizations wish to collaborate to create new models. But given the sensitive nature of data which cannot be shared, such collaboration has been a challenge. This especially applies to industries such as healthcare and finance.

To overcome this challenge, the notion of federated learning is beginning to gain traction recently in these industries. The following are the primary concepts of federated learning:

- An organization can share code, for example, model training code, securely with its partner.

- The code executes securely in the partner infrastructure on the partner data.

- Results (e.g., models) from executing the code are returned to the organization that requested/initiated the execution.

One of the key capabilities needed to ensure the security – right down to the hardware level – of both the model and data, is that of trusted execution environments (TEE) such as Intel SGX. Refer to Federated Learning through Revolutionary Technology (2020) for an example which includes further technical details.

Legal and Regulatory Aspects

We covered some of the primary regulatory aspects around data storage, access, and processing in the previous section on data protection and privacy. Assuming all these aspects are taken care of, and the individual's consent is obtained as needed, there are additional points to be considered when it comes to using the data for data science. In this section, we briefly touch upon the ethical/legal and regulatory aspects *specific* to creating ML models from data.

When Are These Relevant?

For the most part, the aspects covered in this section tend to apply to consumer products, including websites/mobile apps, etc., that are used by a consumer. If your company deals with consumer data, then you would need to expend effort to ensure the necessary regulatory compliances outlined in the following are met by your data science projects and models.

If your projects are purely dealing with nonpersonal data such as sensor readings or data collected about internal operations, etc., then these legal factors could be less relevant.

We would suggest that if you are undertaking a DSI-Prod or a DSBP project,[7] it is usually safer to proactively check all the compliance requirements even if it seems at first glance that you are not dealing with consumer data.

Nondiscrimination

As we have seen throughout this book, data science relies on data, learns patterns from the data, and makes predictions based on the past data. Various ML algorithms may "learn" in different ways,[8] and the resulting models would predict in different ways – but they are ultimately based upon the data that was fed to them during training. If the data itself is biased in some way, then the resulting models too are likely to be biased. There have been several examples of this in the past few years in varied areas of performance of work, financial loans, education, personal preferences, and so forth – refer to O'Neil (2017). The GDPR also outlines these aspects under "profiling," for example, see Recital 71 and Article 22.

---

[7] As these two types of projects are likely to have consumer data.

[8] As seen in Chapter 16.

If a data science model explicitly uses sensitive data such as race, religion, etc., then any biases that are inherent in the humans that created/ prepared the data will be "learned" by the ML algorithms as well. A similar bias would occur if a data science model used other correlated information such as geographic region – this is because some regions may have, say, a higher number of low-income or minority residents. It could be a grave error to regard models that are trained using such data as "objective."

Explainability and Accountability

Regulations such as GDPR Article 12/13 and the US Algorithmic Accountability Act of 2019 cover aspects of accountability in regard to processing data, and decision-making, using machine learning algorithms. For example, if an applicant's loan request is rejected based on a model, the organization is accountable for the rejection (i.e., cannot merely point to a "model" as being responsible) and also needs to be able to *explain* the reason behind the decision.

Even when an organization is well intentioned, one of the primary hurdles to accountability is lack of *explainability*.[9] And the primary hurdle to explainability lies in the technical details of an ML model.

In Chapter 20, we saw the significant variation in the various techniques when it comes to factors such as *attribution* and *interpretability of prediction*. From a purely technical perspective, these are the two primary factors that constitute *model* explainability – which pieces of the data (attributes) influenced the decision/prediction and exactly how the algorithm (ML model) arrived at the final decision/prediction based on the values of those attributes.

Techniques – such as deep learning – that got a low grade on these two factors in Chapter 20, are the most notorious when it comes to *model*

---

[9] There are other ethical aspects to accountability such as an organizations' willingness and drive toward transparency, fairness, etc., that we shall not cover here.

explainability. Such models, which are poor in terms of explainability, are commonly referred to as *black-box models*.[10] In recent years, increasing research is happening in the area of explainability of black-box models. But these techniques are often approximations or estimations, which result in explanations that cannot be trusted to be faithful to how the original model arrives at the predictions. See Rudin (2019) for more details.

We expect the debate around these aspects to continue for several years. Meanwhile, we would recommend that, if you are processing consumer information and personal data, to use explainable techniques to the extent possible, that is, techniques that have a high grade for *attribution* and *interpretability of prediction* in Chapter 20.

Explainable AI: What Is an "Explanation"?

The ideal goal one would like to reach is that an explanation is provided...

> *...to the data subject in a concise, transparent, intelligible and easily accessible form, using clear and plain language...*
>
> —GDPR (Article 12)

This involves much more than merely *model* explainability – achieving this ideal goal can be tricky even for techniques that got a grade of A/A+ for *attribution* and *interpretability of prediction* in Chapter 20. This is because these models are fundamentally mathematical in nature, and explaining their behavior in "clear and plain language," etc., to a data subject could be quite challenging in some cases. Needless to say, it is even more difficult to reach this ideal goal using black-box models (notwithstanding the ongoing research in the area of explainability of such models).

---

[10] Since you only know the predicted value but do not have a simple picture of how it was calculated internally by the model.

Cognitive Bias

We began by looking at Eddington and Einstein in Chapter 1 – let us iterate back now over to them.

> *Eddington's observations … were very inexact and some of them conflicted with others. When he chose which observations to count as data, and which to count as 'noise', that is, when he chose which to keep and which to discard, Eddington had Einstein's prediction very much in mind. Therefore Eddington could only claim to have confirmed Einstein because he used Einstein's derivation in deciding what his observations really were, while Einstein's derivations only became accepted because Eddington's observation seemed to confirm them. Observation and prediction were linked in a circle of mutual confirmation rather than being independent of each other as we would expect according to the conventional idea of an experimental test. The proper description, then, is that there was 'agreement to agree' rather than that there was a theory, then a test, then a confirmation.*

> —Collins and Pinch (1998)

The tendency to actively seek for, and focus on, data and evidence that supports one's preexisting beliefs is referred to as *confirmation bias*.

Recall from Chapter 3 that the monastic culture aims to find eternal truths, while the wild-west culture is fine with short-term, seemingly contingent truths.

Contingent truths are typically not worth having a "belief" in – thus, cowboys are usually less subject to confirmation bias. For example, if they detect a drop in model performance on new data, indicating that the model does not work for those observations, they will not try to defend the model. They will simply retrain using the new observations to build models that represent new short-term truths – it's not such a big deal.

Eternal truths, on the other hand, are arrived at after quite some deliberation and *demand* "belief" – monks invest significant effort in distilling "the truth" and *believe* in it once distilled. Monks may choose to overlook the occasional paltry evidence (observation) that contradicts an eternal truth or examine it in order to prove it misleading/incorrect.

It is unfortunate that the term "confirmation bias" seems to have a negative connotation – after all, the development of all science relies on a *healthy* dose of confirmation bias. But occasionally, a data scientist can be subject to an unhealthy dose of confirmation bias – this can be aggravated by business realities and looming deadlines – which then harms the science and can lead to incorrect conclusions/decisions. For example, a data scientist might reject even good observations that disprove their truth/model, thus leading to incorrect conclusions.

Confirmation bias is a primary example of the gamut of *cognitive biases,* that is, the biases that human reasoning is typically subject to. In addition to confirmation bias, there are numerous other cognitive biases that also play an important role in science, in general, and data science, in particular.

While we have seen several of these biases at work, it is gladdening to see this aspect of data science and machine learning receiving focus in the literature in the past few years. For example, see Kliegr, Bahník, and Fürnkranz (2020) and Miller (2018).

Cognitive Bias and Data Science Projects

In our view, KDD and DSI-Proc projects are typically at risk of being significantly impacted by cognitive biases such as confirmation bias. This is because of various reasons like the goals that are generally targeted in such projects, data science culture typically adopted, etc. At least for these types of projects, it would be prudent to set up peer reviews of the analysis and results – the peer reviews can be conducted by other data scientists and data/business analysts as appropriate.

Conclusion and Further Reading

In this concluding chapter, we covered various practical aspects around executing data science projects. We first saw the four common types of data science projects and some typical traits of each type in regard to the data science process, team structure, reference architecture, etc. We then covered KPIs for evaluating the performance of the data science team.

We then covered various aspects around data quality and data protection/privacy. For more details of these and related aspects, refer to DAMA (2017).

Legal and regulatory aspects around data science are evolving rapidly – we covered some key points around these, including the notion of explainability. For a coverage of GDPR relevant to algorithmic decision-making and right to explanation, refer to Goodman and Flaxman (2017). O'Neil (2017) is a survey of all the bad things that data science and big data have wrought upon humanity. The current swathe of regulations around data and explainable AI is motivated by the types of incidents mentioned in this book.

We then looked at cognitive biases, particularly confirmation bias. The impact of cognitive biases in the context of data science and machine learning is seeing increasing focus lately. Miller (2018) is an excellent coverage of what constitutes an "explanation" and corresponding challenges, including cognitive biases.

References

Collins, Harry and Trevor Pinch. *The Golem: what everyone should know about science, 2nd edition*. Cambridge, UK: Cambridge University Press, 1998.

DAMA. *DAMA DMBOK, 2nd edition*. NJ, USA: Technics Publications, 2017.

Federated Learning through Revolutionary Technology. 6 Nov 2020. <https://consilient.com/white-paper/federated-learning-through-revolutionary-technology/>.

Goodman, Bryce and Seth Flaxman. "European Union Regulations on Algorithmic Decision-Making and a "Right to Explanation"." *AI Magazine* Oct 2017: 50–57. <https://arxiv.org/pdf/1606.08813.pdf>.

Kliegr, Tomáš, Štěpán Bahník and Johannes Fürnkranz. "A review of possible effects of cognitive biases on the interpretation of rule-based machine learning models." December 2020. <https://arxiv.org/abs/1804.02969>.

Miller, Tim. August 2018. *Explanation in Artificial Intelligence: Insights from the Social Sciences.* <https://arxiv.org/abs/1706.07269>.

O'Neil, Cathy. *Weapons of Math Destruction.* Penguin Random House, 2017.

Rudin, Cynthia. "Stop Explaining Black Box Machine Learning Models for High Stakes Decisions and Use Interpretable Models Instead." 2019. <https://arxiv.org/abs/1811.10154>.

Using Machine Learning for Improving Data Quality. n.d. May 2021. <www.cc-cdq.ch/Machine-Learning-for-Improving-Data-Quality>.

Index

A

AB testing, 263
Agglomerative clustering, 80, 119
AI services, 277, 287, 321
Airflow, 166
Akaike information criterion, 298
Algorithmia, 262
AlphaGo, 149
AlphaGo Zero, 150
AlphaZero, 142, 150
Amazon API Gateway, 262
Amazon Comprehend, 277
Amazon DeepRacer, 154
Amazon ECS, 270
Amazon EFS, 138, 170
Amazon EMR, 270
Amazon Forecast, 277
Amazon Personalize, 277
Amazon Polly, 277
Amazon Redshift, 168
Amazon Rekognition, 277
Amazon S3, 167
Amazon Sagemaker Autopilot, 273
Amazon Sagemaker Inference, 262
Amazon Transcribe, 277
Anomaly detection, 91
Anomaly score, 103, 106

Artificial intelligence, 16
    data science approach, 17
    rule based approach, 16
    rule based *vs.* data science, 19
Asimov, 143, 154
Attribution, 290, 292–294, 352
Auto-sklearn, 273
AutoGluon, 273
AutoML, 270–271, 284, 286
AWS Athena, 171
AWS Ec2, 270
AWS Lambda, 261, 262
Azure Cognitive Speech
    Services, 277
Azure Computer Vision, 277
Azure Machine Learning, 273
Azure Synapse, 168
Azure Text Analytics, 277
Azure Video Analyzer for Media, 277

B

Bag-of-words, 70, 175
Bagging, 234
Batch jobs, 285
Bayesian information criterion, 298
BI, *see* Business intelligence (BI)

Printed in the United States
by Baker & Taylor Publisher Services